European Spatial Planning

Edited by Andreas Faludi

Lincoln Institute of Land Policy
Cambridge, Massachusetts

Library of Congress Cataloging-in-Publication Data

European spatial planning / edited by Andreas Faludi.
    p.   cm.
Based on a conference held at the Lincoln Institute on June 29-30, 2001.
Includes bibliographical references.
ISBN 1-55844-153-0 (pbk.)
    1. Regional planning—European Union countries—Congresses.
2. European Union countries—Economic policy—Congresses.
3. Land use—European Union countries—Planning—Congresses.
4. Intergovernmental cooperation—European Union countries—
Congresses. I. Faludi, Andreas. II. Lincoln Institute of Land Policy.

HT395.E82 E88 2002
307.1'2'094—dc21

                                                    2002154080

Project management: Ann LeRoyer, Lincoln Institute of Land Policy
Copyediting: Joseph Ryan
Design, copyediting and production: Snow Creative Services
Printing: Webcom Ltd., Toronto, Ontario, Canada

Contents

Section IV: Conclusion

Foreword

I first became aware of Andreas Faludi quite by chance in late 1999. He was about to offer a module on European spatial planning at the Graduate School of Design at Harvard University, where I was initiating a course on the theory and practice of regional planning. I attended one of Faludi's lectures at Harvard and still remember his starting point, provocative for a Design School course: "Planning is not about design, but about policy."

The global migration of planning concepts has long fascinated me, and I had encountered the first draft of the European Spatial Development Perspective (ESDP) in 1997. I became intrigued with the idea of applying the approach of European spatial planning to the United States. Once having mastered such key terms as *subsidiarity* and *competency* in that new language, Euro-English, I pondered their relevance in the states.

Jerold Kayden (2001, 43) has described the U.S. planning system as follows:

> Listed in order of importance, three levels of government in the United States exercise legal authority over land-use planning and regulation: the local level, the state level, and the national level.... the national government fundamentally does not practice *de jure* or *de facto* national land-use planning and regulation as that term would be specified and understood internationally.

Thus, I had to ask, could a country that had, under its federal system, largely ceded planning authority to the states, which had in turn largely left the job of planning to their local governments, learn from 15 European countries that had agreed to plan across national boundaries?

In search of an answer to this question, my Lincoln Institute colleague Rosalind Greenstein and I determined to bring Andreas Faludi and his story of Europe's "roving band of planners" to a wider American audience. We invited him to present a lecture on European spatial planning at Lincoln House in Cambridge, and he joined us in a discussion with American planners on the revival of the Regional Planning Association of America in New York in April 2000. Then, bracing ourselves for an even deeper immersion in Euro-English, we commissioned this volume, whose development benefited from a panel presentation at the annual meeting of the American Planning Association in New Orleans in March 2001 and a seminar at Lincoln House in June of that year. At the seminar, the papers included here were presented and discussed before a panel of U.S. planners and academics: Robert Yaro of the Regional Plan Association in New York, who wrote the epilogue to this volume; Michael Neuman of Texas A&M University; William Klein of the American Planning Association; and myself.

Klein began the discussion with the following observation, which we do not take to be a final judgment on the marketability of European spatial planning on these shores: "Will this book sell to planners in the United States? The answer as far as I can tell is a definite maybe." The meeting transcript records the colloquy that followed as "(laughter) (simultaneous conversation)." Klein went on to comment that American planners regard Europe as having done a much better job of planning, owing to a better mix of bottom-up and top-down authority. Further, having given away authority to the local government level, Americans were hampered in dealing with larger geographic spaces in metropolitan areas and across state lines, leading to the feeling that Europe is not an example that Americans can copy. Nevertheless, Klein concluded that there are many areas of convergence between U.S. and European planning, centering on struggles over the "proper levels of government to deal with different kinds of decision-making."

Neuman saw further parallels in the U.S. and European planning experience, including our own "roving band of planners" who worked on growth management in the 1960s and 1970s at the municipal scale, and increasingly, at the metropolitan regional scale, leading to the contemporary direction in smart growth planning. Neuman described the recent New Jersey State Plan in the context of the U.S.'s radically decentralized approach to planning as a strategic plan, very much like the European spatial planning perspective: not a local plan, or a land use plan, or a regulatory plan, but a plan of "compatibilization." Each level of government retains its competency, but, through a process of cross-acceptance, the plans of different levels of government are negotiated to be more and more compatible with each other.

Yaro's further elaboration of the nexus (and, in certain respects, the disconnect) between the U.S. and Europe planning situations is included as the epilogue to this volume.

Although a bit chastened by my American colleagues, who certainly don't underestimate the difficulty of applying European spatial planning "on the ground" in the U.S., I am still confirmed in my belief in its intellectual value as a stimulus to transboundary thinking. We accordingly offer this work to all American planners willing to brave the uncharted seas of subsidiarity, competency and spatial strategy, as a first navigational aid.

Armando Carbonell
Senior Fellow and Co-chairman
Department of Planning and Development
Lincoln Institute of Land Policy

Preface and Acknowledgments

North Americans, and planners in particular, sometimes see things in Europe that they miss in their own society. This is not the place to argue about whether they are right. The European visitor, confronted with lively planning debates and the strong commitment of the American planning profession, quickly learns not to be smug. Clearly, Europe does things differently, and with European integration this becomes more evident. A lively interest in European integration exists among U.S. scholars, with distinguished centers of European studies at various universities. Europe's engagement in a form of spatial planning, however, has escaped the attention of many North Americans.

One need not be surprised, since European students of integration do not pay much attention either. Even among European planners, few are aware of this development. European spatial planning is not only new but also a step or two removed from the everyday reality of city planning. More likely, some of those who pay attention are national and regional planners whose work is affected in a more direct fashion.

I was confronted with European spatial planning when completing my efforts, extending over the best part of a decade, to unravel the secret of the success of Dutch national planning. Then, as before, Dutch national planners were actively engaged in promoting European planning, and I decided to follow up my work by focusing on the success and failure of the Dutch.

That work was done jointly with Wil Zonneveld, and it developed into a passion. Among the talented students Wil and I supervised while still at the University of Amsterdam was Bas Waterhout, who was writing his master thesis on the making of the European Spatial Development Perspective (ESDP), and is one of the authors in this book. He could draw on the archives of the Dutch National Spatial Planning Agency, where another author here, Derek Martin, was one of the leading international planners.

Slowly, Wil and I extended our search to Brussels, where I had my first interview with yet another of the present authors, Jean-François Drevet, and to Bonn, then still the capital of the Federal Republic of Germany. Like the roving band of European planners whom we were studying, we too were engaging in networking.

Together with Bas Waterhout, I moved to the University of Nijmegen where I devoted myself to the study of European spatial planning. We engaged in a number of joint projects, among them a book, *The Making of the European Spatial Planning Perspective* (Faludi and Waterhout 2002). We also participated in one of the Interreg IIC projects that Philippe Doucet writes about, called EURBANET, with the research institute OTB of Delft University of Technology (where Wil Zonneveld now works) as the lead partner. Our joint task was to evaluate the ESDP, particularly its application in Northwestern Europe (Waterhout and Faludi 2001; Faludi 2001b). We reestablished contact with two more authors in this book (John Zetter and Jacques Robert), and with other people engaged in European planning, either as practitioners or as researchers. They included Vincent Nadin, who helped manage the work on The EU Compendium of Spatial Planning Systems and Policies (CEC 1997a). Concurrently, I joined a working party of the German Academy for Regional Research and Regional Planning that was exploring the ESDP, and met Arthur Benz.

The Association of European Schools of Planning holds annual conferences, much like its sister organization in North America, the Association of Collegiate Schools of Planning. The transnational planning tracks of these conferences are occasions for scholars who are interested in European spatial planning to meet. Ole Jensen gave several papers at past meetings, chaired by the doyen of academics interested in this field, Dick Williams, author of the seminal work *European Union Spatial Policy and Planning* (Williams 1996). There, and during a visiting professorship at Aalborg University, I came to appreciate Ole Jensen's work, often undertaken jointly with Tim Richardson, now at the University of Sheffield.

The decisive step for this book came when I received an EU Fulbright Fellowship to teach European spatial planning at the Graduate School of Design of Harvard University in spring 2000. Rosalind Greenstein, a senior fellow of the Lincoln Institute of Land Policy, attended some of my classes and invited me to give a luncheon lecture at the Institute. By this time, thanks to Robert Yaro, executive director of the Regional Plan Association in New York, the Lincoln Institute had also invited me to participate in challenging discussions on the future of metropolitan planning. These meetings were chaired by Armando Carbonell, another senior fellow of the Lincoln Institute, who later invited me to offer a seminar on European spatial planning, which was eventually held at the Institute in Cambridge, Massachusetts, on 29 and 30 June 2001.

Prior to that seminar, at the National Planning Conference of the American Planning Association at New Orleans in March 2001, the Lincoln Institute sponsored a special session on European spatial planning, which once again I was invited to organize. With Armando Carbonell as chair, Derek Martin, John Zetter and I presented papers to a packed audience, outlining the Dutch, United Kingdom and German perspectives on European spatial planning. I gave the background paper on the ESDP. Those papers formed the core of a special issue of the journal *Built Environment*, under the title "Regulatory Competition and Cooperation in European Spatial Planning," published in late 2001.

Thanks are due to the Lincoln Institute, above all to Armando Carbonell, whose brainchild this book is, and to the staff of the Lincoln Institute, in particular to Lisa Silva for the organization of the course in Cambridge and to Ann LeRoyer, who has overseen the final editing and production of this book. Thanks are also due to Bas Waterhout who as my editorial assistant has completed many chores, including compiling the comprehensive list of references at the end of this book. It was his idea not only to combine the color maps as an insert, but to let these maps, which come from various authors and other colleagues, tell their own story. We wish to acknowledge Michael Albas, David Geritz, Peter Janssens, Peter Mehlbye, Jean Peyrony, Gerda Roeleveld, Karl Peter Schona and Michel Titecat who kindly assisted in collecting digital versions of the maps, in many cases creating them by their own hands.

Finally, thanks are due to the Rockefeller Foundation for granting me the opportunity to finish the book's editorial work and conclusions at their splendid premises at Bellagio, Italy. There is no more congenial place for this kind of work on the face of the earth!

In the name of all the authors, I proudly present our work, which I believe is at the cutting edge of research on European spatial planning. But why should American planners care? There is intrinsic interest in approaches that appear to be thoroughly different from North American practices. Few U.S. states engage in anything resembling planning (and, if so, under the flag of growth management or smart growth), let alone join forces with each other and the federal government to formulate a joint strategy. To the extent that problems reach across state borders and affect groups of states and perhaps even the U.S. as a whole, perhaps something could be learned from Europe. Better still, the European example could fire the imagination of American planners to formulate approaches better suited to the different circumstances there.

Beyond that matter is the fact that the U.S. and Europe are global competitors. Certainly, the ESDP sees it that way, contrasting the landmass of the U.S. with the differentiated shape of the EU in particular. Other than in the U.S., the ESDP study shows only one larger geographic zone of economic integration in Europe, also called a *global economic integration zone*. The ESDP points out that this leads to imbalances within the European territory, which European policies should rectify, thereby unlocking more of the economic potential in Europe. In this way, the ESDP addresses a central theme of the European Union: its global competitiveness. At the same time, it seeks to integrate social and environmental concerns with the pursuit of economic goals, with the conviction that the drive for competitiveness should be qualified, paying attention to concerns for sustainability and quality of life.

Whether European spatial planning will succeed is for the future to decide. The point of this book is that these issues are addressed here in a planning discourse encompassing the whole territory of the EU. Surely this is worth learning about.

Andreas Faludi
Professor of Spatial Policy Systems in Europe
Nijmegen School of Management
University of Nijmegen
The Netherlands

Section I

European Planning Practices

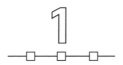

The European Spatial Development Perspective (ESDP)

An Overview

Andreas Faludi

In a cooperative effort, the 15 member states of the European Union (EU) and the European Commission have formulated and are now in the process of invoking a joint European Spatial Development Perspective (ESDP). The document (CEC 1999a) comes in two parts, of which Part A, "Achieving the Balanced and Sustainable Development of the Territory of the EU: The Contribution of the Spatial Development Policy," is discussed in this volume. Part B of ESDP is a technical appendix.

Chapter 1 of Part A concerns territory as a new dimension of European policy, and defines the goal of balanced and sustainable spatial development as reconciling social and economic claims on land with ecological and cultural functions. Chapter 2 deals with European spatial policies (a concept to be explained shortly), singling out three policies as being of particular importance (regional policy; the development of trans-European networks (TENs); and environmental policy) and recommending an integrated and multisectoral spatial development approach. Chapter 3 presents policy options grouped under three spatial development guidelines:

1. Polycentric spatial development and a new urban-rural partnership;
2. Parity of access to infrastructure and knowledge;
3. Wise management of the natural and cultural heritage.

Each of these is broken down into topics and then into 60 policy options. Chapter 4 of the ESDP examines the application of the ESDP on a European and transnational level, and in cross-border and interregional cooperation. Chapter 5 discusses the enlargement of the EU, a topic discussed by Jean-François Drevet in Chapter 8 of this volume, and one likely to dominate future discussions, including spatial planning. European enlargement is a major geographical event surrounded by much uncertainty as to its spatial scope and effects.

The ESDP is a remarkable document. At a national level, planning is far from universally practiced, and where it is practiced, the EU Compendium of Spatial Planning Systems and Policies (CEC 1997a) shows that approaches in the EU's member states vary (see also Faludi 2001a). Additionally, there is perennial conflict between member states looking after their own interests and the European Commission representing the common European interest. What looms in the background are different views about European integration. The concluding chapter here seeks to position spatial planning in this wider context.

This overview has two goals. The first is to explain the concept of spatial planning in the context of European integration. This concept forms the basis for understanding the so-called competency issue, i.e., whether there is or should be a European Community competency for spatial planning. The second goal is to review the process of composing the ESDP (see also Faludi and Waterhout 2002) and to lay the groundwork for the other authors in this book who discuss the various aspects of European spatial planning.

Spatial Planning

Spatial planning is a concept alien to North American planners and to British planners steeped in the "town and country planning" tradition (as in the Town and Country Planning Act). Williams (1996, 57) considers spatial planning to be a Euro-English concept—i.e., non-American and non-British concepts conveyed in English. As English is the most common second language spoken in Europe, Euro English has become the preferred medium of international exchanges in which concepts from various parts of Europe affect each other (Laitin 2000, 7). Feedback effects have occurred, in which Euro English has influenced British English; American English may one day be similarly affected.

The feedback effect is what has happened with the concept of spatial planning. In the eyes of U.K. planners, the strategic thinking that was neglected under the Conservative government is now emulated under the Labor government bent on *Modernising Planning* (DETR 1998). Thus, spatial planning has become a term of good currency in British English (Zetter 2001).

As a concept, however, spatial planning is ambiguous: its meaning shifts over time. Its first mention in the English language was likely in the title of the European Regional/Spatial Planning Charter (Council of Europe 1984), the first European planning document of any description (see Chapter 2). The Council of Europe, on whose behalf it was compiled and published, is an assembly of European parliamentary representatives, currently from 44 countries, and not to be confused with the European Parliament (discussed below). It proved difficult to find adequate concepts while drafting this Charter. In German the title is Europäische Raumordnungscharta. Literally speaking, *Raumordnung* means "spatial ordering." Needham (1988) discusses its Dutch equivalent as standing for public interventions in the spatial order. Williams (1996, 7) uses the term *spatial policy* to refer to such interventions. Thus, spatial policy is "any policy which is spatially specific or is in effect spatial in practice, whether or not it is deliberately designed to be, and any policy which is designed to influence land-use decisions, to be integrated with local planning strategies or to be implemented by local and regional authorities as part of their spatial planning responsibilities" (Williams 1996, 7).

A related concept, *Raumplanung*, literally means the planning of a space or an area, but spatial planning is the common translation. Spatial planning adds an extra dimension to spatial policies: one of deliberateness. After all, spatial policies need not arise out of a plan. According to Needham, this is only the case when three conditions are met. First, the policies must be specifically designed for a certain geographical area. Second, all policies about any specific location must be seen as a coherent whole. Third, the relationships among any one location and others must have been thought out beforehand. *Spatial planning is, thus, the systematic preparation of spatial policies.* For Dutch, and even more so for German planners, the preferred vehicle for this is the creation of a spatial plan. Similar to U.S. zoning ordinances and comprehensive plans, a spatial plan provides grounds for regulating development. Initially, regulating development has been the chief rationale for creating spatial plans. The assumption is that by exposing the reasons for regulatory measures, such plans would remove the odium of arbitrariness from government intervention.

Unlike U.S. zoning ordinances that are controlled locally, European equivalents are subject to approval by state or regional authorities whose control is exercised reasonably and consistently by showing that local spatial plans fit into a broader pattern of planning. Also unlike the U.S., regional and sometimes national governments in Europe create spatial plans, setting out the broader framework into which local plans fit. These levels of government interact variously: Alden (2001) lists five arrangements in the EU; Eser and Konstadakopulos (2000) report that the weights attached to these levels are shifting.

Since this practice interferes with property rights, making spatial plans and taking regulatory measures on this basis must be governed by law. The EU Compendium of Spatial Planning Systems and Policies (CEC 1997a), and the country volumes accompanying it, provide the most comprehensive source on what the powers of making plans and regulating development in EU member states are.

Regulating development is reactive. The initiative for development lies not with the planners but with developers; however, governments also initiate development. The spatial plan is also seen as a vehicle for various branches of government to coordinate their relevant policies. Thus, capital programs and the like must fit in with the plan, the plan must designate land for public services and so forth. In this way, the spatial plan relates to regulating private development as well as to proactive government policies. According to this view the spatial dimension is one of the common facets of all or most government policies, and the spatial plan is a framework for integrating them by way of what is called *horizontal coordination*.

Responsibility for proactive policies is shared among levels of government. Thus, major road links may be a state responsibility, hospitals a regional responsibility and schools a local responsibility. There are also the forementioned European spatial policies discussed in the ESDP. Now, all these levels impact the same territory, calling for *vertical coordination*. The logic of spatial planning is thus seen as the systematic preparation of spatial policies.

Coordination is difficult. Spatial planners must often rely on the regulatory force of statutory spatial plans, which are regarded as the mainstay of planning. Although overall coordination is hoped for, unless spatial plans and spatial planning become the vehicles for articulating government policy overall, this type of planning is essentially regulatory.

In the context of the European Regional/Spatial Planning Charter (Council of Europe 1984), the counterpart to spatial planning was dubbed *regional planning*. This does not refer to spatial planning on the regional level (as in the North American concept of city and regional planning). Here, regional planning stands for the French concept of *aménagement du territoire*, the literal translation being the shaping of the territory, which means not just any territory, but the national territory (Damette 1997). Thus, aménagement du territoire refers to interventions of the national administration to promote development in less favored regions, which is why regional planning appeared to be the appropriate term for this kind of planning. By definition, this is proactive policy. Regulating development does not enter into it.

Apparently, when the Charter was discussed, the gulf between the two concepts was such that invoking a synthetic concept like "regional/spatial planning" was the only way out, at least in the English language version. The conceptual problem persists but terminology has changed. Spatial planning is now an umbrella term. An example is Williams (1996, vii) where the author states that he uses spatial planning as a "relatively neutral and inclusive term for all the various styles and concepts of planning found in the EU, and to encompass all spatial scales from the local to the whole of Europe."

The EU Compendium also invokes spatial planning as an umbrella term, referring to "methods used largely by the public sector to influence the future distribution of activities in space. It is undertaken with the aims of creating a more rational territorial organization of land uses and the linkages between them, to balance demands for development with the need to protect the environment, and to achieve social and economic objectives. Spatial planning embraces measures to coordinate the spatial impacts of other sector policies, to achieve a more even distribution of economic development between regions than would otherwise be created by market forces, and to regulate the conversion of land and property uses" (CEC 1997a, 24).

Under the umbrella of spatial planning, the EU Compendium identifies four approaches, two of which are relevant here. The first is the comprehensive integrated approach, the same as what the Charter describes as spatial planning: a form of planning "conducted through a very systematic and formal hierarchy of plans from national to local level, which coordinate public sector activity across different sectors but focus more specifically on spatial coordination than economic development.... This tradition is necessarily associated with mature systems. It requires responsive and sophisticated planning institutions and mechanisms and considerable political commitment.... Public sector investments in bringing about the realization of the planning framework is also the norm" (CEC 1997a, 36–37). This discussion of what is involved in horizontal and vertical coordination will make clear why the term *comprehensive integrated approach* has been chosen.

The second approach is called the *regional economic approach*, which the Charter has described as regional planning. Accordingly, planning "has a very broad meaning relating to the pursuit of wide social and economic objectives, especially in relation to disparities...between different regions.... Where this approach...is dominant, central government inevitably plays an important role..." (CEC 1997a, 36). So conceived, spatial planning refers to the formulation of some form of spatial strategy, based on an overall appreciation of the national territory and how its constituent parts are positioned relative to each other and also to the wider European and/or global context.

Importantly, the competency to make a spatial plan under the comprehensive integrated approach must be defined by law. After all, regulatory measures that interfere with property rights may flow from such a plan. The formulation of a spatial strategy under the regional economic planning approach, however, does not interfere with property rights. Therefore, it requires no specific competency to be conferred upon the state administration. The competency is implied in the powers to engage in public works, grant subsidies and engage in other policies that help improve the quality of locations. Appreciating the difference between planning as the formulation of spatial strategy to underpin spatial policies, and the comprehensive integrated approach as essentially relying on regulation, is a key to understanding the ESDP process.

Spatial Development

According to Williams (1996, 48), the Dutch wanted the committee to prepare European ministerial meetings to be named the Committee on Spatial Planning. In light of the above, however, the term *spatial planning* suggests a restrictive approach to some. So *spatial development* and sometimes *spatial development policy* became the alternatives. As a consequence, the ESDP avoids the term spatial planning.

In the early 1990s a discussion was held in the U.K. about everything going under the flag of planning (Zetter 2001), which is also why the ESDP has come to be called a spatial development perspective rather than a plan. (Speculating on the future of the ESDP, John Zetter, in Chapter 9 of this volume, assumes that this decision will be reviewed, and he tries out the notion of a European spatial development strategy as an alternative.)

The term *spatial development* has been a hit, not just with the British; the Germans are also unhappy with the restrictive connotations of spatial planning as a concept. To Germans the concept of spatial development signals a new approach, combining the two main planning traditions in Europe: their own and aménagement du territoire. Fürst, Güldenberg and Müller (1994) advocate the use of spatial development policy as a neutral term combining elements of both. A working party of the German Academy for Regional

Research and Regional Planning (ARL) defines spatial development policy as one that "promotes the development of space in accordance with specific general principles...." (ARL 1996, 56–57). Promoting development is said to receive more attention than classic German planning thought. As compared to aménagement du territoire, however, there is more scope for functions and activities other than the purely economic utilization of space.

The Dutch are also embracing the concept of spatial development policy (Netherlands Scientific Council of Government Policy 1999; see also Hajer and Zonneveld 2000). The idea is for planning to become more proactive and to relate to the concerns of the real shapers of the environment, in particular, infrastructure providers. As set out above, the shift to spatial development signals a move away from regulation toward capital programs and the like. And, since the public coffers are notoriously empty, this move also indicates a willingness to engage in a public-private partnership to achieve public goals.

The ascendance of spatial development as a concept notwithstanding, spatial planning continues to be used, for example, in the Study Programme on European Spatial Planning (Nordregio 2000a) or in European Spatial Planning Observatory Network (ESPON), both co-funded by the European Commission.

The Context of European Integration

Having discussed the two main traditions of spatial planning in Europe—regulatory and strategic planning—alongside the emergent spatial development discourse, a short exposition follows on the process and institutions of European integration.

Leaving aside the Council of Europe and the European Coal and Steel Community, European integration started in earnest with the European Economic Community (EEC) established under the Treaty of Rome in 1958. The EEC has assumed new tasks, absorbed new members and restyled itself since then, first as the European Community (EC) and, finally, on 1 November 1993, as the EU, with at present 15 member states (slated to increase to perhaps 27; see Chapter 8). Strictly speaking, the EU is the roof over three pillars, of which the EC is the first and only one with real supranational powers.

Intergovernmental conferences (IGCs) are occasions for major reforms where member states thrash out compromises on European treaties. The last IGC in 2000 has taken steps to keep European institutions on an even keel, the pending accession of Central and Eastern European and Mediterranean states notwithstanding. Among its outcomes has been the decision, on German insistence, of organizing another conference in 2004 to reach a more definitive allocation of powers and responsibilities among member states and European institutions (Hüttmann and Knodt 2000). This has become a major concern germane to the competency issue in European spatial planning.

IGCs culminate in meetings of the European Council, consisting of heads of state and government, which meets on other occasions as well. Summits are held every six months, drawing attention as the high points of EU presidencies that member states hold for six-month terms each.

The best-known European institution is the European Commission, which features the "Eurocrats" at Brussels, seat of the Commission. Their number is surprisingly small, "barely matching the number of administrators of Cologne" (Pond 2000, 9). Currently, they are organized into 24 Directorates General (DGs) and a number of horizontal services, like the Secretariat General. In addition, there are the secretariats of other European institutions, in particular the Council of Ministers, and the administration of the European Parliament meeting at Strasbourg and Brussels, and the European Court of Justice at Luxembourg. There are also special agencies throughout Europe.

A few of the DGs are relevant to spatial planning in that they pursue the spatial policies mentioned. The most important DG deals with regional policy that relates to the "structural funds" good for approximately one-third of EC spending. This DG, called DG XVI (regional policy and cohesion) or latterly DG Regio, is responsible for the Commission input into the ESDP process. References to the Commission mean a small group of Commission officials working in Section A1, called "conception and analysis, regional impact and spatial planning." This in turn is part of Directorate A: "conception, impact, coordination and evaluation of regional policies" of DG Regio.

Next to referring to the Eurocrats, the other meaning attached to the European Commission is that of the College of Commissioners forming the EU "core executive" (Hix 1999, 32), the closest thing to a European government. Unlike governments in democratic states, however, the Commission is not elected by the European Parliament, but is appointed by the member states, admittedly with the European Parliament having some say in the matter. Whether the Commission will ever come close to resembling a democratic government is for the future to tell.

Now the discussion touches upon the pattern of interaction—also called the *Community method*—between the major institutions of the EU. Thus, Community law is adopted, not by the European Parliament (as the analogy with democratic states would suggest) but by the Council of Ministers representing the governments of the member states. As with the appointment of the European Commission under the co-decision procedure, however, the European Parliament now has a say in the matter.

Importantly, the European Commission has the exclusive right of initiative, an important feature of the Community method for EU decision making. Thus, nothing comes before the Council of Ministers, let alone the European Parliament, unless the Commission has proposed it, which makes comparison with national governments even more precarious.

Clearly, the extent and direction of European integration and the positions of European institutions are contested issues. This forms the backdrop for the struggle over European spatial planning. There are the institutions articulating the positions of member states and those representing the forces of integration. The institutions that favor maintaining member state control want to strengthen the former, while those favoring more integration want to strengthen the latter.

First of all, member states call the shots at the European Council, which lays down the main lines of policy. Community law, as such, is adopted by the Council of Ministers. The Council comes in many forms and shapes; in one of its permutations it is almost continuously in session. Voting takes place either unanimously, giving each member state—however large or small, ranging from approximately 80 million to somewhat more than 400,000—the same weight. The alternative is called *qualified majority voting*, a complicated system under which member states, but never two large member states combined, can be overruled.

If the EC, also referred to the Community, had a spatial planning competency, then, on the recommendation of the Commission, the Council in one of its permutations could adopt guidelines or directives, being two forms of Community legislation. Once adopted they would become part of the *acquis communautaire*, a body of Community law for which there is no English term. (Each and every new member state must subscribe to the whole package, running to 80,000 pages, which is why accession taxes the capacities of those concerned.) The Council concerned with spatial planning would also provide an arena for the discussion of European planning matters. In Chapter 9 John Zetter assumes that in due course a regional policy council will be established to take charge of spatial planning, among other issues.

The institutions just discussed are said to represent the intergovernmental element in EU decision making. Other European institutions—the European Commission, the European Parliament and the European Court of Justice—represent the forces of integration. The European Commission, in particular, has the right of initiative. Proactive commissions interpret this as an institutional brief to accelerate the process of European integration (Ross 1995).

One common reflex is to favor strengthening the institutions representing the forces of integration, in particular the European Parliament, the latter to mitigate what is often called the "democratic deficit" in the EU, at least as measured against the standards prevailing in nation states. The underlying assumption is that the EU is a polity. Taking this idea to its logical conclusion would mean that less populous member states would carry less weight than is the case now, at a time when the number of seats in the European Parliament and the number of votes on the Council of Ministers are loaded in their favor. The issue is how a democratic one-person-one-vote system may be reconciled with the rights of territorially defined minorities, as in the U.S., where each state, however large or small, has two senators. Indeed, there have been suggestions to turn the Council of Ministers into something like a senate (and the Committee of the Regions into a third chamber), but so far to no avail. The greatest question is whether the EU will, or indeed should, take the path toward statehood, or whether it represents something altogether different, something unprecedented, and for which the concepts to understand it are still elusive. The concluding chapter in this book pursues these issues further.

European Spatial Planning

Against this backdrop, what could European spatial planning mean? Planning initiated by the European Commission (perhaps prepared by a commissioner for spatial planning), with proposals subject to approval by the Council of Ministers? If so, then—as in all Community matters, via their ministers representing them on the Council—member states would still have the ultimate voice; however, this is sheer speculation. So far European spatial planning has been a matter of voluntary cooperation among member states. This form of European spatial planning has been dubbed intergovernmental.

The reader should note that *intergovernmental* here takes on the altogether different meaning of keeping spatial planning outside the bounds of Community decision making. The reason for doing so is the persistent suggestion that giving the Community a spatial planning competency would remove planning from member states' control. From the above discussion, however, it should be clear that this would not be the case. Admittedly, if spatial planning were to be subject to qualified majority voting, individual member states could be overruled. Also, the Commission would have a role in implementing whatever Community directive or regulation might be issued. The Council of Ministers representing member states, however, would remain responsible.

Whether or not this should occur, what is important here is the distinction between regulatory and strategic planning. Existing state formations have assumed powers of land use regulation. In the U.S., zoning ordinances rest on the legal powers of the state, and Europe has similar arrangements. If European spatial planning were to be regulatory, it would be placed squarely in the context of the contested pattern of relations between member states and the EC. After all, member states would have to relinquish some of their powers to regulate land use.

The above is not the vision of the early proponents of European spatial planning (some of them French). Rather, from the outset they have seen planning as formulating spatial strategy, in the first instance to underpin policy regarding the structural funds. So the competency issue does not arise. After all, under French aménagement du territoire it does not arise either. The point is that experts from other member states steeped in the comprehensive integrated approach understand spatial planning to be regulatory. They also hold that spatial planning must remain a prerogative of the member states. After all, *territoriality* (the control over a well-defined area of land) is one of the defining characteristics of nation states (see Chapter 10). This is why, in ways that will become clear when the ESDP process is described, the competency issue has arisen.

Although published by the Office for Official Publications of the European Communities at Luxembourg, the ESDP is not a Community document, but one based on voluntary cooperation of member states—it remains outside the Community competencies. Nevertheless, the European Commission has had a hand in preparing the ESDP, perhaps with the expectation that in time a spatial planning function would come its way.

The ESDP Process

What follows is a brief outline of the ESDP process. (For a fuller account, see Faludi and Waterhout 2002). Informal meetings of the ministers of the member states responsible for spatial planning have been the high marks in the process. For reference purposes, Table 1 summarizes the venues and topics of these meetings.

The process began in 1989 with a ministerial meeting called by the French Presidency at Nantes. Present was the Commissioner for Regional Policy and the Commission President, Jacques Delors. Strategic spatial planning suited his program of turning the Commission into a strategic actor spearheading European integration. In a speech, Delors alluded to the need for a spatial vision.

Shortly thereafter, a French expert joined DG XVI, who, with a colleague on loan from The Netherlands, became responsible for spearheading Commission planning initiatives. Meanwhile, the European Regional Development Fund (ERDF), the largest of the structural funds, made funding available for preparing what would eventually become the Europe 2000 (CEC 1991) and Europe 2000+ documents (CEC 1994).

The reason the meeting at Nantes (like all meetings thereafter) was an informal affair is said to be that there is no Community competency for spatial planning. The initial meetings, however, consisted of ministers responsible for regional policy and planning. A Community competency for regional policy does exist, but foreign ministers and ministers of economic affairs and of finance want to keep tabs on this second largest spender of Community funds. This is why the French planning minister was prevented from calling a formal meeting, not because there is no Community competency. A lack of spatial planning competency was never the issue.

The Italians organized a followup in 1990, as did the Dutch in 1991, when the Committee on Spatial Development (CSD) was set up. At this time the

☐—TABLE **1**
Venues, Dates and Topics Discussed at Gatherings, 1989–1999

Venue	Date	Topic
Nantes	1989	Start-up
Turin	1990	Uneven development
The Hague	1991	Urban networks, set up Committee on Spatial Development (CSD)
Lisbon	1992	Trans-European Networks (TENs), spatial vision
Liège	1993	Go-ahead for ESDP; member states propose Interreg IIC
Corfu	1994	Working methods
Leipzig	1994	Leipzig Principles
Strasbourg	1995	Scenarios; Commission set to launch Interreg IIC
Madrid	1995	Indicators; start of Interreg IIC
Venice	1996	Commitment to finish ESDP
Noordwijk	1997	First official draft of ESDP
Glasgow	1998	First complete draft of ESDP
Potsdam	1999	The ESDP

Germans were alerted to Commission intentions and started a campaign for European spatial planning as an intergovernmental function. It is important to remember that the Germans conceive of spatial planning as regulatory and embedded in a hierarchical system, emphasizing the level of the *Länder,* the 16 states forming the Federal Republic of Germany.

Federal planning in Germany had long been in the shadow of the Länder, but after German unification some form of overall planning was undertaken. The arena was that of a Standing Conference of Ministers responsible for regional planning, comprising 16 Länder ministers and the federal minister responsible for planning. This resulted in the Guidelines for Regional Policy (Federal Ministry for Regional Planning, Building and Urban Development 1993). German planners wanted to see European spatial planning evolve along similar lines of voluntary cooperation. A more general presumption is expressed by Alfred Gomolka, one-time president of the *Bundesrat*, the upper house of the German Parliament representing the Länder. This presumption, which continues to be a powerful motive of German policy toward the EU, is that German federalism "can be a very useful model for cooperation within the European Community…" (Weigall and Stirk 1992, 194).

By the time the Guidelines for Regional Policy were being prepared, the European Commission had already published *Europe 2000*, so the Guidelines spelled out the German response. Accepting that the Community had specific competencies to intervene in spatial development, they argued against these powers being extended to cover spatial planning. "Endeavors to lay down comprehensive rules and codes for regional policy at the European level must be rejected. Instead, the European regional policy concept, that is, the ESDP, must support the multifarious forces in the individual national and regions, promoting and coordinating cooperation between them at the same time. What we need is not a new super-planning concept on a European scale but the flexible further development of the various forms of coordination" (Federal Ministry for Regional Planning, Building and Urban Development 1993, 20).

By conceptualizing spatial planning as regulatory, the Germans raised the competency issue. And as soon as European spatial planning was conceived in such terms, there was widespread agreement that it should not be a Community competency. Had the issue continued to be framed in French terms, as a formulation of strategy to underpin the delivery of the structural funds and other Community policies, the question of a competency would not have arisen. The Community already had the competency for regional policy, and formulating a spatial strategy could only improve on its transparency and effectiveness. Article 10 of the 1988 regulations governing the European Regional Development Fund allowed the Commission to prepare a prospective scheme for the development of the Community territory and the documents of the Commission, called Europe 2000 and Europe 2000+, were prepared under this provision.

The Germans, above all some of the Länder, do not appreciate the Community role in regional policy, because it imposes restrictions on German policy. Even in the sense of formulating strategy to underpin its regional policy, Community planning would probably have been anathema to some Germans. This is not, however, how the issue was framed; rather, it was framed in terms of control over territory.

This is also why, when the ministers of the member states agreed to form the CSD in 1991, it was decided that the member state holding the rotating European Presidency would chair it. Usually, the Commission would chair the untold number of Brussels committees, so the Commission did not savor this decision, but it acquiesced. The CSD even got the use of facilities extended to ordinary "comitology" committees chaired by the Commission. The Commission also footed the bill for the expenses of a two-member delegation per member state (Faludi, Zonneveld and Waterhout 2000).

As far as the ESDP was concerned, the turning point came in 1993, when, at Liège ministers heeded the call of the Belgian Presidency for such a document. It also asked for Community support for transnational planning, which eventually resulted in the successful Interreg IIC Community Initiative. With the experiences of preparing their Guidelines for Regional Policy accomplished, the Germans hoped to see the ESDP—which they saw as the Guidelines writ large—adopted during their presidency in 1994. They got no further than having the Leipzig Principles accepted and named after the venue of the meeting. In hindsight, it is clear that the principles have been constitutive for the ESDP.

A second French Presidency introduced scenarios in 1995, but national elections stalled the effort. Perceiving the ESDP as a threat to their allocation from the structural funds (of which Spain is the greatest beneficiary), the Spanish Presidency treaded water. At the meeting in Madrid a new Commissioner for Regional Policy sought to straighten out the competency issue by suggesting that spatial planning be seen as implied in the twin goals of the European treaties of economic and social cohesion. Neither this proposal nor the German view (that, once adopted, an intergovernmental ESDP should form a guideline for Community spatial policies) would receive much hearing at the IGC that followed (Selke 1999), so the competency issue remained on the table.

Member states in Madrid warmly received a Commission proposal for a Community Initiative called Interreg IIC which was to co-finance transnational planning efforts. The idea had already been mooted at Liège and discussed at Strasbourg. Money was available, so member states saw no reason to object.

A meeting in Venice took the ESDP process out of the doldrums. At Noordwijk in 1997 the Dutch gained approval for a first official draft (CEC 1997b) to be followed, under the 1998 U.K. Presidency, by the (unpublished) first complete draft. Putting the finishing touches on the work fell to the Germans, and thus, ministers came to accept the ESDP at Potsdam in 1999. However, no vote was taken; the German Presidency simply noted that the process had come to its conclusion. As the ESDP is at pains to emphasize, it is not binding on either the Community or the member states; rather, application of the ESDP is voluntary.

Now that the ESDP is on the books, the Commission appears to be claiming a stronger leadership role. By setting up a working group on spatial and urban development under the Committee on the Development and Conversion of the Regions (which manages regional policy funds), the Commission has brought spatial development into the comitology system via the back door. As chair of this working group, the Commission is able largely to determine the agenda. The CSD continues to operate with two specific tasks that cannot be brought into the comitology: as a forum for discussions with the candidate member states and as a committee for setting up and preparing the European Spatial Planning Observatory Network (ESPON) program. The Commission uses the working group to discuss the integration of the spatial development approach into future structural policies; to elaborate on notions it has introduced, such as *territorial cohesion* (CEC 2000a, 2001; see also Husson 2000; Faludi and Peyrony 2001); and/or *integrated territorial management* (CEC 2000b) as functional equivalents to spatial planning. Connotations of regulatory planning—and with this, the competency issue—are studiously avoided.

Will this action amount to planning being dominated by the Commission? Even in policy areas where there is a formal Community competency, the Commission involves experts from member states. In Chapter 5, Ole Jensen refers to Weiler describing the resulting form of governance as *infranational*. Given the set-up—with the Commission having the right of initiative and member states on the Council of Ministers having the ultimate say, thus requiring consensus—it could hardly be otherwise (Christiansen and Kirchner 2000, 10). The personnel capacity of the Commission is quite small, so, if for no other reason than its dependence on experts from the member states, the Commission would always cooperate with them.

More fundamentally, European decision making always involves a mix of supranational and intergovernmental elements. So the idea that people in the ESDP process appeared to react to—that is, a master plan being imposed from Brussels—is a chimera (Faludi and Waterhout 2002). Perhaps this insight will take hold at some point in the future. Granting the Community limited competency (Martin 2000) would pave the way for European spatial planning to continue as a mixed intergovernmental and communautarian enterprise.

Overview of This Book

This book is divided into four sections: the practice of European spatial planning; various theoretical approaches to its analysis and outcome; the future of the ESDP process; and conclusions, in which the editor seeks to interpret European spatial planning in the light of the literature on European integration.

Chapter 2, "Influencing the Development of European Spatial Planning," is by Derek Martin, head of international affairs at the Dutch National Spatial Planning Agency, and Jacques Robert, a consultant based at Strasbourg. They cover various facets of the development of European spatial planning from expert-led attempts to explore its meaning to the current state of affairs, when politicians are reining in the experts and asserting their leadership role in the process.

One of the main avenues for following the ESDP is the Interreg IIC Community Initiative for transnational planning, currently in the process of being superseded by a similar but wider Community Initiative for transnational cooperation, called Interreg IIIB. Philippe Doucet was a key actor at Liège and subsequently worked as a national expert on loan at the commission. He is now program manager of one of the Interreg programs. In Chapter 3, he reports on "Transnational Planning in the Wake of the ESDP: The Northwest Europe Experience." He also discusses earlier examples of transnational planning in Northwest Europe and the transition from Interreg IIC to Interreg IIIB, including the shifting philosophy behind it, the procedures and the delineation of the area now described as Northwest Europe.

Section Two, "Theorizing European Spatial Planning," opens with Chapter 4, "Polycentric Development: What Is Behind It?" Bas Waterhout, from the University of Nijmegen in The Netherlands, lays bare the assumptions about the substantive policies in the ESDP. He shows that polycentricity is a bridging concept which, in the end, if only for different reasons, all member states could accept. In this sense, it is the most characteristic and most overarching of the concepts invoked in the ESDP.

In Chapter 5, "Imagining European Identity: Discourses Underlying the European Spatial Development Perspective," Ole Jensen from the University of Aalborg in Denmark explores the notion of discourse analysis. He also refers to one of ESDP's follow-ups, NorVISION, the acronym for the spatial vision for the North Sea Area (a parallel document to the spatial vision for the Northwestern Metropolitan Area (NWMA) discussed by Philippe Doucet and also by Vincent Nadin). According to Jensen, the new discourse is based on a complex composite of rationales. The explicit rationales address global urban competition, environmental sustainability and social equity (spatial justice). The implicit rationale is that of re-imagining Europe as a spatial entity with a distinct identity.

In Chapter 6, "Visions and Visioning in European Spatial Planning," Vincent Nadin, a senior researcher at the University of the West of England, explores the notion, often invoked in European spatial planning, of a spatial vision. The point of departure here is the spatial vision project for the Northwestern Metropolitan Area, in which the author has been involved. He shows that this and other visions are not as visionary as they were intended to be.

In Chapter 7, "How to Reduce the Burden of Coordination in European Spatial Planning," Arthur Benz, a political scientist from the University of Hagen in Germany, analyzes decision making on and application of the ESDP as a multilevel process. He asks how the demands on coordination can be brought back to manageable proportions. Coordination must focus on core issues and invoke procedures that allow one to arrive at conclusions, the multitude of actors involved notwithstanding. The chapter discusses selective coordination, and coordination that leaves the autonomy of policy makers at national and regional levels intact. It considers issue-specific positive coordination (simultaneous decisions taken on different policies); negative coordination (policy being checked only for negative external effects); coordination by communication (ideas, arguments) and standards; as well as the use of incentives and benchmarking.

Section Three, "The Future of European Spatial Planning," begins with Chapter 8, "The European Union and its Frontiers: Toward New Cooperation Areas for Spatial Planning," by Jean-François Drevet, a senior Commission official from the Directorate General Regio. He discusses the challenges posed by the shifting and uncertain borders of the EU, and points out that in pursuit of policies as set out in 1993 the EU will see successive waves of enlargement. He discusses the cobweb of cooperation arrangements necessary to prepare countries for accession or to provide substitute arrangements, the goal being the stabilization of the EU environment.

John Zetter, now of University College, London, but formerly the head of the British delegation to the CSD and the CSD chairman for a time, speculates in Chapter 9 on "Spatial Planning in the European Union: A Vision of 2010." In ways that defy summarizing, he backtracks from a meeting of planning ministers at Nicosia, Cyprus (now one of the accession states) purported to be taking place eight years from now. The account of how spatial planning might fare in the years to come, by someone who has been centrally involved in the process, casts light on current difficulties and how they might be resolved.

The concluding chapter, "Spatial Planning and European Integration," by the editor, uses a standard work on European integration, *The Government and Politics of the European Union* (Nugent 1999), as a guide to the complex literature on the subject. This literature often presents positions as polar opposites, such as functionalists putting great store in the forces of integration on one hand and realists emphasizing the dominance of nation states in the process on the other. A growing body of literature, however, analyzes the workings of European institutions and takes a middle ground, invoking concepts that planning writers are more accustomed to, such as networks, discourses and governance. The small but growing academic literature on the creation and application of the ESDP also uses such concepts. From a review of the relevant literature, including the contributions in this volume, the concluding chapter formulates an agenda for reflection and research on European spatial planning.

This introductory chapter concludes with an introduction to "Images of Europe Tell Their Own Story" and a full-color insert of maps organized by topical sections. The maps are reproduced in the respective chapters where they are referenced.

Images of Europe Tell Their Own Story

Maps are the bread and butter of almost any kind of spatial planning. Paradoxically, so far mapmaking has proven one of the most difficult aspects of European spatial planning. There are several reasons for this. One of them is that, as this book shows, European spatial planning is still in its infancy and searching for the most suitable approach. The second reason follows from the first: there is no such thing as a European spatial planner. The planners involved come from various planning traditions that may use and interpret maps differently. A third reason is that policy maps are particularly sensitive because they are clearer than verbal expressions of policy. Where the latter can make use of vague concepts subject to multiple interpretations, the former demand a higher degree of consensus. As a result, notwithstanding several attempts to produce them (see Chapter 4, this volume; Faludi and Waterhout 2002), the ESDP as such does not contain policy maps. Spatial planning without maps, however, is difficult to conceive. Thus, in the wake of the ESDP process, individuals or organizations or even (transnational) combinations of organizations have produced relevant European spatial planning maps.

This insert offers a selection of maps produced in and around the ESDP process and tells the story of European spatial planning through the backdrop, the problems and challenges planners see and the ways they try to give shape to new policies. All maps have been suggested by the authors and are cited in their chapters. The chapter or chapters that cite each map are referenced under the illustration. The insert is divided into sections, each section devoted to a particular subject and containing between two and five maps, mostly placed in chronological order of appearance.

"Images of the EU" contains maps featuring the basics of the EU. It acts as a point of reference.

"Conceptualizing the EU Territory: Evolution" illustrates how the EU has been perceived, or conceptualized, by planners throughout the years. It shows an evolution of thinking about Europe's spatial organization, first as a center with a periphery and then as a more diversified and balanced "Europe of regions," with each region having its own strengths and weaknesses. By giving normative interpretations of Europe, the maps in this section aim primarily at shaping the mental maps of actors. In so doing, they are less factual than the maps in the first section. Or rather, they are based on a set of facts deliberately chosen in order to be able to make a statement. It is these conceptualizations of Europe that form the object of political struggle.

"Dividing the EU into Transnational Areas" deals with the division of Europe into transnational cooperation areas formed mainly to accommodate the initiatives taken by the European Commission to stimulate spatial planning at a transnational level.

"ESDP: Global Economic Integration Zones in the EU and the U.S." contains "Maps of the ESDP." Of course, the maps themselves cannot be found in the ESDP. Rather certain individuals have made them after the approval of the ESDP. In doing so, these individuals have tried to visualize the main rationale behind the ESDP.

The maps in "The EU of the Future?" can be seen as policy scenarios or followup actions of the ESDP trying to give shape to the verbal vision expressed in the ESDP. Although they are not completely imaginary, the maps have no pretensions to represent reality. Rather they aim to provide a challenging contribution to the debate on the future of Europe and the role of spatial planning in it.

"Cooperation Areas Across EU Boundaries" contains maps showing the existing cooperation areas with partners from amongst both the EU member states and the accession states. Cooperation in these areas is likely to contribute to achieving one of the future scenarios presented in the previous section.

"Pioneering in Northwest Europe" deals with policy maps from various types of transnational cooperation in the part of Europe where policy makers are most used to working with such maps and have thus been able to agree upon them.

Images of the EU

─FIGURE **A1**
A Framework for Comparison

Source: CEC (1999, 55)

─FIGURE **A2**
Representing the European Union Territory

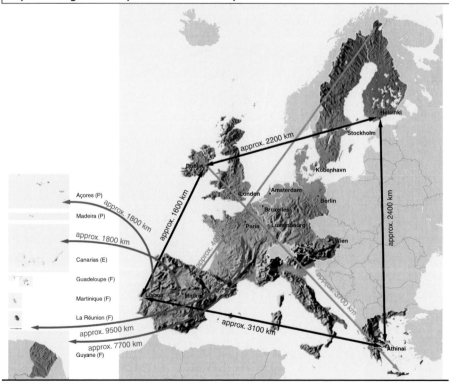

Source: CEC (1999, 56)
See Chapter 5

FIGURE **A3**
Future EU Enlargements

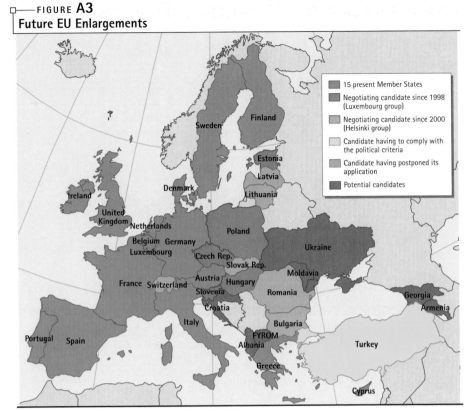

Courtesy of CEC
See Chapter 8

Conceptualizing the EU Territory: Evolution

□──FIGURE **A4**
Three Spatial Conceptualizations of Europe

Source: RPD (1978)
See Chapters 2 and 4

FIGURE **A5**
The Blue Banana Indicating the (Core) Area with Most Cities with More than 200.000 Inhabitants

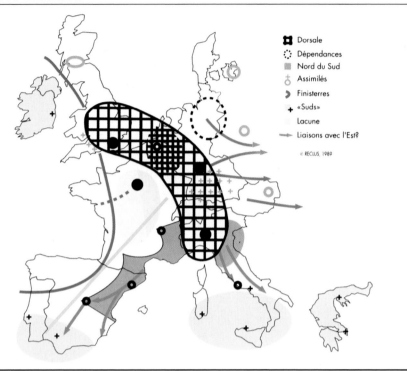

Source: Brunet (1989)
See Chapters 2 and 4

FIGURE **A6**
The Bunch of Grapes Representing a Diversified View of the EU

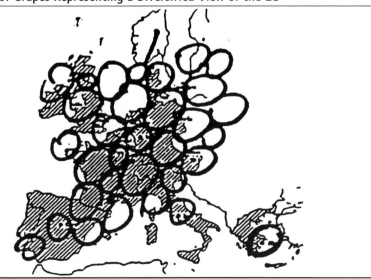

Source: Kunzmann & Wegener (1991)
See Chapter 4

Dividing the EU into Transnational Areas

□─FIGURE **A7**
The Transnational Areas of the Europe 2000 Program 1990–1993

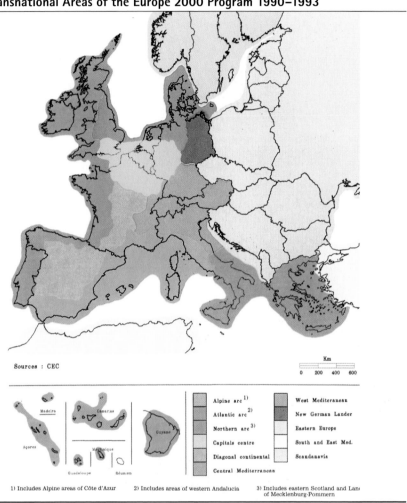

Sources : CEC

Km
0   200   400   600

Alpine arc [1]	West Mediterranean
Atlantic arc [2]	New German Lander
Northern arc [3]	Eastern Europe
Capitals centre	South and East Med.
Diagonal continental	Scandanavia
Central Mediterranean	

1) Includes Alpine areas of Côte d'Azur   2) Includes areas of western Andalucia   3) Includes eastern Scotland and Land of Mecklenburg-Pommern

Source: CEC (1991)
See Chapter 2

FIGURE **A8**
Interreg IIC Cooperation Areas

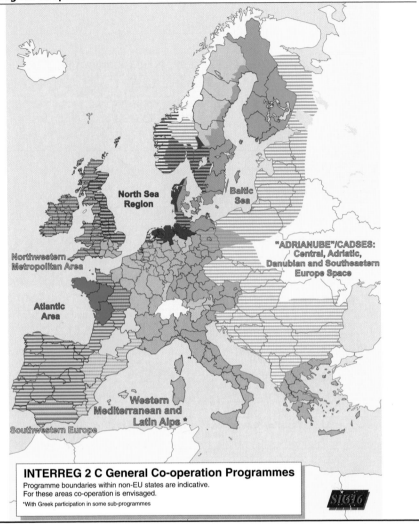

INTERREG 2 C General Co-operation Programmes

Programme boundaries within non-EU states are indicative.
For these areas co-operation is envisaged.

*With Greek participation in some sub-programmes

Courtesy of CEC
See Chapters 2 and 3

─FIGURE **A9**
Transnational Pilot Actions: Cooperation Areas

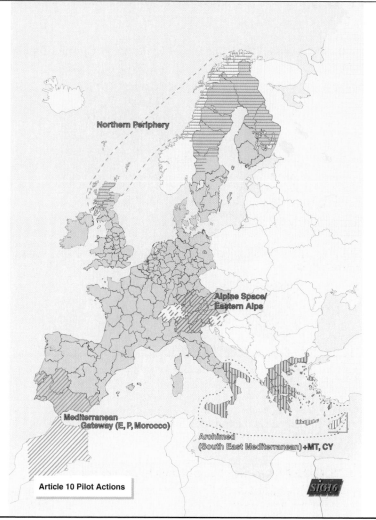

Courtesy of CEC
See Chapter 3

ESDP: Global Economic Integration Zones in the EU and the U.S.

FIGURE **A10**

The "20-40-50 Pentagon," Just One Global Economic Integration Zone in the EU...

Source: Schön (2000)

See Chapter 4

FIGURE **A11**

...Compared with Four Global Economic Integration Zones in the U.S.

Global integration zones in the USA

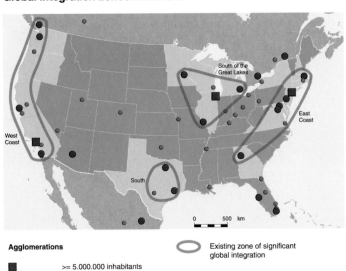

Source: Mehlbye (2000, 757)

See Chapter 4

The EU of the Future?

FIGURE **A12**
Possible Development of New Global Economic Integration Zones

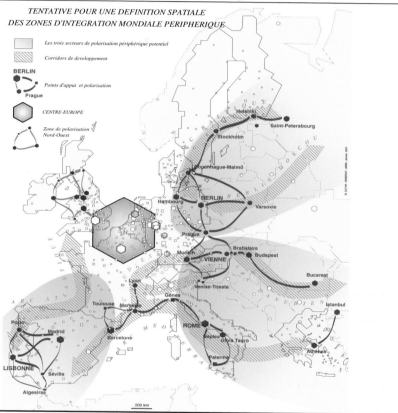

Source: French Presidency (2000b); Guigou (2002)

See Chapter 4

—FIGURE **A13**
Europe as a Collection of Transnational Cooperation Areas in Order to Achieve a Better Urban Balance

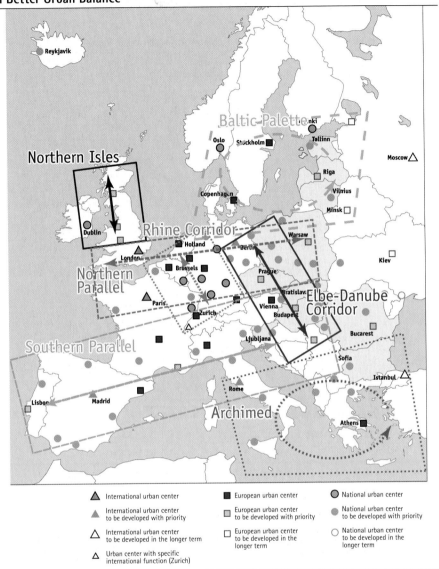

▲ International urban center	■ European urban center	● National urban center
▲ International urban center to be developed with priority	▢ European urban center to be developed with priority	● National urban center to be developed with priority
△ International urban center to be developed in the longer term	☐ European urban center to be developed in the longer term	○ National urban center to be developed in the longer term
△ Urban center with specific international function (Zurich)		

Source: Read (2000, 741)

See Chapter 4

□——FIGURE **A14**

An Invitation to Metropolitan Areas to Cooperate

New European Zones of Metropolitan Cooperation?

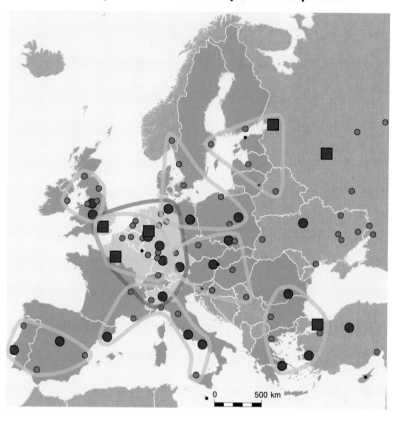

0   500 km

Agglomerations

■   >= 5.000.000 inh.

●   2.000.000 - < 5.000.000 inh.

●   750.000 - < 2.000.000 inh.

•   Smaller capital cities in
      EU Member States and in
      Accession Countries

○   New global integration zones?

○   Existing zone of significant
    global integration

Source for the agglomeration data:
Population Division of the Department of Economic and
Social Affairs of the United Nations Secretariat (1998):
World Urbanization Prospects: The 1999 Revision

Source: Mehlbye (2000, 759)

See Chapter 4

Cooperation Areas Across EU Boundaries

Transnational Cooperation Areas with Partners Outside the EU

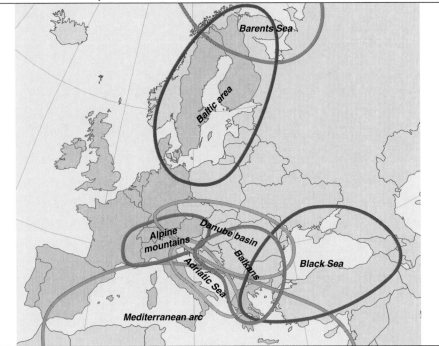

Courtesy of CEC
See Chapters 2 and 8

FIGURE A16
Typology of Border Areas in Central Europe

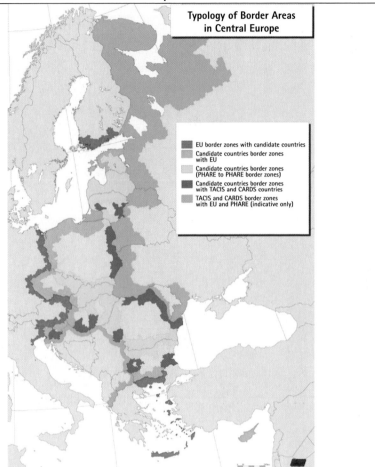

Typology of Border Areas
in Central Europe

EU border zones with candidate countries

Candidate countries border zones
with EU

Candidate countries border zones
(PHARE to PHARE border zones)

Candidate countries border zones
with TACIS and CARDS countries

TACIS and CARDS border zones
with EU and PHARE (indicative only)

Courtesy of CEC
See Chapter 8

Pioneering in Northwest Europe

FIGURE **A17**

Areas of Cross-Border and Transnational Cooperation in Northwest Europe

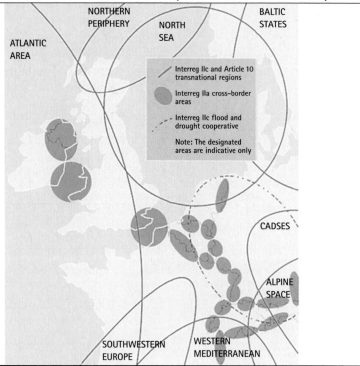

Source: NWMA Spatial Vision Group (2000, 6)

See Chapter 6

FIGURE **A18**

Representing the North Sea Region

Source: VWG (2000b, 14)

See Chapter 5

┌─ FIGURE **A19**
CCC Study: Policy Scenario

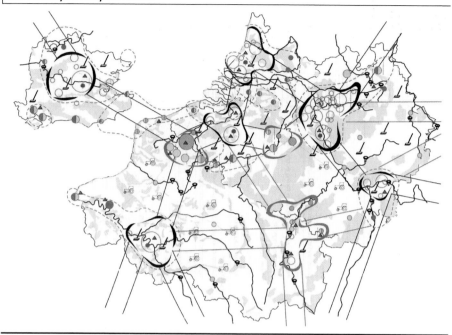

Source: CEC (1996a)
See Chapter 3

┌─ FIGURE **A20**
Second Benelux Structural Outline

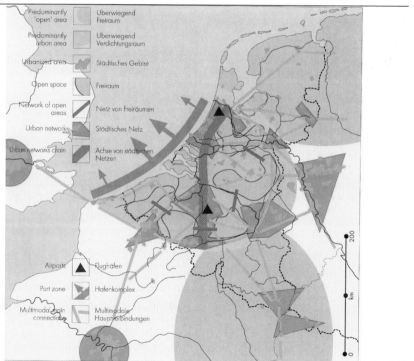

Source: UEB (1997)
See Chapter 3

FIGURE **A21**
A Vision for Northwest Europe: Spatial Vision Diagram

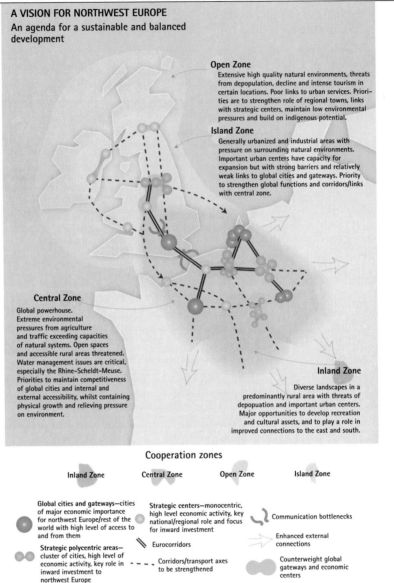

A VISION FOR NORTHWEST EUROPE
An agenda for a sustainable and balanced
development

Open Zone
Extensive high quality natural environments, threats
from depopulation, decline and intense tourism in
certain locations. Poor links to urban services. Priorities are to strengthen role of regional towns, links
with strategic centers, maintain low environmental
pressures and build on indigenous potential.

Island Zone
Generally urbanized and industrial areas with
pressure on surrounding natural environments.
Important urban centers have capacity for
expansion but with strong barriers and relatively
weak links to global cities and gateways. Priority
to strengthen global functions and corridors/links
with central zone.

Central Zone
Global powerhouse.
Extreme environmental
pressures from agriculture
and traffic exceeding capacities
of natural systems. Open spaces
and accessible rural areas threatened.
Water management issues are critical,
especially the Rhine-Scheldt-Meuse.
Priorities to maintain competitiveness
of global cities and internal and
external accessibility, whilst containing
physical growth and relieving pressure
on environment.

Inland Zone
Diverse landscapes in a
predominantly rural area with threats of
depopuation and important urban centers.
Major opportunities to develop recreation
and cultural assets, and to play a role in
improved connections to the east and south.

Cooperation zones

Inland Zone   Central Zone   Open Zone   Island Zone

Global cities and gateways—cities
of major economic importance
for northwest Europe/rest of the
world with high level of access to
and from them

Strategic centers—monocentric,
high level economic activity, key
national/regional role and focus
for inward investment

Communication bottlenecks

Strategic polycentric areas—
cluster of cities, high level of
economic activity, key role in
inward investment to
northwest Europe

Eurocorridors

Enhanced external
connections

Corridors/transport axes
to be strengthened

Counterweight global
gateways and economic
centers

Source: NWMA Spatial Vision Group (2000, 30)
See Chapters 3 and 6

Influencing the Development of European Spatial Planning

Derek Martin and Jacques Robert

European spatial planning has not been a chance development. It has been determined, rather, by the growing needs for forms of planning at the international level during the gradual postwar process of European integration. The internationalization of planning issues has taken place in the wake of the gradual breakdown of nationalistic barriers to trade and the creation of the Single European Market. This economic integration has led, in turn, to a far slower, more hesitant process of political integration. Because of this inherent link to the political process, the development of European spatial planning has been gradual, unpredictable and unplanned, but nevertheless to an important degree determined by political decision making at strategic moments. During those relatively long periods between the moments of political decisions, however, experts from both within (civil servants) and outside (consultants, researchers, academics) the formal decision-making process have been able to exert their influence on the development of European spatial planning. The main distinction between external and internal experts is the relative freedom of the former to produce new ideas and information on the basis of (more or less) objective criteria, and the obligation of the latter to work within political constraints and toward political goals.

The aim of this chapter is to demonstrate the influence of these two types of experts on the development of European spatial planning. It is a story of some 30 years of developing different ideas from different national planning traditions and politico-cultural attitudes toward European cooperation. During that time, the political implications gradually became stronger, the political reins were pulled tighter and the room for experts, particularly external experts, to maneuver to create ideas became slowly more restricted as they were brought more and more into a political framework.

The Institutional Framework

Europe is a complex phenomenon, consisting of a multitude of different governmental and nongovernmental institutions. European spatial planning has taken shape largely within two European institutions, the Council of Europe and the European Community, now the European Union (EU), and within the framework of national and regional governments working together within the context of European integration.

The Council of Europe is an intergovernmental institution set up in 1949 in Strasbourg, France, first and foremost to defend and promote democracy and human rights in Europe. Intergovernmental cooperation within the Council of Europe expanded in the 1960s and 1970s to cover many social and local government issues associated with human rights, including nature protection and regional/spatial planning. Its budget is minimal and its activities restricted largely to organizing conferences and seminars, financing studies and issuing pan-European conventions, for example, on human rights and nature protection. With the breakup of the Soviet empire and the emergence of the new democracies of Central and Eastern Europe, it has expanded to more than 40 members and has regained some of its original role.

The European Community, now the EU, was set up in 1958. The EU has a huge budget to finance a range of highly expensive, supranational policies, in particular agriculture and social-economic structural policies, which, together with other less financially consuming policies such as transport/infrastructure and environment, have considerable spatial impact on European society. The development of the EU out of the European Community in the 1990s symbolized an intensification of cooperation among its present 15 member states.

Within the context of European integration, many countries, regions and local communities work together across international boundaries, sometimes individually and sometimes within the framework of associations of national (e.g., Benelux, Nordic and Alpine countries) and regional or local authorities (e.g., Assembly of the Regions of Europe, Association of European Border Regions, Conference of Peripheral Maritime Regions).

These institutions and organizations represent the main playing field for both the external and internal experts in developing European spatial planning. Their relative importance has changed over the last 30 years (see Table 1), with the Council of Europe being highly influential in the 1970s, and the EU taking over as European spatial planning became more political and policy-oriented

TABLE **1**
Involvement of Various Types of Institutions

	Council of Europe	European Union	Associations of Authorities
Exploring virgin territory	++	−−	+
Emerging political context	0	−	+
Tightening political reins	−	++	+

++ = very significant; + = significant; 0 = neutral; − = insignificant; −− = very insignificant in the second half of the 1990s. Associations of national, regional and local authorities have shown a consistent involvement throughout the 30 years.

As reflected in Table 1, this chapter introduces a three-phase model to describe the development of European spatial planning during this period:

☐ Exploring virgin territory in the 1970s;

☐ The slowly emerging political context during the 1980s and early 1990s;

☐ The tightening of political reins and the beginning of the influence of spatial planning on European policies.

It is within this model that this chapter analyses the role and influence of external and internal experts.

Exploring Virgin Territory

Although there was some interest for the cross-border and international aspects of planning as early as the mid-1950s,[1] particularly within a small circle of Benelux and German planners, the development of European spatial planning began at the end of the 1960s. At that time the first cross-border planning commissions were set up among the Benelux countries and the old Federal Republic of Germany. These densely populated and relatively more developed parts of Europe were confronted with the greatest need for international cooperation in spatial planning. The same period also witnessed a growing interest in other European countries. The time was ripe for exchanges of experience and discussions on different aspects, including the cross-border aspect, of spatial planning. This was also the time when member states of the Council of Europe decided to set up a European Conference of Ministers responsible for Regional Planning (CEMAT), with the Federal German government holding the first CEMAT conference in Bonn in 1970.

For many years thereafter, European spatial planning remained virgin territory with total freedom for "the expert" to explore European spatial planning. The results were then the subject of exchanges of ideas at conferences and bilateral meetings among politicians from neighboring countries. Such exchanges probably influenced planning practice in the different European countries, but they had no implications for planning policies at the European level.

Exploring Themes: Pioneer Activities Within the Council of Europe

The 1970s and early 1980s were characterized by seminars, conferences, studies and other forms of intergovernmental cooperation, inspired, above all, by the Council of Europe. The relatively low financial and political status of the Council of Europe made the working climate favorable for the production of objective, innovative and forward-looking information and concepts by experts.

During the 1970s four CEMAT meetings were organized under the auspices of the Council of Europe. The first Bonn conference in 1970 laid down the fundamental principles of planning at the European level and identified major European regions requiring different international approaches: moun-

---

[1] The Conference of Regions of Northwest Europe (CRONWE) was the most noteworthy early association in the 1950s (see also Chapters 3 and 4, this volume).

tain, remote rural, industrial redevelopment, peripheral and frontier regions. Later conferences looked deeper into the specific needs of frontier regions (La Grande Motte, France 1973), urbanization and planning (Bari, Italy 1976) and the management of rural areas and the balance between town and country (Vienna 1978). Civil servants within the administrations responsible for these conferences were involved in drawing up the political resolutions, but these texts were based solely on the ideas and material supplied by consultants and academics.

Within the Council of Europe, a number of different bodies treated spatial planning issues. The framework of CEMAT and its Steering Committee for Regional/Spatial Planning provided a series of thematic seminars organized by different working groups. The topics treated were diverse, dealing not only with all the above topics of the ministers' conferences, but also with complementary, technical subjects such as long-range forecasting methods and computerized cartography.

Besides CEMAT, two other Council of Europe bodies[2] looked at spatial planning issues from the perspective of regional and local authorities. In the 1970s they also initiated a series of conferences aimed at raising interregional issues related to the development and planning of specific areas of Europe. These conferences looked at the specific planning needs of peripheral coastal regions, border regions, mountain regions (Alps, Pyrenees) and islands, by using external experts to prepare recommendations. Their contributions were published in the study series, Local and Regional Authorities in Europe, and distributed to the ministries of the member states (in most cases the ministries of the interior) responsible for supervising regional and local authorities.

Opening Shots: Pioneer Activities in the European Union

In the 1970s the European Community had no real interest in matters relating to spatial development or planning. The Treaty of Rome, the basis for EEC policy, contained no provisions on spatial planning, so as an institution it was not mandated but it was free to finance studies. The first and only significant initiative was taken in 1973 by the Directorates General (DGs) for regional policy and environment of the European Commission to jointly finance a "Prospective Study on Physical Planning and the Environment in the Megalopolis in Formation in Northwest Europe" (ERIPLAN 1975; see also Figure 1). The Club of Rome motivated this initiative, which provided an early premonition of what would be known as *sustainable spatial development*. This highly innovative initiative, however, remained for many years an occasional affair.

Assisting National and Regional Governments and Interregional Organizations

External experts involved in the European organizations often worked for regional and national governments and interregional organizations interested in the international aspects of spatial planning. Clearly this was because such regional associations and national governments were inclined to commission

---

[2] The Steering Committee for Regional and Municipal Affairs and the Standing Conference (now called Congress) of Local and Regional Authorities of Europe.

□──FIGURE **1**
Three Spatial Conceptualizations of Europe

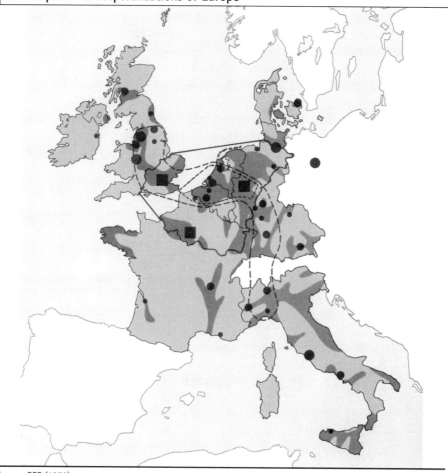

Source: RPD (1978)
See insert Figure A4 for a color version of this map.

studies on transnational or cross-border issues by recognized experts. Their numbers, however, were limited.

Studies were carried out for national bodies on spatial planning issues in the border regions for the German federal ministry responsible for spatial planning (Robert and Istel 1980) and the National Spatial Planning Agency (RPD) of the Netherlands (Robert 1981). A second category of studies analyzed the position of specific regions in the global context of European integration. The French National Agency for Regional Development and Spatial Planning (DATAR) commissioned a study on the maritime functions of the lower Seine area in the Northwest European context, with the objective of investigating the potential of the ports of Le Havre and Rouen.

Other commissioned studies were of a comparative nature. National and regional governments needed information on policies in neighboring countries. For example, during the 1970s the Dutch government promoted the development of "growth centers" to contain suburbanization, and was interested in the way public finance is used in other countries to achieve similar objectives. It commissioned a comparative study to investigate this issue and to formulate proposals for a more concentrated and better coordinated financing of the Dutch growth centers (Robert 1976).

This interest in spatial developments at the European level within national planning administrations gave civil servants incentive to produce ideas for ways national planning policies could be involved with international developments. Again, the administrations in the northwestern corner of Europe were particularly interested. In 1978 the Dutch National Spatial Planning Agency published a pioneering work on international spatial developments and trends and the territorial implications of European Community policies. Attempts to interest the European Commission, however, failed.

Summing Up the Early Days

During the 1970s there was no agenda and certainly no political impetus for developing European planning. The impetus was for exchanging ideas and experiences and broadly discovering a common ground. During these exchanges, mostly within the framework of the Council of Europe but also bilaterally between neighboring countries, there were a small number of expert consultants and academics—almost exclusively from France, Germany, the U.K. and the Benelux—who provided the first ideas, mostly in the form of studies. The only role of civil servants was to translate this material into political resolutions. The first pioneering work in this virgin territory was therefore carried out mostly by groups of experts formed by chance from outside the national planning administrations, who were often linked to or even sometimes worked for border regions and European interregional organizations.[3] These experts were mainly responsible for turning a general interest in national planning administrations into knowledge and awareness of the possible political implications of cross-border, transnational and European spatial planning.

The Emergence of the Political Context

External experts clearly began to sow seeds within certain national administrations, so much so that during the next phase civil servants began to acquire their own expertise. Since they were working in a political environment, it automatically meant that a political context was introduced. The virgin territory was slowly becoming colonized.

Political Negotiation Increases

Toward the end of the 1970s the discovery of common goals and planning principles, through the experts' work and the exchange of ideas and experiences, raised political awareness on the potential of European spatial planning.

---

[3] Apart from Jacques Robert, Von Malchus, Kunzmann, Ernecq, Pierret and Ricq spring to mind.

The idea of elaborating a European spatial planning scheme was launched by experts in the late 1970s (Robert 1979). This approximated a master plan for Europe, not to determine land use at the European level but to establish lines of policy that would then apply to the whole of Europe. This ideal was out of step with political reality, however, and it appeared that civil servants and their political bosses were beginning to tame the enthusiasm of the experts.

The U.K. organized a fifth CEMAT conference in 1980, analyzing the results achieved during the 1970s, and assessing the prospects of spatial planning in Europe. Again, the main contributions, not just the analyses but the more strategic contributions, were by external experts (Robert 1980). This ministerial conference kept alive the politically more acceptable aspects of the scheme, which eventually became the European Regional/Spatial Planning Charter mentioned earlier, which introduced the term spatial planning into the discussion. It was decided to elaborate the concept, and the Charter was finally adopted at the sixth CEMAT conference in Torremolinos, Spain, in 1983, quite a long time for the creation of a five-to-six page document, but this was a political process. Civil servants were responsible for negotiating its content. On matters of substance, the Charter does not contain anything particularly new. It sets out the main characteristics and objectives of spatial planning and how (via coordination and cooperation) to achieve them. Although no new expertise was needed, consensus was. The Charter was significant because it was the first political consensus document on planning in Europe. It was a "lowest common denominator of planning" in all democratic countries of then-Western Europe, and as such became influential, especially in those countries in Southern Europe still developing their planning systems.

Civil Servants Become Involved in Substance

After adoption of the Charter the political context of European spatial planning was established. Inspired both by the work done within the Council of Europe and by the increasing need for cross-border cooperation in many border regions, particularly in Northwest and Central Europe,[4] the first half of the 1980s saw an increase in direct involvement by national, regional and local (border area) administrations. This led to a gradual increase in expertise in cross-border and European planning within these administrations.

A good example of this is found within the Dutch National Spatial Planning Agency. During the early 1980s the level of knowledge and understanding of cross-border and European spatial planning within the agency increased significantly, since considerable work was done in this area. The first Benelux outline plan was written entirely by civil servants working in the Secretariat General of Benelux in Brussels and in the national administrations. No external experts were used, although the ideas they produced in the 1970s, and new ideas being developed by Benelux students and academics, did have an indirect influence on what was written.

---

[4] Until 9 November 1989, "Europe" meant non-Soviet Western Europe.

The seventh CEMAT, held in The Hague in 1985, dealt with decision making in spatial planning. It had an element both of exchanging experiences in planning practice (the theme of decentralization) and of the more political theme of cross-border cooperation. Every member state contributed a paper, written largely by civil servants, on the decentralization of planning. Conference papers on cross-border cooperation were also written by experts within the Dutch and French administrations, and a third paper on the implementation of the Charter was written by an expert within the Spanish administration. A fourth paper attempting to extend the political boundaries of European spatial planning was written by the chief planner in the national Luxembourg administration. Their roles clearly had changed from simply translating information from external experts into political resolutions to formulating ideas for the further political development of European spatial planning.

Toward the end of the 1980s, however, as national planning administrations began to develop their own expertise, the political influence of the Council of Europe began to decline, as the EC under Jacques Delors became stronger. One of the activities cut back was spatial planning. At the eighth CEMAT in 1988 in Lausanne, Switzerland, it was interesting to see the behavior of different countries, whose administrators and politicians had come to recognize the added advantages of cross-border and European spatial planning. On one hand, the Luxembourg minister, under the influence of his Euro-idealistic civil servants, pushed the idea of the European planning scheme in an isolated and pointless battle. On the other hand, the Dutch and French administrators convinced their ministers to discuss a new initiative within the EC, coinciding with the reform of regional economic policy of 1988. The influence of the external expert within the Council of Europe decreased, but it was reemerging elsewhere.

The EC Discovers the Territorial Dimension

When the European institutions of the European Community (now the EU) became involved in spatial development, political interest (as opposed to the exchange of experiences) in spatial planning increased. This was first and foremost because the need for European spatial planning was becoming stronger as spatial planning issues became more international, but also because the EC had earmarked huge budgets for its regional economic policy.

Some interests had been expressed earlier in the 1980s within both the European Commission and the European Parliament, but these had not taken hold. Thus, P. H. Gendebien, a Belgian member of the European Parliament, produced a report in 1983, advocating for a European planning scheme and an important role for European regions and institutions, seen in certain respects almost as a "fourth administrative layer of government." The report was above all a political statement, but given the depth of the analysis and arguments in its 60-odd pages, it is unimaginable to think that Gendebien was not assisted by some sort of expertise. Whatever the case, the content was political *Fantasy Island*.

A second example of increasing interest within the European institutions was a Dutch civil servant who worked with several external experts at the

Environment Directorate General of the European Commission, trying to introduce planning as an instrument of European environment policy, for example,
in coastal management and nature protection. The work failed because there
was no political interest in what was considered to be too complicated to
implement. All that emerged from this collaboration of internal and external
experts was the setting up of a remote sensing land use database (Corine Land
Cover) with a standard nomenclature for all of Europe. This database is still
being used to good effect today.

After the reform of the European Regional Development Fund (1989),
the new regulation provided the possibility to the European Commission of
financing transnational spatial development studies. The Commission took this
up and started the Europe 2000 Program in 1990. The setup of this program
reflects a new-found form of cooperation between internal and external expertise. Two civil servants within the French and Dutch administrations, both of
whom previously had developed a large degree of expertise on cross-border
and European planning, were brought into the European Commission to set
up and develop this program. It involved studies aimed at improving knowledge of transnational spatial development and at exploring the possibilities
of a more holistic, integrated and territorial approach to regional economic
policies. These studies were meant to serve longer-term policy goals. The situation was totally different from the virgin territory of the 1970s. The combined
spatial planning and political insight of the two civil servants (and one or
two permanent European civil servants who became involved) into what was
needed to achieve these goals provided the basis for the subjects to be studied.
These were then put out for tender and carried out by international teams of
consultants and academics, but were under strict instruction and supervision
of the civil servants.

The studies covered specific subjects, such as the spatial effects of the Channel tunnel linking Great Britain to the European mainland or new location
factors for firms in the European Single Market. The main focus, however,
was a series of integral studies of transnational areas: the Atlantic Arc, the
Central Capitals Region, the Alpine Arc, the Continental Diagonal, the New
Länder, the Mediterranean Region, and the North Sea Region. The subject,
focus and approach of these studies were determined by internal civil servants;
the research and the more detailed ideas were provided by teams of external
consultants and academics. The prospective study for the Atlantic Arc, for
example, coordinated by Jacques Robert, involved a network of university
professors (in regional economics and geography) from Portugal, Spain, France,
Great Britain and Ireland. The Central and Capital Cities Region was led by
a well-known international consulting firm assisted by specialists from each
country involved.

The Europe 2000 Program provided a lot of new insights and ideas, and it
started political minds working, both within the European Commission and
within national and regional planning authorities (see Figure 2). Following the
1991 publication of the Europe 2000 report, a second report was initiated in
1993—Europe 2000+—this time with a closer link to the more political process

FIGURE **2**
The Transnational Areas of the Europe 2000 Program 1990–1993

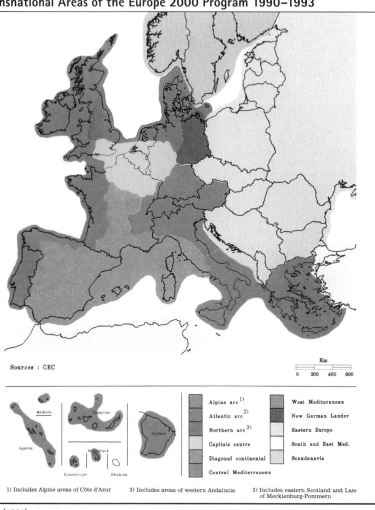

Source: CEC (1991)
See insert Figure A7 for a color version of this map.

that finally resulted in the production of the ESDP. The Europe 2000+ report was done under the instructions of civil servants of the European Commission by a network of experts coordinated by the consultant author, working in close contact with national civil servants. The network of approximately 40 experts was much more heterogeneous than before, comprising research institutes and consulting firms as well as a number of individual experts, mainly university professors.

Since then, two further transnational studies have been carried out: the Danube study and the Black Sea study (see Figure 3). The main objective is to integrate macrospatial issues relating to Central and Eastern Europe, given the EU policy of assisting the former Soviet satellites in protecting their fragile democracies. The set-up for these studies was similar to the Europe 2000/2000+ Program.

□—FIGURE **3**
Transnational Cooperation Areas with Partners Outside the EU

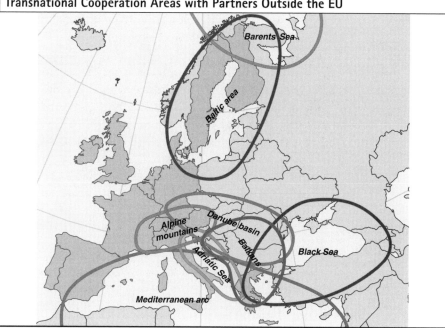

Courtesy of CEC

See insert Figure A15 for a color version of this map.

Summing Up the Second Phase

The 1980s witnessed a growing interest in and knowledge of European spatial planning among what was still a quite limited number of civil servants responsible for developing the political context and policy relevance of activities that emerged in the early 1990s. They were able to use the services of an expanding number of consultants and academics interested in the European dimension of spatial planning, who did the research and provided new information, insights and ideas. The civil servants, with the go-ahead from their political bosses, provided the strategic policy and political framework. It was a period of intense effort, growth of knowledge, an emerging clarity of purpose and the beginnings of an effective cooperation between internal and external experts, which would become increasingly intensive and intricate.

Tightening the Political Reins

The early 1990s saw planners working intensively on the ESDP, and once again relations between civil servants and consultant experts changed.

Influencing Political Initiatives Within the EU

The 1993 decision to produce the ESDP meant that the political context of European spatial planning was truly set. How the document was written reflects a further shift in relations between external and the internal experts.

From the end of 1993 to the spring of 1996, different ESDP working documents had been written under the supervision of the national spatial planning administrations of the different EU presidencies,[5] involving different forms of cooperation between their own civil servants and external experts. The draft ESDP was written by European Commission civil servants, including Philippe Doucet, a Belgian civil servant, now the program manager of the Northwest Europe Interreg IIIB program and one of the authors in this volume; and by civil servants in the Dutch, Luxembourg, Italian and Irish planning administrations. The Luxembourg, Irish and Italian administrations used external consultants simply due to lack of personnel (Martin and Ten Velden 1997). The role of these consultants, however, was one of virtual civil servants, sometimes literally taking the place of the latter in negotiations. It is interesting to note that most of these consultants are still involved in European spatial planning and all but one have become civil servants. Thus, civil servants took the lead in the ESDP process, but they used a whole range of material from Europe 2000/2000+ and previous presidencies. External experts played a major role in writing this material; however, it was under the supervision of their civil servant colleagues.

The ESDP has led to an EU cooperation program called Interreg (see Chapter 3), which promoted and assisted transnational spatial development in roughly the same transnational areas as those initiated by the Europe 2000 program (see Figures 2 and 4). This extension was approved in 1996 and in a second implementation period as of 2001 will continue to 2008. The writing of the operational programs (OPs) for these transnational cooperation areas reflects a shift from external to internal experts, but also such an intensification of cooperation that the distinction between the two categories of experts was becoming irrelevant. The process of writing the OPs was in the hands of civil servants in the national administrations involved, assisted by external experts where necessary. Calling on the latter's assistance was no longer due to a lack of knowledge or expertise of the material being dealt with, however, but rather mostly due to the lack of time or capacity. European spatial planning needed more human resources in the planning administrations, whereas those administrations had been cutting back the number of civil servants consistently since the first half of the 1980s.

Discussions are currently taking place on how to adapt EU regional economic policy to absorb the challenge of enlargement, a topic discussed elsewhere in this volume. One of the ideas is to introduce the strategic territorial dimension, put forward in the ESDP, to ensure EU-funded regional investments (which will be concentrated in the new, poorer member states) continue to promote the spatial economic cohesion of the EU. This idea is entirely political and there is little room for external expertise to develop it futher. The necessary research work, for example, identifying new indicators for eligibility for funding, will be carried out by a network of research institutes and consultants under the strict instructions of civil servants. The fundamental research

---

[5] Every member state is president of the EU for six months, on a rotation basis. As Chapter 1 in this volume has shown, during this period it was Belgium, Greece, Germany, France, Spain and Italy.

FIGURE **4**
Interreg IIC Cooperation Areas

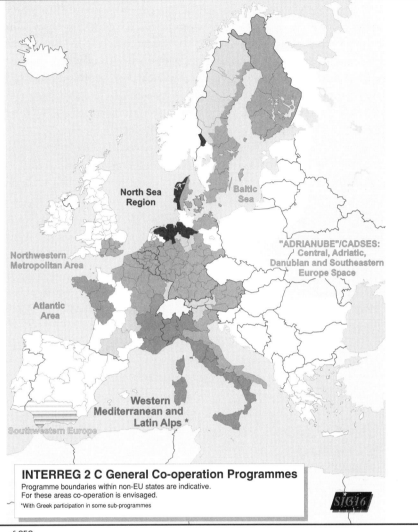

Courtesy of CEC
See insert Figure A8 for a color version of this map.

necessary for such shifts in policy, for example, on the spatial impact of EU policies, has been carried out by consultant experts.

Still Influencing Regional Interest Groups

During the 1980s and 1990s the European interregional organizations, which played an important role in providing the original external European spatial planning experts in the early years, grew in numbers and influence representing different groupings of regional authorities: border regions, peripheral maritime regions, ultra peripheral regions, islands, mountain regions and so forth. Given their character, their interest in the development of European spatial planning is obvious. Expert contributions to these organizations were and remain diverse in nature.[6] They comprise the elaboration of strategic studies aimed at collective political actions of the regions concerned, and they give advice on decision making about EU policies. For example, the Département des Alpes Maritimes commissioned two studies, one on the international functions and potential of the Côte d'Azur metropolis, the Nice agglomeration (Robert 1996); the other on the potential for cooperation within the Latin Arc, including Spain, France and Italy (Robert 1999; see also Figure 5). The National Association of Finnish Regions commissioned a study, at the time of Finland's accession to the EU, on the identification of strategic elements for a successful integration of Finnish regions in the EU (Robert 1996). Other activities related to the preparation of conferences and to editing publications.

Regional interest groups now have quite a strong influence on the shaping of development priorities for the specific types of areas they represent. This influence is due to an effective interaction among the external experts, and the political insight and expertise of the people working in these organizations. This interaction provides strategically timed political activities, such as adoption of

---

[6] Jacques Robert has been associated, from the beginning, with the emergence and development of such organizations. He has advised the Conference of Peripheral Maritime Regions for more than 20 years, and was a long-time member of the scientific committee of the Association of European Border Regions.

□——FIGURE **5**
The Blue Banana Indicating the (Core) Area with Most Cities with More than 200.000 Inhabitants

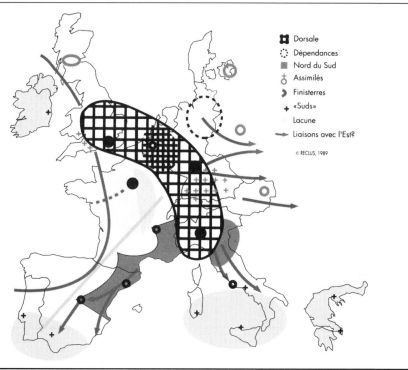

Source: Brunet (1989)
See insert Figure A5 for a color version of this map.

resolutions transmitted to the European institutions and direct contacts among politicians, backed up by research and solid arguments.

Spatial Planning in Greater Europe: Back to the Future

With the need to assist the emerging and vulnerable democracies in Central and Eastern Europe after the collapse of the former Soviet empire, the Council of Europe found new life in the 1990s, in its original field of activities: human rights and the development of democracy. Most of the ex-Soviet states and satellites of Central and Eastern Europe rapidly became member states of the Council of Europe. Against this background, from 1995 onward, substantial activities were again devoted to spatial planning issues in the context of CEMAT, which had been eclipsed by the EU's work around the ESDP.

On German initiative, CEMAT decided to formulate "Guiding Principles for Sustainable Spatial Development of the European Continent." The document, which both updated and elaborated the European Regional/Spatial Planning Charter of 1983, was adopted by the ministers of the member states in September 2000 in Hanover. These guiding principles are similar to the ESDP, but are geographically much wider in scope and less constrained by the scope of EU policies. The Congress of Local and Regional Authorities of Europe is also active in raising awareness and assisting in transfers of know-how to Central and Eastern Europe.

The preparation of the guiding principles reenacted the kind of interaction between civil servants and external experts from the 1980s. Jacques Robert was commissioned by the German federal ministry responsible for spatial planning, to prepare the guiding principles not only on its behalf as the presiding member state, but on behalf of all member states. His role was to write draft texts, to present his work at meetings of member state representatives and to incorporate their observations into the revised draft. The guiding principles were prepared smoothly and finally adopted unanimously at the twelfth CEMAT in Hanover, Germany, in September 2000. The ease of this process is explained by the fact that the experience of the civil servants representing the new democracies of Central and Eastern Europe was still rather rudimentary. Additionally, the EU member states gave relatively low priority to this work, knowing that the guidelines were of limited political significance, and that they would follow the lines as set out in the ESDP.

Internal and External Experts: An Effective Interaction

The development of European spatial planning has in no small way been influenced, even determined, by the interaction between external and internal experts. They have built up a long-term working relationship that has changed considerably but has always remained complementary and mutually supportive.

When the virgin territory of European spatial planning was being explored, the external expert had a lot of leeway. There was little expertise within the national administrations, although an understanding of this new facet of spatial planning began to take root among a select few civil servants.

In the emerging political context of the 1980s and early 1990s, this growing internal expertise was put to good use, and cooperation between internal and external experts was smooth. The consultant, civil servant and politician interacted in a creative, evolving process. As the political context crystallized, however, there was a shift in the lead role from external to internal experts, and consultants were used more to do specific work under the explicit orders of administrations.

With the writing of the ESDP, when the political reins were tightened in the mid- to late-1990s, civil servants who had strategic political and policy insights and a considerable knowledge of European spatial planning began, under the instructions of their ministers, to give even more direct guidance. The external experts, however, have continued to make enormous contributions, particularly those under permanent contract to the smaller national administrations, functioning as virtual civil servants. A further tightening of the political reins will continue, given the possible absorption of spatial planning thought into EU policies (and spending), and the continued necessity to develop cross-border and transnational cooperation among the countries of Europe.

The Different Roles

The role of the consultant has above all been that of a creator of ideas, both at the Council of Europe and later during the EU years. Consulting for the EU, however, has a rather different character from consulting for the Council of Europe (see Table 2).

The studies commissioned by the European Commission have had a much larger budget, necessitating teamwork, and they had a political goal, making the nationality of consultants a factor to be considered. Moreover, in calling for studies, the European Commission pays particular attention to homogeneous multicountry coverage. Territorial studies must take into account regional diversity and provide precise information. For all these reasons, studies are generally carried out not by single experts but by research and consulting networks. The composition of the team must reflect not only the geographical diversity of the area studied but the various relevant disciplines as well.

Examples of this approach include the prospective study on the Northwest European megalopolis, the transnational study for the Atlantic Arc and the

TABLE **2**
Different Roles of Internal and External Experts

External Expert	Internal Expert
Creator of ideas and concepts	Developer of ideas into policy
Researcher	Process animator and controller
Adviser	Negotiator between supporters and opponents
Moderator and go-between	Intermediary between facts and policies
Additional human resource	Decision maker (politicians)

preparation of the Europe 2000+ report. In such networks, the task of the lead coordinator, coping with the diversity of approaches, working styles and languages in the different countries, is particularly challenging. Networks must be flexible enough to enable innovative contributions from various experts, but they must also be coherent enough to deliver clear and realistic political messages.

The role of external experts is also multifunctional, resulting from the fact that a major function of independent experts is the production of studies aimed at facilitating public decision making. The work of experts, however, has a number of indirect impacts outside the circle of those who have commissioned them. The Europe 2000+ report, for example, which was translated into all EU languages, was used not only to develop European spatial planning; from the national down to the local level, it was also a tool used to better position one's territory in Europe and to adapt spatial strategies accordingly. The report was arguably more influential at national and regional levels than it was at the EU level, although it was published as an official communication of the European Commission.

External experts serve the role of go-between in the vertical transfer of information. They must detect innovations and new issues and bring them to the attention of the European administrations. This role also works in the other direction, since local and regional authorities are also keen to be informed about new initiatives taken by European or transnational bodies. This transfer of knowledge is also relevant, to a certain extent, among the various DGs of the European Commission, where it serves horizontally, as there is no standing coordinating body on spatial planning issues within the commission. The DG responsible for regional policy recently commissioned a major study on the territorial impacts of various EU sector policies, the findings of which are now being discussed with the member states to see how policies could be adapted. When DGs do not agree, independent experts may also act as moderators in producing joint documents. This happened, for instance, in the case of Community Policies and Spatial Planning, a document for the ESDP forum in February 1999, the preparation of which involved 19 DGs.

Finally, particularly in recent years, when the numbers of civil servants in most EU countries have been cut back considerably and the amount of work on European spatial planning has increased, external experts have been called in more often as an additional human resource, acting sometimes as virtual civil servants.

The role of the civil servant/planner between the external consultant and the politician was, first of all, one of process control. They translated information and ideas provided by external experts into political resolutions and recommendations, then guided the emerging political framework on which further ideas, elaborated by the external expert, were based. When external experts threatened to become too idealistic, such as with the European planning scheme and Charter, the civil servant/planner put on the brakes, separating applicable from inapplicable ideas. When faced with political reluctance and cynicism from sector interests, the civil servant/planner found ways to enable the process to continue. Thus, the internal expert has also been a process stimulator and animator.

A second important role is that of negotiator among supporters and opponents of European spatial planning, ensuring that the various national views on European spatial planning slowly merge into a consensus view. In this role the civil servant/planner has also aligned the political goals of national administrations with those of the European Commission. The ESDP process particularly depended on this role, given the great diversity of views on what the ESDP should or should not be.

The civil servant/planner also has an intermediary function advising the political boss while providing strategic insight and advice to the minister. At the same time they are transmitters of political parameters to the experts. Finally, the civil servant/planner has developed into an important creator of new substantive ideas by translating sometimes vague political goals into practicable concepts, for example, developing European spatial planning as a part of regional policy in the Europe 2000/2000+ Program, by defining the transnational areas. They have developed politically realistic ideas for advancing the development of cross-border, transnational and European spatial planning by transforming ideas and concepts into politically acceptable proposals. The civil servant/planner has provided information on the situation in his or her own country for comparative studies, and, when the political reins were tightened, provided the ideas and written the more political texts, such as in the case of the ESDP and the operational programs of the Interreg initiative.

The influence of both types of experts depends on the political will to pursue new policies and to give civil servants freedom to explore them, either by themselves or with the help of external experts. The role of the politician (regional politicians, ministers and commissioners) is essentially that of decision making. Regional politicians from the border regions have always been in the forefront of European spatial planning and have been responsible for many initiatives. At the national level the national interest, more than anything else, has determined the attitudes of politicians. In the early years, the Benelux countries, France and Germany were interested in pursuing the international dimension of spatial planning because they were confronted, more than other countries, with cross-border issues. Ministers from these countries took initiatives, therefore, instructing their civil servants to develop ideas and cooperation. At the European level, the three commissioners involved in the emerging European spatial planning through the 1990s to today—the Scot, Bruce Millan; the German, Monika Wulf-Mathies; and the Frenchman, Michel Barnier—represent an increasingly positive attitude toward European spatial planning, from a somewhat reluctant permission to the development of ideas, through critical acceptance to the present day enthusiasm.

The Development of Ideas and Concepts

Fundamental to the influence of the internal and external experts in developing European spatial planning are the ideas and concepts they have brought forward. European spatial planning has progressed through the creation of new concepts and ideas. These are essentially important in a multinational context where each planning culture uses its own concepts, which often are colored by specific national or institutional characteristics and are therefore mutually incompatible.

Developing new European concepts produces several effects: it draws the attention and energy of representatives of the national planning authorities toward future-oriented issues, and creates a common language as an essential tool for international communication among experts. Thus, new concepts created at the European level quickly penetrate the media and political circles. They are a way of conveying policy intentions to national and regional authorities and also to society at large. A number of the new planning concepts produced by European institutions have become popular indeed.

A constant concern of the external expert has been to produce new concepts, both as innovative strategic elements and as communication tools in a multicultural planning world. This can be illustrated by three examples in which Jacques Robert was personally involved.

When asked to write the synthesis report of the study on the Northwest European megalopolis, the challenge was to explain how urbanization interferes with ecological functions. The approach chosen was deliberately dialectical. Although urbanization appeared to be much stronger than the resistance capacity of open space, the conceptual framework was based on the dependence of urban regions on open spaces. All indicators and trend analyses were redefined so that the multifunctional role played by open space appeared as a major element for protection and enhancement. Although the dependence of urban regions on open space now sounds obvious, 30 years ago it was not.

When CEMAT decided to elaborate the guiding principles, Jacques Robert was asked to work on the text. In the first draft, a major chapter was devoted to challenges emerging from the new tasks of spatial planning at the continental scale, resulting directly from the new political and economic context in Central and Eastern Europe. The German chair considered this important enough to incorporate the term *continent* in the title of the guiding principles. For the first time, spatial planning at the scale of the European continent was introduced as a new concept and recognized by a European institution. It was then rapidly adopted by planning circles, including outside those Council of Europe.

The preparation of the Europe 2000+ report presented the opportunity for introducing a number of spatial planning considerations relating to transnational spatial interactions. It was necessary to create a distinction in terms of objectives between European spatial planning and EU regional policy, which is based on the pursuit of economic and social cohesion. Counteracting territorial desegregation caused by globalization trends and organizing a higher degree of territorial interdependence through more consistent networking proved a valuable strategy for European spatial planning. This was called *spatial cohesion*, and has been transformed by politicians into *territorial cohesion*, now an established concept, referred to in the Treaty of Amsterdam and currently being elaborated on by civil servants in the prenegotiations to the new round of regional policies after 2006.

Such new ideas would never have had the effect they did, however, without their acceptance by the civil servants of their role as intermediaries. This shows why the key word in this analysis is *interaction*. The considerable influence of both external and the internal experts has been due to their interaction, their mutual understanding and the complementarity between their different roles. These roles are becoming less distinct as consultants play the role of civil servants and many civil servants have joined the private sector while continuing work on European spatial planning. Without the internal expert, the external expert would have been a voice in the wilderness; the internal expert without the external expert would never have been able to push the boundaries of innovation on which the development of European spatial planning has so depended. Together, however, their influence has been considerable.

Transnational Planning in the Wake of the ESDP

The Northwest Europe Experience

Philippe Doucet

A key idea underlying the ESDP is that cities and regions in Europe are increasingly interdependent. Decisions or actions taken in one area may have a significant impact on spatial development in other, sometimes distant, areas. The national territory has (or should have) long ceased to be the only relevant frame of reference for spatial development policies. In river basins, for example, the fate of downstream regions has always been determined by what happens in upstream regions of foreign countries. The development of new major infrastructure such as a tunnel under a mountain range (e.g., Alpine crossings) or cross-strait fixed links (e.g., Channel tunnel; Øresund bridge) may dramatically affect traffic flows, environmental resources and economic development in far-distant regions. Such instances of interregional dependency are numerous. If not new, this phenomenon has nonetheless been considerably amplified in recent years by European integration and globalization.

Early Experiments: Benelux, CRONWE and the CCC Study

This growing interdependence has progressively led to the recognition of the need for cooperation among local, regional and national authorities of neighboring countries. Arguably, Northwest Europe (NWE) has been at the forefront of this awareness-raising process, especially within and around the Benelux area.

The Benelux Structural Outline

Traditionally at the crossroad of international trade exchange and transport flows, the Benelux members (Belgium, The Netherlands and Luxembourg) have virtually no natural inland borders. The core region (the Benelux Delta) encompasses the estuaries of three major transnational rivers: the Rhine, Meuse and Scheldt. The Benelux countries therefore had good reason to cooperate on transnational spatial planning more intensively and at an earlier stage than did the rest of the EU.

In 1975 a joint strategic planning document, the Benelux Structural Outline, was drawn up and formally approved after a decade of intensive work (Union Economique Benelux 1986). It appears to be the first transnational spatial planning document ever produced in Europe. This pioneering document was superseded by a Second Structural Outline, dated May 1996 (Union Economique Benelux 1996; 1997; see Figure 1).

The Conference of Regions of Northwest Europe

Another forerunner of transnational spatial planning in Northwest Europe, the Conference of Regions of Northwest Europe (CRONWE), pioneered a coordinated approach in this field from the late 1950s onward. Initiated in 1955 as an international scientific association, CRONWE was run by a board composed of senior planning officials from five (later six) Northwest European countries and regions, including the three Benelux countries, some West German *Länder* and northern French regions. Counties of southeastern England joined the association in the early 1970s. Through a series of publications, seminars and public conferences, the CRONWE experiment raised awareness in the planning community on a wide range of key spatial development issues in Northwest Europe.

FIGURE **1**
Second Benelux Structural Outline

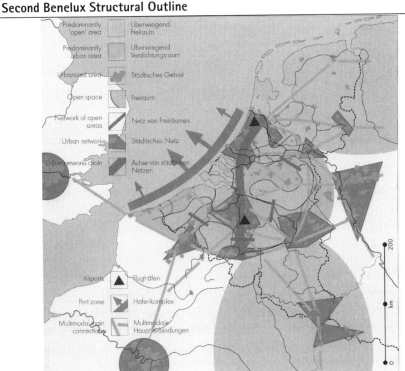

Source: UEB (1997)
See insert Figure A20 for a color version of this map.

The CCC Study

The CRONWE proceedings inspired a study published by the European Commission, known as the Central and Capital Cities (CCC) area (CEC 1996a). This was one of the seven transregional studies produced by the commission to underpin the drawing-up of its Europe 2000+ report (see Chapter 2). As its name suggests, the CCC area is home to a number of capital cities, including London, Paris, Amsterdam, Brussels, Luxembourg and Bonn (the German federal capital at the time). The concentration of command functions, economic power, markets, international airports and seaports and other major infrastructure, as well as knowledge-based industries, is so impressive in the CCC area that it is generally regarded as Europe's main powerhouse.

The CCC study, however, pointed to a number of challenges facing the region: an aging population; the need for regeneration in old manufacturing industry areas; traffic congestion; unsustainable mobility; urban sprawl and related degradation of environmental resources; other environmental threats induced by factory farming and the tourism industry; deprivation and social exclusion in inner cities; and increased internationalization of the economy (at both EU and global levels).

Six metropolitan areas or systems were identified as key components of the CCC settlement pattern: the U.K. southeast and the French Ile-de-France region (respectively centered around London and Paris); the Flemish Diamond (with Brussels, Antwerp and Ghent as major centers); the Randstad region (Amsterdam, The Hague, Rotterdam and Utrecht); the Rhine-Ruhr area (Duisburg, Essen, Dortmund, Düsseldorf, Wuppertal and Cologne); and the Rhine-Main area (Frankfurt, Wiesbaden-Mainz and Darmstadt) (see Figure 2).

A major finding was that the above six metropolitan systems, despite experiencing population and physical decline—at least in their inner cores—in recent decades, now face the prospect of renewed growth. Rather than complementing each other, however, they compete. Increased polarization in these major centers may jeopardize sound, balanced spatial development of the CCC area as a whole, by marginalizing other regions located outside the major Euro-corridors that link the large metropolitan areas. In reaction to these threats, the study made a case for various planning responses, including cooperation between metropolitan areas (to better position themselves in the global context) and the integrated development of three counterweight, cross-border metropolitan systems around Lille, Liège and Luxembourg.

The Interreg IIC Quantum Leap

The informal council of ministers held in Liège in November 1993 is generally regarded as the ESDP kickoff (see Chapter 1). The ESDP, however, was not the only item on the agenda. Significantly, the Belgian Presidency also raised the question of widening cross-border cooperation (Belgian Presidency of the Council of Ministers 1993, 33–43).

FIGURE 2
CCC Study: Policy Scenario

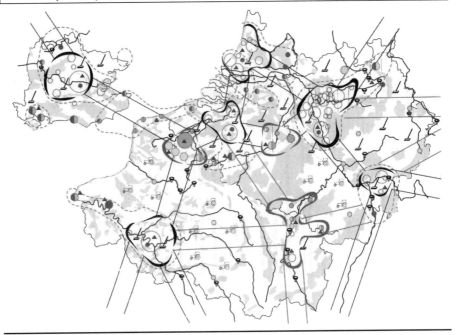

Source: CEC (1996a)
See insert Figure A19 for a color version of this map.

From Interreg to Interreg II

As for cross-border cooperation, a dramatic shift has taken place in Europe over the past five years. In the early 1990s, cross-border cooperation in its narrow and official meaning—that is, cooperation among local authorities and other partners on both sides of a common national border—was already a well-established practice. Defined as such, its geographic scope was limited to border zones, a minor part of the European territory. Moreover, spatial planning was often addressed in cross-border cooperation schemes as merely one among other possible items (see Table 1).

Many such schemes had been co-funded by the European Regional Development Fund (ERDF) during the programming period 1989–1993 of the EU structural funds, within the framework of the Interreg Community Initiative.

Near the end of this programming period the new Interreg II Initiative was under preparation and the Belgian Presidency was aware of the main policy options of the European Commission to reshape the assistance allocated to cross-border cooperation over the following period, 1994–1999. As no significant extension of the geographic scope was on the agenda, the Belgian Presidency, supported by several delegations at the informal council meeting, made a timely case for a new style of cooperation to be carried out in wide transnational areas, with a strong emphasis on spatial development issues.

At the time, this move did not please the European Commission, whose immediate reaction was lukewarm. The Interreg II Initiative, confining coopera-

□—— TABLE **1**

EU Regional Policy and Cohesion / Interreg: Some Key Facts

□ Since 1989 EU structural funds operations have been carried out in multiyear programs over three successive programming periods: 1989–1993; 1994–1999; 2000–2006.

□ According to the *concentration principle,* a number of regional objectives are pursued in predetermined eligible areas. Among these, Objective 1 has been defined as economic adjustment of regions whose development is lagging behind. By far the main beneficiaries of structural funds—regions eligible for Objective 1—are those where the GDP per head is less than 75 percent of the EU average.

□ Traditionally, the bulk of resources appropriated for regional development by EU structural funding has been allocated to mainstream programs defined and carried out by national and regional authorities under the supervision and with financial assistance of the EU.

□ In contrast to these mainstream programs initiated nationally, Community Initiatives are sets of programs of particular relevance for the European Community and therefore undertaken at the initiative of the European Commission. Interreg is probably the best known and the most richly endowed Community Initiative. Interreg, Interreg II and Interreg III, respectively, were launched during the first, second and third programming periods mentioned above.

□ Interreg, Interreg IIA and Interreg IIIA are or have been about cross-border cooperation, that is, among local authorities and other local partners on both sides of a common national border; Interreg IIB was devoted to the completion of large energy networks.

□ Interreg IIC and Interreg IIIB are or have been about transnational cooperation, that is, among partners from regions belonging to the same large, geographically contiguous, cooperation area.

□ Interreg IIIC supports interregional cooperation, that is, cooperation among not necessarily neighboring and sometimes far distant regions from all over the European continent.

tion to programs among neighboring border areas, was thus kept unchanged. As a gesture of good will, a limited amount of ERDF funding was allocated to a few pilot schemes called *transnational cooperation pilot actions.*

The member states quickly moved to draw up the ESDP. In September 1994, the Leipzig Principles were adopted. This outline of the future ESDP placed great emphasis on transnational cooperation, which was believed to be the most appropriate area for putting the new ESDP ideal into practice (Informal Council of Spatial Planning Ministers 1994, 19).

On 1 January 1995, M. Wulf-Mathies, the new commissioner for regional policy and cohesion, took up her duties. Her commitment to deepen the Commission's involvement in European spatial planning was clear from the start. She succeeded in persuading the College of Commissioners to adopt the new Strand C of the Community Initiative Interreg II—in short, Interreg IIC—devoted to transnational cooperation on spatial planning.

The Interreg IIC Guidelines

The official Interreg IIC Guidelines, published in July 1996, established a clear link between transnational cooperation programs and new thinking on European spatial planning developed in the publications Europe 2000 and Europe

2000+ as well as in the ESDP strategy outlined in the Leipzig Principles. Interreg IIC was meant to:

- help restore the balance between different areas of the European Union;
- foster transnational cooperation initiated in this field by member states and other authorities with responsibilities for spatial planning;
- improve the impact of community policies on spatial development; and
- help member states and their regions take a preventive and cooperative approach to the problems of water resources management posed by floods and drought (CEC 1996b, 23, Art. 5).

Three main categories of programs were foreseen: spatial planning and transnational cooperation measures; spatial planning and transnational cooperation against flooding; and spatial planning and action against drought. The inclusion of the second category was triggered by the disastrous floods in winter 1994–1995. It was to be the reference framework of the Interreg Rhine-Meuse Activities (IRMA) flood mitigation program, involving the Dutch, Belgian, Luxembourg, French, German and Swiss regions of the Rhine and Meuse river basins (see Figure 1) with the largest budget of all Interreg IIC programs. The drought-related programs of the third category concerned Mediterranean member states. Only the programs of the first category were expected to deal with spatial planning in the broad sense of the word.

Two major requirements were imposed in the Guidelines: to base programs on a joint strategy and to establish a joint management structure. Lacking clear definition, however, these two concepts were understood differently from one program to the other, depending on the administrative culture of the member states involved.

Seven programs in the first category were launched: Baltic Sea Region, North Sea Region, Northwestern Metropolitan Area, Atlantic Space, Southwestern Europe, Western Mediterranean and Latin Alps, and CADSES (Central European, Adriatic, Danubian and Southeastern European Space) (see Figure 4). Four transnational cooperation pilot actions (initiated by the Commission in 1994) were to be carried out in parallel, with considerably less ERDF funding: Northern Periphery, Mediterranean Gateway, Eastern Alps, and Archi-Med (Central and Eastern Mediterranean Space) (see Figure 5).

The NWMA Program: Coping with the Transnational Cooperation Challenge

With Northwest Europe as the focus of this chapter, the following discussion expands on the Interreg IIC Northwestern Metropolitan Area (NWMA) program experiment.

The NWMA Cooperation Area

At the dawn of the Interreg IIC Initiative, the groupings of regions identified by the European Commission for its transregional studies were expected to serve as reference for delineating the Interreg IIC cooperation areas. Therefore all

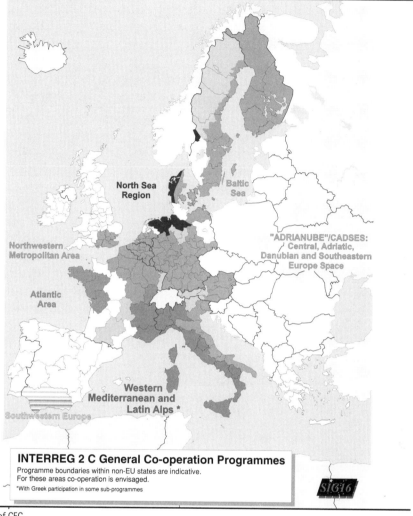

Courtesy of CEC
See insert Figure A8 for a color version of this map.

regions included in the CCC area first thought of cooperating within the same area, which they regarded as the scene of their common spatial development framework.

Yet, not each of these original study areas were equally suitable for cooperation. This proved to be true in various parts of the European continent. Out of the eleven Interreg IIC and pilot action cooperation areas listed above, only five (Baltic Sea Region, North Sea Region, Atlantic Space, Western Mediterranean and Latin Alps, and Archi-Med) come close to matching one of the transregional study areas previously defined by the European Commission (compare Figures 4 and 5 with Chapter 2, Figure 2, discussed on page 25). Not surprisingly, these five groupings correspond to maritime rims where

FIGURE **5**
Transnational Pilot Actions: Cooperation Areas

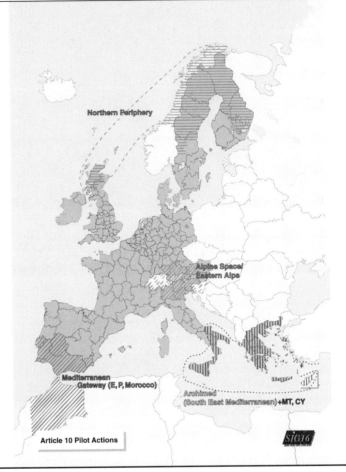

Courtesy of CEC
See insert Figure A9 for a color version of this map.

specific cooperation mechanisms had already been put in place by a remarkably influential interregional lobby, the Conference of Peripheral and Maritime Regions (CPMR).

Although originating in the CCC area, the NWMA represented a considerable extension. As shown in Figure 1, these two areas are as similar on the continent as they are dissimilar on the other side of the Channel (where all the British Isles were included). This unexpected extension had its origin in Ireland's determination to join the NWMA. This attitude, albeit paradoxical, was very sensible for such an atypical country. All Irish regions are eligible under Objective 1 of the structural funds. Along with dozens of other CPMR regions, Ireland reputedly belongs to the club of poor and peripheral areas. Recently, however, Ireland, dubbed the "Celtic Tiger" for its impressive economic recovery, has demonstrated its capacity to catch up with the thriving regions of the European core. Was there a better way to confirm this than by including Ireland in the NWMA?

Appealing though it was to Dublin, this option was resisted by other governments involved. They were reluctant to welcome to their common approach a country they had never thought of associating with, one built on the community brought to light by the CCC study and the CRONWE legacy. The Irish government, supported by the European Commission, nonetheless managed to persuade the other NWMA partners to change their minds. The main argument put forward was that synergy among complementary regions was more desirable for an ERDF-funded transnational cooperation program than a homogenous but rather selfish common ground established among prosperous regions.

All the same, the move proved disruptive, especially in the U.K. It was first envisaged to limit the extension to metropolitan areas (Midlands, Lancashire and Dublin) outside of the CCC area, but this option, unacceptable for other British regions, was rapidly foregone. Eventually Ireland and the U.K. were included in their entirety. The U.K. government insisted, however, that, despite the inclusion of numerous rural areas, metropolitan development should remain a key dimension of the NWMA program.

The outcome of this negotiation—the newly defined NWMA—was one of the widest and most populous Interreg IIC cooperation areas, encompassing the whole of Belgium, Ireland, Luxembourg and the U.K., as well as parts of France (nine regions), Germany (four Länder) and the Netherlands (nine provinces); and it was home to 143 million inhabitants. After a preparatory phase initiated in 1997 the NWMA Interreg IIC program was officially adopted by the European Commission in June 1998 (CEC 1998).

The NWMA Program Strategy

To contribute to general aims such as sustainable development and increased spatial, economic and social cohesion, four measures (i.e., categories of operations for which a certain amount of funding is appropriated in the program budget) were set out in the NWMA program, each pursuing various strategic objectives.

- ☐ *Measure 1. Urban and Regional Systems:* Strategic objectives: competitiveness of and complementarity among metropolitan regions, better balance between these and medium-sized towns, promotion of the quality of life in cities, social integration and job creation in deprived urban areas, prevention of urban sprawl and protection of open space.
- ☐ *Measure 2. Infrastructure and Communications:* Strategic objectives: reduction of traffic congestion, promotion of energy-efficient transport means, reduction of unnecessary travel and promotion of information and communication technology (ICT).
- ☐ *Measure 3. Natural Resources and Cultural Heritage:* Strategic objectives: protection, enhancement and management of natural resources, the open countryside and the cultural heritage.
- ☐ *Measure 4. Technical Assistance:* This was devoted to the overall management and promotion of the program.

Moreover, the four measures were meant to contribute to a common strategic objective: the development of a long-term Spatial Vision for the area providing the basis for cross-sector cooperation in the field of spatial planning. To this end, a specific Spatial Vision project had to be carried out.

The total program budget amounted to Euro 56.634 million, including Euro 31.392 million in ERDF funding.

The NWMA program was drafted shortly after the first official draft ESDP had been published (CEC 1997b), and the ESDP/Interreg IIC natural synergy had already been widely acknowledged. The ESDP and Interreg IIC were regarded as two sides of the same coin: the theory and principles of the former were to be tested and applied by the practice of the latter, in a dynamic and iterative synthesis process. Thus, quite logically, the first three measures of the NWMA program (see Table 2) mirrored the policy guidelines for the spatial development of the EU set out in the ESDP (CEC 1999a, 11). This is not specific to the NWMA, since the same parallelism can be observed in most other Interreg IIC programs. It was the first time in the history of EU structural funds that a document on spatial planning—informal, nonbinding and unofficial though the ESDP may appear—proved so influential.

The NWMA program, however, was still far from representing a joint planning strategy, nor was it meant to be one. In many respects it remained more akin to ordinary regional policy programmatic documents. For example, neither real planning targets nor spatially differentiated planning objectives were defined. Instead, the strategic objectives were applied uniformly to the cooperation area as a whole.

The NWMA Program Management Structure

A monitoring committee and a steering committee, comprised of representatives of the seven member states involved and their regions, were set up to supervise the management of the program and select project applications. Moreover, the program was run by a joint technical secretariat based in London, and the entire ERDF funding was transferred to a joint bank account.

This may appear quite logical for such a transnational undertaking, yet not every Interreg IIC program was run on the same basis. In many cases, especially in southern Europe, preference was given to virtual secretariats (a smokescreen for a network of national institutions), and to a handling of the ERDF funding at the national level (i.e., one distinct bank account in each member state).

☐—— TABLE **2**

NMWA Measures and ESDP Policy Guidelines

NWMA Measures	ESDP Policy Guidelines
Urban and regional systems	Development of a balanced and polycentric urban system and a new urban-rural relationship
Infrastructure and communication networks	Securing parity of access to infrastructure and knowledge
Natural resources and cultural heritage	Sustainable development, prudent management and protection of nature and cultural heritage

This exemplifies the reluctance of national bureaucracies to embark on genuine transnational cooperation and adopt the style of working entailed. Even in Northern Europe, setting up transnational management structures for programs such as the Baltic Sea Region, the North Sea Region and the NWMA, though finally effective, turned out to be a sensitive exercise. The decision on the location of the NWMA program secretariat, for example, gave rise to fierce competition in a rather hectic atmosphere.

The NWMA Program Achievements

At the NWMA program launch, transnational cooperation among European public bodies was virtually virgin territory. Many regions and other potential project partners had little or no experience in international contacts. The preparation and implementation of a successful Interreg IIC project was no simple matter. Some of the many difficulties to be overcome included setting up an international partnership (with partners from at least three different countries), defining a credible action plan and project budget, and negotiating a project convention to secure efficient cooperation mechanisms and the solvency of partners.

Even more difficult were the hurdles rising from the wide variety of national cultures, languages and administrative practices in the NWMA. All involved in NWMA cooperation ended up realizing that the technical preparation of a project is nothing more than the tip of the cross-cultural communication iceberg. A critical ingredient of successful transnational cooperation in Europe, often overlooked at the outset, is the will to promote a patient mutual understanding among different cultures. Transnational cooperation is probably one of the most fertile seedbeds of European identity that, in Castells's opinion, remains to be built (Castells 1998; see also Chapter 5).

The NWMA steering committee selected no less than 45 projects (reviewed in NWMA Secretariat 2000), involving 369 partners. Among the wide range of spatial development issues addressed were:

☐ polycentric urban regions in the European context;
☐ the prospect for inward investment in major cities of the NWMA;
☐ transnational market areas of new economic activities (e.g., factory outlet centers);
☐ the future of major transnational development corridors;
☐ out-of-town open spaces;
☐ sustainable mobility (waterways, greenways, urban mobility management);
☐ cooperation among airports;
☐ multimodal freight in major Euro corridors;
☐ the spatial impact of ICT;
☐ the integrated management of landscapes and natural resources;
☐ integrated strategies for coastal zones.

Partnerships comprised public and private bodies, with a vast majority of regional authorities (161 partners in total). Other types of partners included local authorities (85 partners), regional development agencies, national authorities, universities and nonprofit organizations, along with some private consultant agencies. The scope for further cooperation has become immense, considering the size of the network created by the various project partnerships among which coordination mechanisms have been set up.

Proceeding by trial and error was unavoidable in such circumstances, where a totally new style of working had to be invented. Yet these years of NWMA cooperation, as well as similar experiments of other Interreg IIC programs, will arguably represent a major breakthrough for spatial development policies in Europe, and for European integration itself.

The Spatial Vision

One of the 45 NWMA projects, the Spatial Vision, merits particular attention. The project partners were the seven NWMA member states, led by the Rijksplanologische Dienst (National Spatial Planning Agency) of the Dutch government.

The project was spearheaded by the Spatial Vision Group, a think tank comprised of officials and experts from the seven member states and the NWMA secretariat. This group met regularly from 1998 to 2000, assisted by an international consortium of consultants led by the University of the West of England (see Chapter 6). The resulting document, A Spatial Vision for Northwest Europe, was published in September 2000 (NWMA Spatial Vision Group 2000).

The Spatial Vision is meant to stimulate the emergence of a coordinated transnational approach to spatial planning in the cooperation area. It identifies key priorities for future transnational cooperation, including an input to the preparation of the Northwest Europe Interreg IIIB program, but also a long-term strategy.

At this stage, however, the NWMA Spatial Vision remains a modest outline and has not as yet been validated. It represents a first attempt, neither statutory nor official, of what could one day become an ambitious transnational strategy. In the same vein as the ESDP, it will be an ongoing process, not a rigid master plan. Nevertheless, the Spatial Vision should not be confused with a mini-ESDP, let alone a mere remake of the ESDP applied to the NWMA. Instead, it should be seen as an interface between the theory and principles of the ESDP on one hand, and the operations carried out in the framework of long-term transnational cooperation on the other. The Spatial Vision is intended to become a strategic tool of the aforementioned ESDP/Interreg dynamic synthesis. A permanent cross-fertilization process, therefore, must occur between Interreg transnational projects and the Spatial Vision.

The Spatial Vision is made up of four sections. Section 1, "Planning into the Twenty-First Century," provides the Spatial Vision rationale and explains why transnational cooperation on spatial development is needed. Section 2, "Northwest Europe Today," identifies key issues in the area. Section 3, "A Vision for Northwest Europe," outlines the spatial strategy, revolving around six vision principles illustrated by a Spatial Vision diagram. Section 4, "Actions: Implementing the Spatial Vision," looks at practical ways of carrying the vision forward. The six principles put forward in Section 3 include:

1. enhancing the global role of NWE's metropolitan areas;
2. ensuring more fairness in the distribution of prosperity in NWE;
3. maintaining high levels of access to and from NWE;
4. improving internal access and mobility in a sustainable way;
5. reducing NWE's global environmental impact; and
6. protecting and creatively managing the natural and cultural heritage.

Like the NWMA measures, these vision principles accommodate the ESDP's fundamental policy guidelines. These have been considered, however, from two distinct angles: the relationships between Northwest Europe and the rest of the world (odd-numbered principles); and the spatial development of the cooperation area as such (even-numbered principles).

This twofold approach bears witness to the Spatial Vision Group's determination to focus on issues of real transnational relevance: those linked to the interdependency among distant regions that cannot therefore be properly tackled without transnational cooperation. Thus, the external dimension is critical. Indeed, confining territorial development policies strictly to the NWE area in isolation would be no less absurd than doing so within national boundaries.

As rightly emphasized by Vincent Nadin (Chapter 6), this focus on transnational issues is a specific feature of the NWMA vision (compared with similar documents produced by other Interreg IIC programs). It reflects the Spatial Vision Group's eagerness to apply the celebrated subsidiarity principle to the full.

Section 3 of the Spatial Vision also includes a diagram (see Figure 6), outlining a geographically differentiated picture of priorities for territorial development in the various subregions of the cooperation area.

This rather risky exercise had been envisaged at the EU level in 1997 in the first official draft of the ESDP (the Noordwijk draft, CEC 1997b), but the Potsdam ESDP (CEC 1999a) left the question unanswered. This cannot be left out of a genuine territorial development strategy, however, and this is the challenge the Spatial Vision dares to address.

Transnational Cooperation Comes of Age: Interreg IIIB Takes Over from Interreg IIC

In the 2000–2006 programming period of the EU structural funds, the relative weight of Community Initiatives has been significantly reduced to some 5 percent of the total budget, compared with 9 percent during the 1994–1999 programming period. Fewer Community Initiatives have been launched, however, and the funding earmarked for the popular Interreg Initiative has noticeably risen from Euro 3563 million for Interreg II to Euro 4875 million for Interreg III.

A new Strand C, devoted to interregional cooperation, has been introduced. Strands A and B are meant to prolong the cross-border and transnational cooperation initiated over the past years. Thus, rather misleadingly, Interreg IIIB has taken over from Interreg IIC.

The Interreg III Guidelines published by the European Commission are anything but complacent about the Interreg experience until then. Acknowledging that "significant steps have been made toward joint cross-border programming and program management in many cases," the Guidelines also point to "parallel projects on each side of the border" (CEC 2000c, Art. 5, 143–146). This suggests that several past cooperation schemes hardly deserved the name because they consisted of regional development operations carried out in isolation by

FIGURE 6
A Vision for Northwest Europe: Spatial Vision Diagram

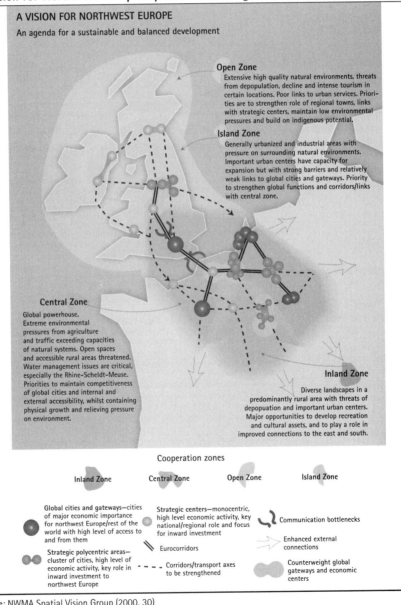

Source: NWMA Spatial Vision Group (2000, 30)

See insert Figure A21 for a color version of this map.

each of the neighboring regions officially involved without pursuing genuinely common benefits. A caricature of this approach is seen in two roads built in Spain and Portugal parallel to their common national border, the last straw for a cooperation scheme.

A bi- or multilateral partnership is a necessary but not a sufficient condition for real cooperation to take place. The European Commission has seen a variable amount of cooperation in the Interreg IIC programs. The main challenge assigned to Interreg III is building on the positive experiences of genuine cooperation developed by some of these (CEC 2000c, Art. 6, 143–147).

To achieve this end, a joint strategy and a joint management structure are once more seen as two key prerequisites. This was already formulated in the Interreg IIC Guidelines, but in rather vague terms; therefore, the issue was worth elaborating on. Not only does a formal joint strategy have to be drawn up for every Interreg III program, but "the operations selected…must also be clearly cross-border/transnational *in nature*" (CEC 2000c, Art. 7, 143–147; emphasis added).

As far as the management structure is concerned, five bodies must be set up, including a managing authority, a paying authority, a joint technical secretariat, a monitoring committee and a steering committee. The latter two committees were already a well-established tradition in past structural funds programs. A joint technical secretariat existed for some Interreg IIC programs, but only in Northern Europe. Willy-nilly, all Interreg IIIB programs have been required to adopt this model. As suggested by Faludi (2001b, 674), "the NWMA is now a model for others which is in itself a demonstration of the community method of allowing experimentation, picking out the arrangements that succeed, and formalizing them at the first opportunity."

The managing and paying authorities are innovations introduced in the new regulation applying to structural funds. Bodies with a legal status must be appointed by the member states to manage the structural funding of a program and to effect the related payments. The procedure is quite straightforward for mainstream programs but rather tricky for Interreg programs.

Ten Interreg IIIB programs have been launched all over the European continent: Western Mediterranean, Alpine Space, Atlantic Area, Southwest Europe, Northwest Europe, North Sea Area, Baltic Sea Area, CADSES, Northern Periphery and Archi-Med. The Alpine Space excepted, all these cooperation areas derive from one of those defined for the previous programming period (see Figures 4 and 5).

The Ambitious NWE Program

On 3 May 2001 a draft Northwest Europe Community Initiative Program (CIP) (International Working Party NWE, 2001) was formally submitted to the European Commission. The NWE cooperation area is an extension of the former NWMA: four new French regions (Brittany, Pays de la Loire, Franche-Comté and Alsace), Baden-Württemberg and part of Bavaria in Germany, and 15 Swiss cantons have been incorporated. The extended cooperation area encompasses the entire Rhine and Meuse river basins, which allows prolonging the activities undertaken by the Interreg IIC IRMA Program (see above for the Interreg IIC Guidelines).

The NWE Program Strategy

The fundamental aim of NWE cooperation is "to contribute, through an innovative and integrated approach of transnational cooperation on territorial issues, to a more cohesive, balanced and sustainable development of the European territory, and of the NWE area in particular" (International Working Party NWE 2001, 24). This clearly echoes the ESDP message, as well as that of the NWE Spatial Vision, the external dimension of which is encapsulated by the expression "development *of the European territory*, and of the NWE area in particular" (emphasis added). This indicates an unambiguous determination to contribute to an overall approach in symbiosis, not in competition, with the other regions of Europe.

The NWE strategy revolves around five thematic priorities:
1. An attractive and coherent system of cities, towns and regions;
2. Internal and external accessibility;
3. Water resources and prevention of flood damage;
4. Other natural resources and cultural heritage;
5. Territorial integration across seas.

Priorities 1, 2 and 4 are nothing other than the ESDP leitmotifs, as were the three main measures of the NWMA program. Noteworthy is the fact that the detailed presentation of these priorities owes a great deal to the NWE Spatial Vision principles. Arguably then, this Vision has already proved influential, despite its tentative nature and before any formal steps have been taken for its validation.

Priority 3 is clearly a newcomer; its inclusion was justified by the high transnational relevance of water resource management and to offer prospects of extending the IRMA cooperation. Priority 5 represents another innovation: it equally echoes the NWE Spatial Vision, where establishing better links between the British Isles and the continent is key.

The NWE program will capitalize on the positive pioneering NWMA experiences, but there is also broad agreement on the need to move into higher gear. The main NWMA activities (i.e., apprenticeship in mutual comprehension among national cultures, initial joint studies, initial exchanges of experience) were and remain necessary, but cooperation can no longer be limited to these. This has explicitly been stated in the NWE Community Initiative Program (CIP). A project limited to a mere exchange of experience, for example, will no longer be eligible for ERDF support.

Significantly, some investment projects are foreseen. They imply reduced ERDF grant rates and usually a complex financial setup, which might have recourse to borrowing from the European Investment Bank and other institutions. All this should allow transnational projects to gain momentum in Northwest Europe while conferring more credibility on the cooperation program.

Such fresh impetus, though emphasizing concrete results, will not prevent the NWE partners from refining the strategic approach at the program level, including the pursuit of the Spatial Vision. The NWE CIP underlines the need to develop an appropriate structure for long-term cooperation on spatial planning, liberated from the time constraints rising from the structural funds programming periods. This structure will include a "standing, efficient and dynamic forum" bringing together the authorities concerned on a regular basis, with the Spatial Vision on the agenda (International Working Party NWE 2001, 30).

The NWE Program Management Structure

The total ERDF funding allocated to the NWE program amounts to about Euro 330 million, with total eligible costs worth Euro 654 million. This is the largest budget allocated to an Interreg IIIB program. Compared with the Euro 31 million ERDF funding of the Interreg IIC NWMA budget, the increase is spectacular; however, this sum is still rather modest, in light of the immense cooperation area and the great diversity of topics dealt with in the NWE CIP. Hence the importance of encouraging concrete and innovative projects, including those with a leverage effect offering real spinoffs.

Another important requirement is setting up an efficient management structure. As indicated, it must be comprised of five bodies, as required by the Interreg III Guidelines. For two of them, the monitoring and the steering committees, the NWMA practice will be further pursued. The same will apply to the program secretariat but with significantly increased staff resources: the new NWE team is expected to include about 16 employees, compared with the five dedicated to the NWMA program. Establishing two new bodies, the managing authority and the paying authority, proved extremely sensitive. After protracted discussion it was decided to entrust the Nord-Pas-de-Calais Regional Council and the Caisse des Dépôts et Consignations (a French public bank) with the relevant responsibilities.

Nord-Pas-de-Calais ranks among the most European-minded of French regions, with its capital, Lille, in northern France. Since the NWE secretariat will act as the managing authority's staff, it was decided to move it from London to Lille. Boldly supported by the U.K. government, this relocation is a revealing signal. Nord-Pas-de-Calais is typically a restructuring region of old manufacturing industries. Its recent economic recovery epitomizes the ideal policy agenda of many such regions in the NWE. In addition, Lille is at the core of the London-Paris-Brussels triangle, in a strategic position to act as a counterweight metropolitan area in the NWE system of cities (see Sassen 2000, 45). It is hard to imagine a more meaningful expression of the NWE partners' will to put the celebrated ESDP polycentric model into practice.

What Next?

Admittedly, transnational cooperation initiated by Interreg IIC and IIIB can be regarded as a major step forward in EU spatial development. True, when considering the time constraints and the complexity of the issues addressed, project and program partnerships faced a difficult challenge and their success in delivering quality results was variable. Yet, the very launch and implementation of Interreg IIC programs was in itself a remarkable, unprecedented achievement. As successor Interreg IIIB programs are still in the startup phase, the time appears ripe to raise two main questions. First, what can be expected of transnational cooperation in the years to come? Second, and more specifically, how is this cooperation likely to interact with the ESDP process?

The Future of Transnational Cooperation

What has been discussed here about the NWMA/NWE experience applies equally to other Interreg IIIB programs. European transnational cooperation is at a crossroads: practices acceptable in the experimental Interreg IIC stage should no longer be so thereafter. Concentrating on the promotion of cross-cultural mutual understanding and exchange of experience among partners—even on issues the transnational relevance of which may be questioned—was probably a necessary step in the learning process. But Interreg IIIB, if limited to that, would lose its credibility.

Put more positively, Interreg IIIB programs are now challenged to provide evidence of their specific added value. This entails delivering tangible results to the common benefit of cooperating partners, preferably on issues of real transnational relevance. There is no other way to confirm the need for cooperation than to achieve what cannot be successfully undertaken by programs of the mainstream under Objectives 1 and 2 of the structural funds.

Moreover, the Interreg IIIB purpose is twofold; not only is transnational cooperation at stake, but also spatial planning, the very subject of the exercise. Interreg IIIB programs are also expected to yield a specific added value, which is often questioned by skeptics. The aim should be to generate common understanding and political will about a long-term spatial strategy and its progressive implementation. This implies going far beyond the classic programmatic approach of regional policy schemes, generally limiting the allocation of funds to thematic priorities for the lifetime of the program. Spatial planning means considering the program as a step in a longer-term strategy and complementing the thematic priorities by spatially differentiated objectives. This is tantamount to answering the highly sensitive question: what needs to be done and where?

To make progress, maps are essential. Those provided in the NWE Spatial Vision, in particular the vision diagram, are a first and modest attempt, as are similar documents produced by other Interreg IIC programs. Critical to the credibility of the Interreg IIIB programs will be their capacity to further elaborate on this first outline. This should be pursued in two ways: first, a more detailed geographic picture of the policy options (zooming in on the diagram and its basic thematic layers); second, a quantification of the related objectives, where they lend themselves to quantification (which in planning means agreeing on targets).

Such an approach may appear extremely ambitious for a program on transnational cooperation. Sticking to the current combination of regional policy programming and hazy spatial diagrams, however, would arguably equate the latter to mere rhetoric. After all, global environmental targets, for example on carbon dioxide emissions, have been agreed to in Kyoto. Why should it be unrealistic to do so at a transnational level, on questions such as the modal split on various transport axes, areas of land designated to extend the green infrastructure, the degree of containment of urban sprawl, and so forth?

For now, transnational cooperation on spatial planning has succeeded in generating real enthusiasm as well as some skepticism. A rumor has circulated within and around European Commission circles: after the current programming period 2000–2006, transnational cooperation might become a central focus in future EU structural funds programs. It would no longer be confined to the Interreg Community Initiative. Instead, a real transnational dimension would be introduced into mainstream programs.

This rumor is not groundless. The recent Second Report on Economic and Social Cohesion (CEC 2001), a flagship publication of the European Commission, includes some considerations that will be noticed. Of particular interest is the following passage about programming actions after 2006.

> In a first step, the Commission could set out a global strategy comprising the different economic, social and territorial dimensions in partnership with the member states at national and transnational levels with a view to identifying priorities including those of particular Community interest.... Afterwards, programming would be decentralized to the appropriate level, for example at regional, urban or transnational level (CEC 2001, xxxv).

Noteworthy is the double mention of the transnational level. The territorial dimension, along with the traditional economic and social dimensions, is also referred to in this excerpt and throughout the whole report. A detailed section, entitled "Territorial Cohesion: Toward a More Balanced Development," has been deeply inspired by the ESDP and related studies.

The above considerations about the future of the structural funds, however, have been deliberately written in an interrogative mood. Far from concluding at this stage, the Commission deemed it more appropriate to launch a public debate. There is little doubt that the outcome will depend on whether Interreg IIIB programs will become success stories.

Cooperation: Makeshift or a Catalyst?

In Chapter 9, John Zetter's witty, forward-looking scenario speculates on one possible course of events. As with any back-to-the-future exercise, the purpose of this highly stimulating view of the ESDP process over the forthcoming decade does more to highlight than to conceal the great uncertainty that remains. For the time being, the question of the status of EU spatial development policy remains unanswered. For a long time the process has been wallowing in a sea of informality, not wanting to breach the gates of EU institutions. As Faludi, Zonneveld and Waterhout rightly point out, this informality has been perceived by some delegations of the Committee on Spatial Development as a major threat, leading to "a danger of the ESDP process fading out of existence (2000, 130)." Anything that has a bearing on national territory (as spatial planning does by definition) will long remain a private backyard of sovereign member states, which remain the basic components of the EU quasi-confederation.

As Andreas Faludi and John Zetter suggest in this volume, the debate on the possible inclusion of spatial planning as a formal community competency in the Treaty on the European Union appears pointless. Another question makes much more sense: how should the obvious communautarian (or supranational) dimension of European spatial development be accommodated in the policy-making process? Far from answering this question, the Potsdam ESDP, by its very existence and current status, lends credence to a misleading and selfcontradictory thesis: that a mere intergovernmental method is appropriate to tackle issues of a supranational nature, including the integration of spatially relevant EU policies. Little progress can be expected in coming years if a more communitarian method fails to prevail over the current intergovernmentalism. And this entails the ESDP being recognized as an official EU document.

What can be expected of the Interreg IIIB transnational cooperation in such circumstances? Two scenarios appear equally possible.

The first scenario could be dubbed *makeshift cooperation*. Somehow, the partners involved in a cooperation program are not far from behaving as local authorities do, absent an elected regional tier of government: they cooperate in a tailor-made and unofficial association of counties, districts or municipalities, acting as a de facto region, but with poor legitimacy and reduced efficiency. They simply make do with the lack of an institutionalized region. Those opposing the creation of regions worthy of the name will exploit any modest or partial achievement of the association to underpin their favorite thesis: there is no real need for a regional strategy, let alone for a supralocal authority. Bringing the debate from the supralocal to the supranational scale, intergovernmentalists would be delighted to apply the same reasoning to transnational cooperation on spatial planning. Why should the ESDP be given a formal status, why is an official EU approach to spatial development needed, given that pragmatic transnational cooperation suffices to get things done?

The second scenario is likely to emerge as soon as the first reveals its limits. It could be named *cooperation as a catalyst*. In this case, bodies involved in transnational cooperation end up realizing that joint action, stimulating and relatively efficient though it may be, cannot be regarded as a panacea. Not everything can be solved at this level, not in the least because of the relative arbitrariness of cooperation area boundaries. For example, many strategic development Euro-corridors (Rotterdam-Warsaw, Copenhagen-Milan, and so forth) are not included in their entirety in one of the current Interreg IIIB cooperation areas. More importantly, the identification of such axes or any other priority areas for European spatial development cannot reasonably take place at transnational level; an EU or even a continental approach is needed.

That said, the transnational level remains extremely relevant in this second scenario. If not the ultimate level for decision making, it remains an irreplaceable interface between supranational and regional spatial strategies. Thus, transnational visioning could turn out to be an extremely powerful awareness-raising tool, a unique opportunity to involve those who should have been given a greater say in the ESDP process so far, particularly the regions. This involvement will speed up rather than delay, as the first makeshift scenario would, the process leading to the recognition of the need for a genuine European spatial development policy.

Section II

Theorizing European Spatial Planning

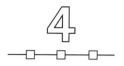

Polycentric Development

What Is Behind It?

Bas Waterhout

Polycentric development is the only substantive spatial planning concept in the European Spatial Development Perspective (ESDP) with the potential to integrate the interests of the many parties involved. Indeed, it will become clear that polycentric development has already formed this bridge among the perspectives of the member states.

In an unbalanced continent like Europe, with only one economic core area in the northwestern countries, interests diverge. With the Single Market and European Monetary Union both aiming to create a Europe-wide level playing field, competition among cities and regions will inevitably intensify. The situations of various cities and regions, however, are not the same (CEC 1999a), and spatial planners think they can help to alleviate this problem.

This is not the first time planners have tried to address the larger European scale (National Spatial Planning Agency 2000). In 1955 Northwest European planners met at the Conference of Regions of Northwest Europe (CRONWE) (see Chapter 3). Inspired by the concept of a megalopolis introduced by Jean Gottman (1961), CRONWE also identified its study area as a megalopolis, or at least in the process of becoming one. At the European level the European Conference of Ministers responsible for Regional Planning (CEMAT) has met since 1964 (see Chapter 2). In 1986 a veritable structural outline for the Benelux countries saw the light of day. Common to these initiatives was the conceptualization of Europe as a core and periphery (see Figure 1). Modest achievements in the Benelux area aside, however, none of the initiatives was successful in influencing policy (Zonneveld and Faludi 1997; De Vries 2002).

Since 1989 the ESDP process has been under way with Directorate General Regio (see Chapter 1). For the first time the member states have been able to formulate a joint spatial planning document, the most promising attempt so far to put spatial planning on the European policy map. The ESDP planners,

This research is based in part on work done jointly with Andreas Faludi in the context of EURBANET, a project in the framework of the Community Initiative Interreg IIC for the Northwest Metropolitan Area. The research institute OTB at Delft University of Technology was the lead partner.

FIGURE 1
Three Spatial Conceptualizations of Europe

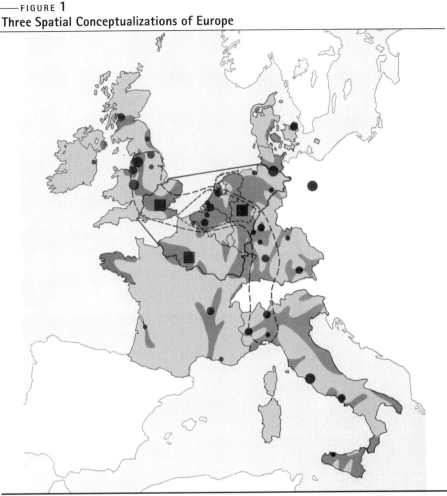

Source: RPD (1978)
See insert Figure A4 for a color version of this map.

however, have no real instruments to give their policies teeth. Their only chance is to formulate ideas that the outside world finds interesting. Fortunately, the underlying objectives of the ESDP correspond with those in the EU treaties: economic and social cohesion, competitiveness and sustainability. Whether this attempt will be enough to attract the interest of the outside world, however, remains to be seen. What is needed is something new, something that stirs up enthusiasm, like polycentric development.

The analytical concept policy theory is used in this chapter to explain the reasoning behind polycentric development. In doing so, the world behind the plan must be analyzed, invoking two archetypes of spatial conceptualization of Europe: the "Blue Banana," which portrays Europe with a core and periphery, and the "Bunch of Grapes," which reflects a more diversified view of Europe. The chapter discusses how polycentric development has been taken up after the completion of the ESDP, examines these archetypes and ends with some conclusions.

Policy Theory: A Joint Construct

Reconstructing policy theory means laying bare the causal, final and normative assumptions involved in proposing or adopting a specific policy. In a widely read paper, Hoogerwerf (1984, 495) introduced the concept of *beleidstheorie* in Dutch, but not without first referring to other authors who invoked the same idea. For academic as well as practical purposes he claims the assumptions underlying policies are interesting to examine.

The complex assumptions underlying a policy theory consist of various elements, including assumptions about characteristics of the phenomena concerned and others about the relationships among these phenomena. The latter in particular give policy theory the character of a theory (Hoogerwerf 1984, 501). Hoogerwerf distinguishes three types of relationships:

- □ Principles and norms, either among one another, or between principles and norms on the one hand and the existing or expected situation on the other hand (normative relationships);
- □ Cause and effect (causal relationships);
- □ Ends and means (instrumental or final relationships).

Polycentricity, as used in the ESDP, involves all of these relationships. The assumptions behind them can be broken down into conclusions and arguments. The Dutch literature refines this further (Pröpper and Reneman 1993), but here, the distinctions above will suffice. The conclusions are what the policy under consideration, in this case the ESDP, states. They form the reference point for the reconstruction of the policy theory. The policy analyst's task is to reveal the arguments behind these conclusions, to say why the policy makers have concluded that the policy in question is the one they should adopt.

Since there is no established model for reconstructing a policy theory, the analyst can encounter various problems. One complicating factor is that policy makers are not always aware of the assumptions they make. In many cases the policy theory is perhaps just the unintended outcome of a complex process of interaction among various stakeholders. This certainly has been the case with the ESDP. It is clear that the final policy document provides an insufficient basis for understanding the policy theory behind it. Once again, the final text acts as the reference point for reconstructing the policy theory because it represents the conclusions of a process. What should be borne in mind, however, is that these conclusions are the result of compromises that, if only up to a point, have succeeded in satisfying the concerns of all participants in the process. In European spatial planning, where one is dealing with strategic policies, one often finds a strong correlation among the multi-interpretability of a policy text and the complexity of the process that has led to it (Teisman 2000).

Thus, every stakeholder and every addressee can and must translate the often vague and abstract policy conclusions into terms amenable to their situation. (This may be true for any sort of text; see Faludi and Korthals Altes 1994.) In reconstructing a policy theory, one needs to explore the world behind the plan where various actors pursue various interests. As shown in Chapter 1, the world behind the ESDP includes 15 EU member states and the European Commission interacting with each other in a highly politicized context.

Polycentricity: The Core Concept in the ESDP

Before turning to the world behind the ESDP, this section discusses the chief outcome of the ESDP process as well as the key conclusion of the policy theory: polycentricity. Davoudi (1999, 368) comes to the same conclusion: "One of the most central yet least clear concepts in the ESDP is the concept of polycentricity." A second key conclusion is the concept of application, which has more to do with procedures and is not the object of this chapter.

Why is polycentric development a key concept? Because it stands for a balanced, sustainable form of development of the European territory, terms that figure in the subtitle of the ESDP: "Toward Balanced and Sustainable Development of the Territory of the European Union." This subtitle encapsulates the three objectives underlying the ESDP:

□ Economic and social cohesion;
□ Conservation of natural resources and cultural heritage;
□ More balanced competitiveness of the European territory (CEC 1999a, 10).

A second reason stems from ESDP's Chapter 3 on policy aims and options for the territory of the EU, which sets out the policy options for European spatial development under three spatial development guidelines:

□ Polycentric spatial development and a new urban-rural partnership;
□ Parity of access to infrastructure and knowledge;
□ Wise management of the natural and cultural heritage.

The ESDP variously refers to polycentricity but makes no explicit study of it, so the concept remains vague. In the second half of 2000, however, the French Presidency (2000a) made the concept the focus of its attention. The outcome was an analysis of ESDP policy options from the perspective of polycentricity. As usual in the ESDP process the document is based primarily on the answers of CSD delegations to a questionnaire. On this basis, the French document points out that polycentricity relates not only to the first but also to all three spatial development guidelines stated above.

Polycentricity also can be defined on the continental, national and regional, and urban and peri-urban scale, where the ESDP deals with functional relations among towns and rural areas, and with cooperation within metropolitan areas. The French document is concerned first and foremost with the continental and transnational scale as the most appropriate for any overall consideration of the ESDP. This scale is what political options (1) and (2) of the ESDP are about:

□ "Strengthening of several larger zones of global economic integration in the EU, equipped with high-quality, global functions and services, including the peripheral areas, through transnational spatial development strategies."
□ "Strengthening a polycentric and more balanced system of metropolitan regions, city clusters and city networks, through closer co-operation between structural policy and the policy on the Trans-European Networks

(TENs) and improvement of the links between international/national and regional/local transport networks (CEC 1999a, 21)."

These two options are based on the notion that

> [t]he concept of polycentric development has to be pursued, to ensure regionally balanced development, because the EU is becoming fully integrated in the global economy. Pursuit of this concept will help to avoid further excessive economic and demographic concentration in the core area of the EU. The economic potential of all regions of the EU can only be utilized through the further development of a more polycentric European settlement structure. The greater competitiveness of the EU on a global scale demands a stronger integration of the European regions into the global economy (CEC 1999a, 20).

Strengthening several world-ranking economic integration zones is the response to the present, monocentric spatial structure of Europe. After all, the ESDP identifies "only one outstanding larger geographical zone of global economic integration: the core area of the EU, the pentagon defined by the metropolises of London, Paris, Milan, Munich and Hamburg" (CEC 1999a, 20). In this pentagon, about 50 percent of the EU's total GDP is produced by 40 percent of the EU citizens on 20 percent of the total area of the EU (CEC 1999a, 8). Hence the "20-40-50 pentagon," as a German expert called a map he produced after the event (see Figure 2). This is considered to be a problem. The distribution of such zones in Europe "differs from that of the USA, for instance, which has several outstanding economic integration zones on a global scale: West Coast (California), East Coast, Southwest (Texas), Midwest" (CEC 1999a, 20). Figure 3 offers an interpretation of the more balanced distribution of economic integration zones in the USA.

Achievement of a more polycentric development depends on cooperation and promotion of complementarity. The ESDP is clear about who should cooperate with whom, but not about how this can be attained.

> [W]ays and procedures must be found to enable cities and regions to complement each other and cooperate.... As well as city networks at regional level, the need for complementing cooperation also applies to city networks at interregional, transnational or even European level.... Promoting complementarity...means simultaneously building on the advantages and overcoming of disadvantages of economic competition.... However, complementarity should not be focused solely on economic competition but be expanded to all urban functions, such as culture, education and knowledge, and social infrastructure (CEC 1999a, 21).

The document of the French Presidency elaborates on the same theme. Accordingly, a more balanced spatial organization of Europe is all the more necessary because hyperconcentration results in diseconomies, including congestion, pollution, property inflation and the negative impacts on peripheral areas. Like the makers of the ESDP, the French regard stimulation of new global economic integration zones in peripheral areas and coastal zones as the fundamental ESDP strategy. At the level of the whole European continent, this is what polycentricity amounts to: stimulating areas outside the existing core to aspire to the status of global economic integration zones.

FIGURE 2
The "20-40-50 Pentagon," Just One Global Economic Integration Zone in the EU...

Source: Schön (2000)

See insert Figure A10 for a color version of this map.

FIGURE 3
...Compared with Four Global Economic Integration Zones in the U.S.

Global integration zones in the USA

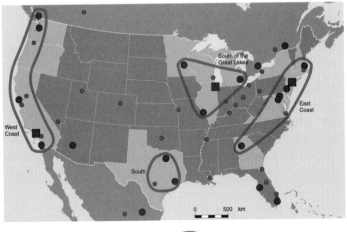

Source: Mehlbye (2000, 757)

See insert Figure A11 for a color version of this map.

Combining Interests

This section explains how the concept of polycentricity came into the ESDP. Two well-known metaphorical conceptualizations of the organization of the European territory are the Blue Banana (Brunet 1989) and the Bunch of Grapes (Kunzmann and Wegener 1991; Kunzmann 1998) (Figures 4 and 5). These may be considered as archetypes of how to conceptualize the spatial organization of Europe. The first represents a one-dimensional view, considering only indicators like densities and economic performance. The view of Europe underlying the allocation of structural funds, in particular those under Objective 1, is a good example (Figure 6). The second represents a more subtle, more diversified view, taking account of more indicators. It demonstrates a willingness to look closely at individual regions and their specific characteristics. Economic performance is just one dimension, neither more nor less important than others. In a schematic way, the Bunch of Grapes illustrates physical and cultural diversity in Europe.

There is another difference as well. The Blue Banana shows the situation as it is, while the Bunch of Grapes represents an idea of how Europe should develop. In policy theory, this normative relationship underlies the policy conclusions of the ESDP.

FIGURE **4**
The Blue Banana Indicating the (Core) Area with Most Cities with More than 200.000 Inhabitants

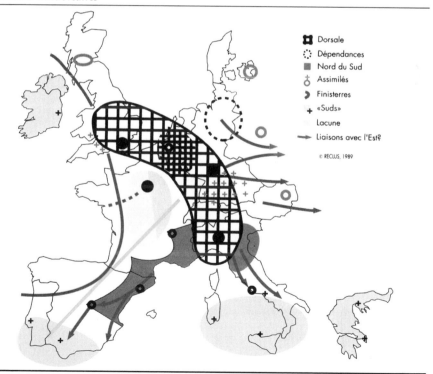

Source: Brunet (1989)

See insert Figure A5 for a color version of this map.

FIGURE **5**
The Bunch of Grapes Representing a Diversified View of the EU

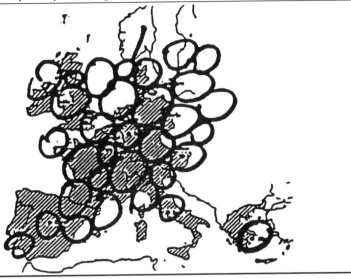

Source: Kunzmann & Wegener (1991)
See insert Figure A6.

The Italians held the first meeting after Nantes, and set the process on a track of cohesion thinking (see Chapter 1). A long-time recipient of EU funding, the Italians conceptualized Europe as the Blue Banana with a core and a periphery. In their 1990 Presidency document, the Italians simply spoke of a circle with a radius of 500 km around Luxembourg as the core. They pleaded for a cohesive policy to remedy the continuing division of Europe into a center and periphery, and they linked this to an investment strategy for the structural funds based on a one-dimensional view of Europe (Presidenza consiglio dei Ministri 1990). Clearly, with the Single Market in the offing, they feared further deterioration of their economic position in relation to the northwestern part of the European Community.

Many others shared this view of prosperous regions benefiting more from the Single Market than those less favored. The disappearance of the Iron Curtain and the opening up of new markets led to even greater disparities. So the Italians set the ESDP process on a track of assuming a causal relationship between the Single Market and increasing disparities which from then on would dominate the proceedings. Consequently, the focus was mainly on developing final relationships aimed at economic and social cohesion.

As could have been expected, however, member states located in the core of Europe were eager to shift attention to their concerns, and they introduced a new discourse with final relationships aimed at a different goal. Thus, a year later the Dutch Presidency brought attention to the problems in Europe's highly urbanized core and to European global competitiveness. The Dutch drew inspiration from their Fourth National Spatial Planning Report (Ministry of Housing, Physical Planning and the Environment 1988) and from a follow-up study, Perspectives in Europe (Verbaan et al. 1991). The latter focused on

---FIGURE **6**
Objective 1 Investments, 2001–2006

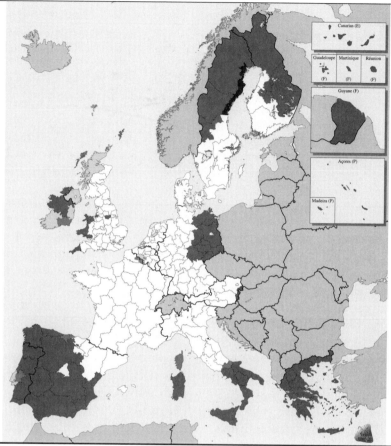

Courtesy of CEC

Northwest Europe while trying to identify suitable spatial planning strategies. The study was translated into English and disseminated among the member states, but failed to have much influence because of the singularly Dutch viewpoints it represented (National Spatial Planning Agency 2000).

Both documents had a strong economic bias. "Spatial planning should aim at supporting and accommodating modern trends in society and economic development. Good use must be made of the endogenous potential of cities and regions" (Verbaan et al. 1991, 127; translation by this author). Economic development, in this view, depended on numerous criteria like cultural and natural heritage, quality of water, air and soil, diversity and many others that are often subsumed under the term *quality of life*. As Table 1 shows, while the Italians invoked the normative principle that European spatial planning policy should support economic and social cohesion, the Dutch started from a different normative position.

The complementary causal relationship was that European global competitiveness largely depended on the well-being of its core area. At least this was what had been learned from the domestic situation in the early 1980s, when

TABLE 1
Italian and Dutch Policy Theories

	Italian Presidency (1990)	Dutch Presidency (1991)
Normative relationship	European spatial planning aims at social and economical cohesion	European spatial planning aims at accommodating modern trends in society and economic development
Causal relationship	Single Market will increase disparities between core and periphery	Europe's economic performance depends on the well-being of its core area
Final relationship	Peripheral regions must be better linked to the core and their development should be encouraged by inward invest-ment strategies	Problems in the core need to be addressed and regions outside the core should use their endog-enous potential and be linked to each other and the core

The Netherlands suffered from severe economic recession (Zonneveld 2000). As a reaction the Dutch pursued a national policy called "regions under their own steam," based on the view that regions, especially peripheral ones, needed to make better use of their endogenous potentials. A fundamental belief was that the national economy depended to a large extent on the well-being of its economic core, the Randstad. By way of analogy, it was assumed that this also applied to Europe (see Table 1).

The Dutch and Italian policy theories summarized in Table 1 represent the two diametrically opposing views on which member states took positions. To formulate a joint spatial planning strategy, these two views had to be merged.

The Dutch took great strides in this direction. In their Presidency document, Urban Networks in Europe (Ministry of Housing, Physical Planning and the Environment 1991), they forged a link between their own interests and the principle of social and economic cohesion. In a European context they learned that the latter (before the ESDP process planners had no international experi-ence) could never be neglected. What they proposed was to develop urban networks throughout Europe. One of many incarnations of polycentricity, according to the Dutch, this concept could capture both the objectives of cohe-sion and competitiveness, and would also legitimize more balanced attention to prospering and lagging regions.

The Dutch based this approach on existing spatial conceptualizations of Europe by Brunet and the Europe 2000 report (CEC 1991). These included the Blue Banana and an emergent core zone, the Sunbelt (Schmidt and Sinz 1993), which formed an arc from Valencia and Madrid in Spain via Barcelona and Marseilles in France to Tuscany and Venice in Italy (see Figure 4). Note, however, that its development potential does not go unquestioned (Tönnies 2001). Moreover, the Dutch had a differentiated view of Europe's spatial organization. Not all regions in the core were doing well, nor were all regions outside the core lagging. By linking the primary urban regions of Europe to each other and by linking secondary urban networks to them, regions outside the core were expected to become more competitive, thus improving Europe's competitiveness as a whole (see Figure 7).

The Portuguese Presidency (1992) continued along the same lines. Inspired by their own location, the Portuguese emphasized inadequate connections from the periphery to the core. In 1993 the Danish stressed the importance of a high-quality environment. All these objectives were described partly or fully in European infrastructure networks, urban networks or a European urban network consisting of various levels of integration and with a new rural-urban relationship. The terms decentralization, deconcentration and redistribution (of seaports and airports) were also used. The Danish and the Dutch in particular had carefully worked out their preferences, combining them with those of others, into a strategy wherein the concept of polycentric development (or a similar concept) played an important role.

After four-and-a-half years of discussions, almost all objectives of various member states were combined under the concept of polycentric development, which also had become central in the Leipzig Principles of 1994. These principles, officially named Principles for a European Spatial Development Policy, were the product of the Committee on Spatial Development (Bundesministerium für Raumordnung, Bauwesen und Städtebau 1995). They represent interim conclusions of the ESDP process setting the agenda for future discussions.

The Leipzig document identified two of the three fundamental goals in the ESDP: economic and social cohesion and sustainable development. The Dutch attempt to introduce the issue of competitiveness was less clearly visible.

FIGURE 7
Urban Network in Europe

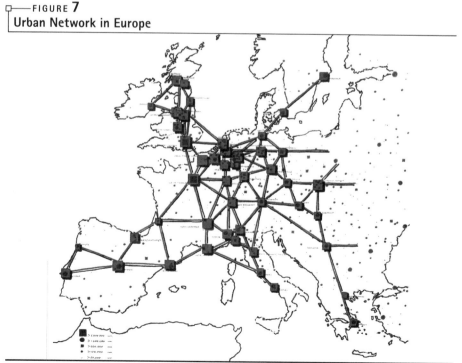

Source: Ministry of Housing, Physical Planning and the Environment (1991)

By then the three spatial development guidelines, including the one on balanced polycentric development, also had been developed. The Leipzig document took an intermediate position between the Blue Banana and the Bunch of Grapes. The Blue Banana was the point of reference and the Bunch of Grapes, although not explicitly stated, was the desired outcome. Developing a polycentric system of cities in Europe was seen as a way of bringing the periphery closer to the core, but there was as yet no suggestion as to how to realize something akin to the Bunch of Grapes.

From then on the context changed. In comparison with the late-1980s and early-1990s the prospects for European integration worsened. The communautarian approach lost out to the intergovernmental approach. Growing reluctance surfaced about transferring competencies to the European Community. Furthermore, there was more conflict over the Community budget. Reacting to Agenda 2000, the net contributors in the EU grew more concerned about their financial burden (Laffan 2000, 739).

The successive French, Spanish and Italian presidencies witnessed these effects, so there was little progress. The status of the CSD and of the ESDP in the making was unclear, thus causing additional problems. The moot point was whether the ESDP (if it would ever come to pass) should influence the structural funds, which was especially relevant for the Southern Europeans led by Spain. The Spanish government took note of the ESDP process and limited the mandate of its delegation to a minimum. Other member states also grew more reluctant, albeit less overtly.

With another presidency in the offing the Dutch were determined to end the wavering. Joining the delegation of DG XVI, they introduced a set of new working principles. Relieved that the discussion would finally come to an end, the other delegations agreed to let the troika (the previous, next and present presidency plus the Commission) write the document. Based on previous presidency and CSD documents, the troika succeeded in preparing a succession of drafts. Finally in June 1997 at Noordwijk the Dutch Presidency proudly presented the first official draft ESDP (CEC 1997b). Before the approval of this Noordwijk document, however, two debates relating to polycentric development were needed.

The first concerned a simple and apparently innocent map (Figure II.1 in the Noordwijk document, CEC 1997b). It shows the shape of the EU, the distances between Greece and Ireland and Finland and Spain, population densities, and natural physical barriers like seas and mountain ranges. The version of the map that went before the CSD was the same as the map that finally made it into the Noordwijk document, the difference being that the published version failed to depict the core of Europe (see Figure 8), because the latter did not please member states from Southern Europe. The proposed map reflected a center-periphery model of Europe (an early version in the files even carried this title), with a juxtaposition of strong and weak regions. In the beginning it had been Southern Europeans who had identified disparities as the central issue. To represent this on a map, however, was controversial. In the end, leaving the core of Europe off the map (Figure II.1, Noordwijk document, CEC 1997b), the shape of the European territory in the first official draft represented a compromise. Apparently, the Blue Banana thinking was no longer acceptable.

A second debate about competitiveness was occurring simultaneously, and may have amplified the first. Since the meeting under the Dutch Presidency in 1991, the issue of competitiveness had been crowded out by that of cohesion. Compared to the problems in the core, the problems in the periphery were much greater and this may be the reason. The Dutch, whose planning philosophy had not changed, however, reintroduced the issue of competitiveness. Located in the core of Europe, they could be trusted to do so.

The Dutch and the other troika members (Ireland and Luxembourg) proposed a third basic goal to the ESDP, namely competitiveness within the European territory. This may have made southern member states unhappy about the elliptical shape on the map discussed above. Nevertheless, the Spanish delegation was unhappy with the formulation of this third goal. Well aware of Dutch ideas, they probably judged the concept of competitiveness dangerous, in that it could have led to Northwest European claims on the structural funds. Contrary to Dutch thinking, cohesion countries often argue that European competitiveness as a whole depends on the quality of the competition among its regions, which is what cohesion policy is designed to stimulate. Consequently, Spain proposed the addition of the word *balanced* before competitiveness,

FIGURE **8**
Elliptical Shape Indicating the Core

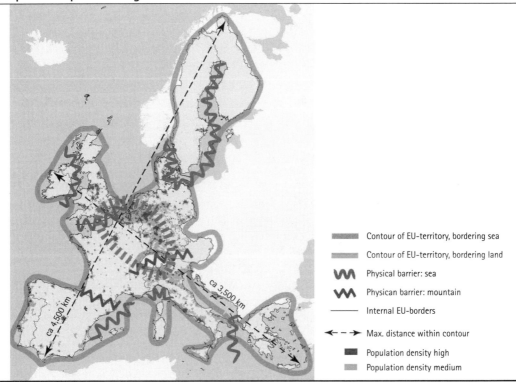

▬▬	Contour of EU-territory, bordering sea
▬▬	Contour of EU-territory, bordering land
᙭	Physical barrier: sea
᙭	Physican barrier: mountain
──	Internal EU-borders
◄- -►	Max. distance within contour
■	Population density high
▦	Population density medium

Source: Archives of the Dutch National Spatial Planning Agency; Faludi and Waterhout (2002)

so the third basic goal of the ESDP became "balanced competitiveness within the European territory."

Balanced competitiveness surely has a more polycentric ring to it than simply "competitiveness within the European territory." Since the Blue Banana thinking had been rejected, the ESDP planners moved closer to the philosophy behind Europe as a Bunch of Grapes. There was still no solution, however, as to how to portray Europe in its true shape—that of a center and a periphery—while simultaneously discussing cohesion strategy and strategies for improving Europe's competitiveness. Cohesion and competitiveness were still mutually exclusive when related to a core-periphery model. The concept of polycentricity alone could not solve this dilemma, nor did the addition of the qualifier "balanced" before competitiveness. Both objectives were considered necessary, however, and therefore the makers of the first official draft of the ESDP chose not to visualize the shape of Europe.

After Noordwijk, the ESDP process went smoothly, and the Noordwijk document provided a sound basis for further elaboration. After the 1998 meeting in Glasgow, where the complete draft ESDP was approved, it was up to the Germans to bring the process to a conclusion under their presidency in May 1999.

Precisely who made the proposal—whether the Germans or the Commission officials on the troika (Commission officials always participated in troika meetings)—is not clear, but during this period a solution was finally found: the concept of polycentric development combined with the development, based on their endogenous potential, of global economic integration zones. The European territory in the ESDP is described in the vein of the Blue Banana, with a core, the pentagon, and a periphery. The ESDP vision (described verbally only), however, reflects more the idea of the European Bunch of Grapes with several core zones. In this way, the EDSP bridged the gap between the two archetypes of European spatial conceptualization: the Blue Banana and the European Bunch of Grapes.

Polycentric Development: A Bridging Concept

Polycentricity is the outcome of a political, rather than a theoretical, debate between two normative viewpoints. As such, the viewpoints have not changed, rather they have been linked together by invoking the concept of polycentricity. As a consequence, the exact meaning of the concept in practice remains vague. Research in 1999 pointed out that even among the members of the CSD there is no common understanding of polycentricity (Waterhout and Faludi 2001). This is hardly surprising, given the suboptimal conditions under which the CSD operates, leaving little room for open discussions and mutual learning. "To be acceptable to delegates, concepts invoked in the work of the CSD have to be broadly defined" (Waterhout and Faludi 2001, 107).

The literature on European integration shows broad concepts accommodating different objectives meant to avoid deadlock. "A...way to reach a consensus in bargaining processes is to settle for a framework decision, phrased in such vague terms as to allow actors with diverging views to interpret it according to their individual interests" (Héritier 1999, 17). Indeed, from the outset the ESDP was meant to be a framework.

Vague concepts might thus be unavoidable in European policy making. Considering its heterogeneous composition and the complex institutional setup involving 15 member states and the Commission as it does, it could hardly be otherwise. In such an environment, "regimes around which actors [sic] expectations can converge are needed: the European Community puts a premium on the ability to provide convincing policy concepts and their interpretation" (Eising and Kohler-Koch 1999, 275).

Eising and Kohler-Koch refer to belief systems revolving around broad orientations toward solidarity and reciprocity and the search for consensus, following the consociational ordering principle. They distinguish among three types of concepts and principles. First, substantial concepts relate to policy content, the goals to be attained and the instruments to be employed. Second and third, procedural and distributive principles pertain to the EC system as such. An example of the former is subsidiarity and of the latter is the cohesion principle. Clearly, polycentricity is a substantive concept, but it also includes elements of a distributive concept. Such concepts are necessarily vague, and "their normative relevance as well as their prescriptive elements are often disputed and subject to divergent interpretations...." (1999, 277). Bridging concepts, therefore, are needed to reconcile differences.

> Even within the European Commission or individual member state governments, actors are in need of bridging concepts. Being responsible for different tasks within the administration, they identify with exclusive policy philosophies. Environmental policy is a good example of how a common denominator had to be found to break a deadlock. 'Sustainability' was the formula used by environmentalists within the Commission in order to present their strategies in a way which was also acceptable to their colleagues form other DGs.... (1999, 278–279).

This is an example of an attempt to formulate what Kohler-Koch (1999, 30) calls *hegemonic concepts*. It is also what the makers of the ESDP have attempted to do by supplying persuasive concepts to gain the ear of policy makers. To gain acceptance, however, they had to invoke flexible and even amorphous concepts like that of a polycentric system of cities in Europe. If successful, such albeit generalized bridging principles form the basis for further cooperation.

Polycentric Development Being Taken Seriously

With the ESDP on the books, polycentricity received much attention from policy makers, European-wide cooperation networks, consultants and academics. Debates on polycentricity at the regional and transnational scale intensified (see Dieleman and Faludi 1998; Kloosterman and Musterd 2001; Albrechts 2001; Houtum and Lagendijk 2001), and a new debate on polycentricity has begun at the continental level. Three documents are of importance: the French Presidency document discussed above; its followup (French Presidency 2000b);

and the Second Report on Economic and Social Cohesion (CEC 2001). All have drawn inspiration from the ESDP. In fact, the French Presidency documents are direct followups to it.

The first document aimed at a better understanding of the concept of polycentricity. Taking an approach based on agglomeration rates and gateway functions, the second French document identifies potential global economic integration zones. It has been drawn up by a small group of independent consultants commissioned by the French planning agency DATAR, and presented to the CSD in December 2000. Going far beyond usual practices in the ESDP process, where mapmaking proved impossible, the document offers a tentative long-term spatial vision of Europe complete with maps (see Figure 9). Whether this second document will have a followup remains unclear.

The third policy document, the Second Report on Economic and Social Cohesion, is a flagship report of the European Commission (CEC 2001). Important is Part 1.3 (Territorial Cohesion: Towards a More Balanced Development), written by DG Regio officials of the same unit as was previously involved in the ESDP process. Interestingly, the ESDP is used to legitimize the

□—FIGURE **9**
Possible Development of New Global Economic Integration Zones

Source: French Presidency (2000b); Guigou (2002)
See insert Figure A12 for a color version of this map.

view of DG Regio. The focus here, however, is mainly on the challenges of the eastern enlargement of the EU (see also Chapter 8, this volume). Polycentric development is seen as the best way to achieve a more balanced territory. The report does not present a strategy, however, as does the ESDP by introducing the concept of global economic integration zones, let alone a spatial vision for Europe over, say, 20 years. What it promises is to lift the concept of polycentricity out of the small world of the ESDP and introduce it into all Directorates General of the European Commission. In turn, they can go further by interjecting it into other EU policies.

More bottom-up initiatives come from other cooperation networks and advisers. An example of the first is the Metropolitan Regions Exchange network (METREX), comprising 36 European metropolitan regions and almost 60 individual authorities. It considers Europe as "a number of transnational areas within which there are, or could be, strong polycentric metropolitan relationships" (Read 2000, 740; see Figure 10). This situation forms a sound basis for further development toward a better urban balance. An example of the latter is an alternative development perspective for Europe (Figure 11) meant to inspire actors within the megalopolises indicated. It was drawn up by Peter Mehlbye (2000), an independent consultant who formerly was involved in the ESDP process, first as an official of the Danish Ministry of Environment and Energy and later as a national expert at DG Regio. What is important here is that both examples are witness to some belief in the possibilities of a polycentric approach.

Academics have always been interested in polycentricity at the regional scale, but now, in the wake of the ESDP, they also focus on development at the scale of Northwest Europe or even the EU as a whole (see Kunzmann 1998; Böhme 1999; Richardson and Jensen 2000; Richardson 2000; Krätke 2001; Copus 2001; Ache 2001). At the same time, there is a lot of skepticism. There is the feeling that polycentricity is the outcome of a debate on normative relationships. In the ESDP, however, it is being presented as an instrument, a final relationship. To make matters worse, it is based on questionable causal relationships. At the very least, the ESDP fails to provide empirical evidence. These issues make the usefulness of a polycentric approach questionable.

It is exactly the bridging function of the concept of polycentricity that makes Krätke (2001) doubt its value. According to him "the ESDP might partly be judged as an 'idealistic' approach, particularly with regard to the notion of combining competitiveness and cohesion" (Krätke 2001, 106). He argues that current economic developments intensify competition among cities and regions and that, from a regional economic perspective, the European urban system can be understood as a system of competing locations. Competition, he argues, results in winners and losers. Thus "strengthening the competitive position of certain centers in the European urban system does not automatically entail a lasting improvement in the competitiveness of the pan-European urban system" (Krätke 2001, 107).

Copus (2001) warns that, as a consequence of the political tensions in the ESDP process with civil servants acting within limited mandates, the theoretical

FIGURE 10

Europe as a Collection of Transnational Cooperation Areas in Order to Achieve a Better Urban Balance

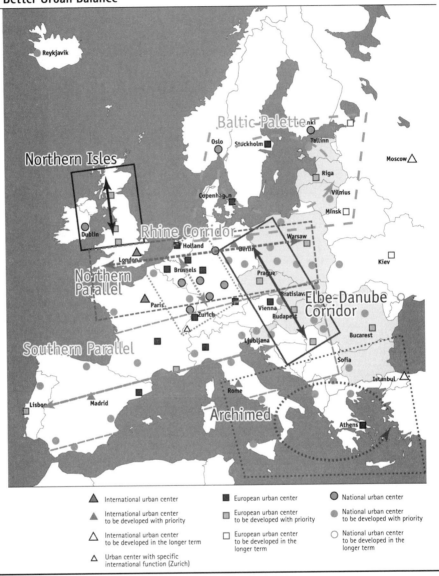

Source: Read (2000, 741)

See insert Figure A13 for a color version of this map.

underpinning of the ESDP and especially the concept of polycentric development is rather weak. Some of the proposals in the ESDP to promote polycentric development "are closer to 'ends' rather than to 'means', and no theoretical arguments are provided to make the case that such activities will stimulate the desired forms of 'polycentric development'" (Copus 2001, 549).

The concept of global economic integration zones receives critical attention from other authors as well. For instance, Ache (2001) devotes an entire paper to discussing whether the concept of global economic integration zones is viable.

┌───FIGURE 11
│ An Invitation to Metropolitan Areas to Cooperate

New European Zones of Metropolitan Cooperation?

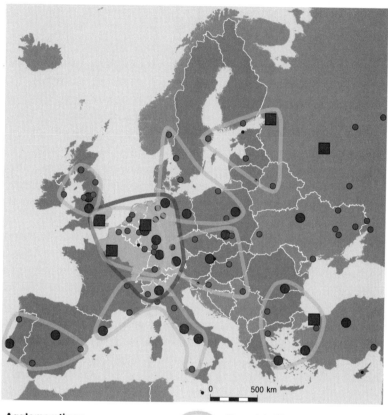

Agglomerations

■   >= 5.000.000 inh.

●   2.000.000 - < 5.000.000 inh.

●   750.000 - < 2.000.000 inh.

•   Smaller capital cities in
    EU Member States and in
    Accession Countries

New global integration zones?

Existing zone of significant
global integration

Source for the agglomeration data:
Population Division of the Department of Economic and
Social Affairs of the United Nations Secretariat (1998):
World Urbanization Prospects: The 1999 Revision

Source: Mehlbye (2000, 759)
See insert Figure A14 for a color version of this map.

One of his conclusions is that images such as the pentagon can be extremely powerful, but that there is a danger of oversimplification. Krätke, for his part, is of the opinion that the idea of "[d]eveloping additional world economic integration zones outside the core area of the EU would appear unrealistic in the light of the existing imbalances" (Krätke 2001, 110).

It would be easy to quote more such comments on global economic integration zones, and on the ESDP, but to do so would go beyond the scope of this chapter. Suffice it to say that most authors try to help fill the theoretical vacuum. Some explicitly call for more critical research (Richardson and Jensen 2000), which is exactly what the makers of the ESDP—arguing that it is just a first simple step in an ongoing process—have aimed for.

Conclusion

After 10 years of discussing European spatial planning, in the absence of any competitors, polycentric development has become the key substantive concept in the ESDP. It serves as a bridging concept welding the views of various key actors together, thereby giving them sufficient incentive for staying in the game. To fulfill this role, the interpretation of the concept needed modification. Thus, the ESDP interpretation is different from that used in a national context, in that the concepts of endogenous development and global economic integration zones form part of the package deal. According to the French Presidency document, polycentricity contributes to all three ESDP objectives. Furthermore, by spanning the continent, it may also bind all European regions together.

In the ESDP polycentricity is seen as the vehicle for moving toward a Europe that, in the long term, develops from a highly centralized territory (indicated by the Blue Banana) to a balanced territory (symbolized by the Bunch of Grapes). The Bunch of Grapes represents an ideal and the ESDP vision lies somewhere en route to that end. The ESDP vision, however, is couched in terms of cohesion and competitiveness, which are diametrically opposed normative principles held by different groups of member states that have shaped the ESDP discussions. Thanks to the concept of polycentricity forming a bridge, both objectives could finally be integrated in the ESDP, keeping the process on an even keel. Polycentricity is thus much more the outcome of a debate on normative issues, rather than on causal and final relationships. Its prime function is to keep member states in the process, while providing an instrument for reaching the situation described by the Bunch of Grapes.

In the original meaning of the Bunch of Grapes, sustainability and diversity also have played important roles. They do so in the ESDP as well. From the perspective of polycentricity, however, their role in the ESDP debate has been minor. Because of the normative debate on cohesion and competitiveness, with polycentricity as the outcome, the ESDP also has an urban bias. Polycentricity is first and foremost a concept relating to urban development. Given the theoretical vacuum in the ESDP debate, it is doubtful whether polycentricity will be the right instrument for reaching these objectives. There has been no alternative concept on sustainability and diversity, however. As the French Presidency document has shown, the belief is that polycentricity will also automatically serve these interests. Whether this assumption is justified from the ESDP discussions remains unclear. It must not be forgotten that, in the first instance, polycentricity is the answer to the competing interests of member states about cohesion and competitiveness.

Thus, polycentricity is a vague concept. In a European context, however, precisely because of their multi-interpretability, bridging concepts provide the basis for further cooperation. At least politically, polycentricity fulfills this function. Credit for this should go to the small group of ESDP planners who showed courage, stamina and creativity. They paved the way for further elaboration of polycentricity as a concept. From the perspective of understanding how polycentricity works, the evolving academic debate on causal and final relationships underlying the concept is welcome. From the perspective of influencing European policy making, it is also positive to see that within the ESDP process, followup actions are being taken and that the Second Cohesion Report incorporates the ESDP and polycentricity. With polycentricity as the subject of an academic debate, while forming the basis for further cooperation, the conclusion here is positive in that, just as its makers intended, the process continues.

Imagining European Identity
Discourses Underlying the ESDP

Ole B. Jensen

> If meaning is linked to identity, and if identity remains exclusively national, regional or local, European integration may not last beyond the limits of a common market, parallel to free-trade zones constituted in other areas of the world. European unification in a long-term perspective, requires European Identity.... So, by and large, there is no European identity. But it could be built, not in contradiction, but complementary to national, regional, and local identities.
>
> *Castells 1998, 332–333*

Addressing questions about Europe is a complex endeavor. With the new breed of spatial visions emanating from the complex institutional web of the EU, one witnesses the emergence of a new discourse on European space. This complex conglomerate of spatial representations works as a new way of facilitating rationales as diverse as European economic growth, environmental sustainability and social equity. Furthermore, such notions bear on an implicit rationale of representing and reimagining European identity.

This chapter first looks into the conceptual and analytical toolbox of the growing, heterogeneous discipline of discourse analysis. The emphasis is on the importance of the representation of spaces and places. Then the chapter moves into empirical territory with a short account of the European Spatial Development Perspective (ESDP). In a brief excursion away from this "mother document," a discussion of the European North Sea Region (NorVISION) serves as an illustration of this new breed of spatial representations. Extracted from these documents is the main thesis of this chapter: three explicit rationales—global urban competition, environmental sustainability and social equity/spatial justice—and one implicit rationale, reimagining European identity.[1] This then leads to unraveling the rationales and meanings of the discourses underlying the ESDP. These concluding remarks will also touch on the potential interest of this topic to a North American planning audience.

The author wishes to thank Dr. Tim Richardson, Department of Town and Regional Planning, University of Sheffield, for research collaboration from which this chapter benefits.

[1] The distinction between explicit and implicit here refers to what can be read off the discourses very explicitly and what needs more thorough (implicit) interpretation.

Representing Space: On Discourses and Discourse Analysis

Dealing with discourses and analysis here refers to a heterogeneous body of theory. The plethora of discourse perceptions and conceptualizations, however, will not be the focus; rather, earlier writings on this topic (Jensen 1997; Richardson and Jensen 2000) will be taken as a point of departure. Thus, a discourse will be understood as "an entity of repeatable linguistic articulations, social practices and power-rationality configurations." Accordingly, the analysis is divided into three analytical spheres: language, practice and power rationality. A main feature of this particular approach to discourse analysis is that it is different from the approaches worked out on a strictly linguistic basis. Seen this way, any given discourse attempts to gain hegemony by means of a particular reality and knowledge conceptualization. Thus, discourses aspire to be acknowledged as the natural perception of reality. They imply an institutionalization and fusion of articulation processes and practice forms, the outcome of which are knowledge and rationality forms and subject positions from which to undertake legitimate social actions. These points will be elaborated below.

Language/Articulation

The question of representation deals with how particular themes, events or objects are described and articulated in words, images and pictures. The objects of study are thus the linguistic expressions and the images of discourses often articulated through powerful metaphors, key concepts or strategic graphical representations and maps. Answers are sought about how particular actions, institutions or physical artifacts are represented in the language and pictures, for example, of policy documents. Furthermore, the ways in which policy themes are addressed in language illustrate how a particular theme can be the object of policy and planning. Thus, different ways of exploring framing space lead to different requirements for spatial knowledge to be gathered and analyzed in particular ways to feed and support different spatial representations. Words not only describe the world but also contribute to establishing arenas for talking, reasoning and acting. Thus, the use of words draws lines between legitimate and illegitimate uses of language. Since words are set into action by social agents in institutional settings, such arenas do not consist of language and images alone.

Social Practices

As any given discourse seeks to be accepted as "the natural perception of reality" (hegemony), languages and images must be placed within the context of a real-life policy process where different interests compete over the shape of policy and where different spatial visions are the objects of contest. Apart from the illusory separation of language and practice, the basic idea of including agents and institutions in discourse analysis draws on the idea that spaces and places do not present themselves but are expressions of power relations embodied in strategies, discourses and institutional settings. Thus, institutional settings of discourses are both a necessary condition of the existence of a given discourse and a structure offering social agents specific places from where to act and construct identities (subject positions).

Rationales

Discourses frame and represent spaces and places, and thus express a specific power-rationality configuration.[2] Any given discourse carries within it (implicitly or explicitly) a set of basic norms and values governing its attempts to realize its view of the world. This amounts to putting the question of power in the center of the analysis. Construed in a productive way, power is seen here as the foundation for social action, as well as a form of potential control and coercion. Thus, different rationales—with their distinctive horizon of values and norms that guide social actions—are implicitly acts of power in that they are attempts to govern which sort of social actions are to be carried out and which are not.

In the wake of these three analytical dimensions, a few more methodological comments are in order before proceeding to the analysis. First, any given discourse should be understood not as revealing an eternal essence, but as an analytical structure that the analyst can discern in a particular debate (Hajer 2000, 137). Therefore, the use of the key concept of discourse, either in the plural or in the singular, is a question of the level of analysis. At one level one can apply the singular in the sense that there is a new discourse in the making, on European spatial development. Nevertheless, one can also use the plural, as in the title of this chapter. When used in both ways, discourses must be understood as being nested. For example, on a general level one finds a European discourse made up of complex cross-references to many different ideas and texts (intertextuality). Within this, a complex process of cross-fertilization takes place through drawing heavily on other discourses, for instance discourses of global urban competition, environmental sustainability, social equity and European identity. Thus, in the conceptualization of discourse used here, such layered or nested discourses express specific rationales in the wake of framing their objects.

Furthermore, it must be emphasized that the discourse conception of this particular approach subscribes to the point of view that a discourse-analytical framework is "substantially empty" (see Jessop 1990 for a similar point). Thus, it might be used to analyze how specific rationales are articulated, on what grounds and in what institutional settings. A theory of discourse, however, does not say anything in particular about the European urban system, for example, or the ways that contemporary transformation processes of space and place are developing. In dealing with the contemporary material changes of space, therefore, another theoretical framework is needed.[3]

---

[2] For the sake of simplicity, the word *rationale* here is seen as synonymous with the less-straightforward concept of "power-rationality configuration" (see Richardson and Jensen 2000 for an elaboration of this concept).

[3] This is understood in line with the epistemology of *critical realism*, a position within the theory of science that seeks to grasp the relation between discourse and materiality in a dialectic way (Sayer 2000).

One could say that the discourse-analytical framework is used to study how something is constituted as an object of knowledge-formation and planning, whereas theories of spatial transformation are used to study what is created and under which material and societal conditions. Thus, a comprehensive discourse analysis of spatial visions also must address the object in question, in this case spaces and places. Since there is insufficient space to develop this point, and notwithstanding the importance of theories of spatial development (see Castells 1998; Harvey 1996; Massey 1993; Urry 2000 for such analyses), the focus here is strictly on the discourse theme. From this brief overview of discourse and discourse analysis, the chapter moves into empirical territory, looking first at the development of a new vision for European spatial development.

The European Spatial Development Perspective

The European Spatial Development Perspective (CEC 1999a) presents three explicit rationales: global urban competition, environmental sustainability and social equity (spatial justice), and one implicit rationale: reimagining European identity. As Andreas Faludi explains in Chapter 1 of this volume, the Potsdam document represents the latest phase in a decade-long attempt to prepare the ground for European spatial planning as a field of policy (see also Bengs and Böhme 1998; Eser and Konstadakopulos 2000; Faludi 2000a; Faludi et al. 2000; Jensen and Jørgensen 2000; Williams 1996). The ESDP is a vision covering the territory of the EU (Figure 1).

Language/Articulation: The ESDP Document

The core ESDP policy goals center on a policy triangle of economic and social cohesion, sustainable development and balanced competitiveness, iterated in the final document (CEC 1999a, 11) as:

☐ development of a balanced and polycentric city system and a new urban-rural partnership;

☐ securing parity of access to infrastructure and knowledge;

☐ sustainable development, prudent management and protection of nature and cultural heritage.

Although the importance of social cohesion and sustainable development is highlighted, the rationale of economic competitiveness is nevertheless dominant (Davoudi 1999). This is evident, for example, from the way the notion of balanced regional development is linked to the issue of global economic competitiveness (CEC 1999a, 20). The powerful core region of Europe is framed as a model for other EU regions. This is pursued by the new concept of "dynamic global economic integration zones" that should be created in other regions to imitate and duplicate the prosperous core (CEC 1999a, 20), in spite of severe problems with traffic congestion, which the ESDP recognizes do not contribute to the sustainability objective. For weaker regions outside the proposed dynamic global economy integration zone, the approach is to widen the economic base and carry out economic restructuring (CEC 1999a, 22).

FIGURE **1**
Representing the European Union Territory

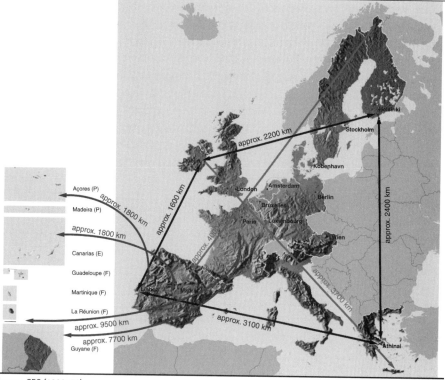

Source: CEC (1999, 56)

See insert Figure A2 for a color version of this map.

The document acknowledges the importance of rural areas and stresses the importance of the development of a new urban-rural partnership—in which rural areas are not merely seen as the hinterlands of the metropolises and cities (CEC 1999a, 24)—although it emphasizes urban and metropolitan areas. This is especially the case where the issue is linking cities through an effective infrastructure. The ESDP treats enhanced mobility as a critical priority for securing economic development within an overall spatial strategy of harmonization (CEC 1999a, 26).

Briefly dealing with the words and images of the ESDP, two points can be made. The first is the rise of a new vocabulary, including words and concepts like polycentric urban systems, balanced competitiveness, dynamic global economic integration zones and mobility as accessibility. Furthermore, in the almost 10-year long gestation process leading to the ESDP, one finds that the most characteristic metaphors of urban spaces and places are those of gateways, engines, spearheads and hearts. Within the ESDP policy process, the second point relates to the much-contested question of maps and graphics. Thus, one finds a new way of picturing space and territory, termed *infographics*. This way of representing space is a double strategy of presenting empirical evidence and rhetorically underlining the basic ideas of the discourse.

Social Practices: ESDP Institutions and Agents

Even though the ESDP has real effects in shaping policy discourses (Davoudi 1999; Jensen and Jørgensen 2000), it must prove its ability to survive and perhaps develop into a mature and legally binding EU policy field. Given the legal status of this policy field, it comes as no surprise that the transnational level is seen as the most important when it comes to possible actions under the umbrella of the ESDP (CEC 1999a, 35). It is at this level that one finds the initiatives under the Interreg Community Initiative, activities that since 1996 have proven to be the de facto field of implementation of the ESDP rationale and policy. Interreg is thus the entry point for divergent spatial visions (Faludi 2000a, 256; see also Chapter 3, this volume). Interreg IIC enables cross-border transnational planning initiatives among national and European levels within the context of megaregional perspectives and visions that are subsumed under the ESDP framework. Furthermore, the new (and better funded) Interreg IIIB program states that recommendations made in the ESDP must be taken into account, and the program especially encourages drawing up spatial visions at the transnational level (Inforegio News 1999).

As a further attempt to facilitate the institutionalization and legitimacy of the ESDP rationale, the Potsdam document proposes that member states take into account the policy aims and options of the ESDP in their respective national spatial planning (CEC 1999a, 44). Countries like The Netherlands and Denmark have already begun this exercise (Dutch National Spatial Planning Agency 2000; Faludi 1998; Jensen 1998). In the words of the ESDP:

> It is proposed that member states also take into consideration the European dimension of spatial development in adjusting national spatial development policies, plans and reports. Here, the requirement for a 'Europeanisation of state, regional, and urban planning' is increasingly evident. In their spatially relevant planning, local and regional government and administrative agencies should, therefore, overcome any insular way of looking at their territory and take into consideration European aspects and inter- dependencies right from the outset. (CEC 1999a, 45)

This is a straightforward message to the member states: they should tune into this new Europeanization of state, regional and urban planning to over- come any insular way of looking at their territory. Such a message is unlikely to be accepted easily as representing a neutral and objective point of view, however, thus leading to the question of multiple social agents with divergent interests, agendas and powers.

That a vision of the EU territory reflects conflicting views and agendas should come as no surprise. During its gestation period, various interests have been expressed about the ESDP, one of the classic differences being between a South European and a North European view. Rusca (1998) identifies the south- ern attitude as one of specific concern for the cultural heritage and identity of places. This divergence has often been attributed to differences in planning and administrative culture between north and south. This might be the case, but a more realist account is the financial benefit linked, for instance, to the structural fund initiatives that are subsumed under the overall rationale of the ESDP. The southern concern goes deeper, however, with fears that implementation of the

ESDP could lead to a reduction in overall EU funding (Dutch National Spatial Planning Agency 2000, 7). This fear is further nurtured by the prospect of relatively poorer newcomers entering the EU (Rusca 1998, 47).

Furthermore, there appears to be a new move within the Nordic countries to articulate specific Nordic interests in the ESDP. Some analysts have even gone as far as suggesting a "Nordic ESDP," based not only on the contemporary similarities among these countries (i.e., strong regional and local government planning), but also on the historical legacy from the Kalmar Union (Böhme 1998; 1999). The issue here is whether the ESDP expresses an urban center-periphery model that focuses on the central growth area, thus neglecting the more peripheral and rural Nordic countries (Böhme 1998, 78). Another dimension of a potential Nordic position on the ESDP refers to the Nordic style and tradition of planning as a participatory and democratic exercise, expressed as a fear of centralism and federalism in the wake of the ESDP process (Böhme 1998, 83). There will most certainly be tensions in the wake of the question of the enlargement of the EU. Here signs are materializing that show the contours of a south versus east demarcation.

Another expression of underlying tensions and power struggles that shape the ESDP can be found in the series of transnational seminars held during the ESDP consultation process. From April 1998 to February 1999, the Directorate General for Regional Policy in the European Commission (DG XVI), drawing on input from experts, civil servants and politicians, held nine semipublic seminars. Only two of these meetings, held in Berlin and at Lille, France, will be considered here.

At the opening seminar in April 1998 in Berlin, when the ESDP was introduced (DG XVI 1998a), the politicians in particular took a more high-minded view than the planners, as expressed in the statement from Eduard Oswald, the German Minister for *Raumordnung, Bauwesen und Städtebau* (Regional Planning, Building and Urban Development). He saw the ESDP as part of the process of building European unity on the basis of common cultural basic values (Oswald 1998, 3); his is an outspoken illustration of the identity question. At the seminar in Lille, opposing views were given about the democratic legitimacy of spatial visions. The Danish National Planning Director Niels Østergård clearly expressed the Danish nation state's support of strategic urban nodes in the new global competition (Østergård 1998, 3). Meanwhile, a Swedish politician expressed the opposite rationale, a critique of "European growth bananas" mapped on an insufficient planning basis (Nilsson 1998, 3). This is a voice, however, that does not come through in the ESDP. Rather, following the seminars, DG XVI published a summary highlighting the general consensus among participants on the ESDP's rationale (DG XVI 1998b, 1).

On the issues of institutionalization and practices, the creation of the intergovernmental forum of high-ranking civil servants in the form of the Committee on Spatial Development (CSD), the authors of the ESDP, raises questions of both transparency and national sovereignty. Since it was established in 1991 the CSD has managed to present itself as a forum of de facto policy makers was well as as a unique informal body with an obscure supranational tint due to of the secretarial role fulfilled by DG XVI (Faludi et al. 2000). The CSD has thus become an institution over which neither national nor European politicians have full control. This is not in the least due to the infranational character of the CSD. Infranationalism in the EU has been defined as second-order governance involving commissions, directorates, committees, government departments and so forth. These organizational layers exhibit medium-to-low levels of institutionalization, have the character of a network, practice an informal style and, last but not least, have low actor- and event-visibility and process-transparency (Weiler 1999, 275). These features have made the CSD, working in the "cracks and holes" that occur in large organizations like the EU, into a potent instrument for the implementation of the ESDP rationale. In doing so, however, infranationalism could result in a weakening of political control and in increased autonomy at the administrative level. Furthermore, where this situation has led to agenda setting about the orientation and spending of the Community Initiative Interreg IIC, the result appears to imply less control by the member states and increased managerialism and reliance on expertise.

Studies of the Interreg IIC North Sea Region (NSR) confirm this to be the likely outcome of such organizational and political processes (Jørgensen and Williams 1998, 4). Danish municipal and regional politicians involved have been explicit that planning under Interreg IIC should not be subject to Danish requirements for public participation. Realistically speaking, however, the question of democracy should be framed as transparency rather than direct participation. Thus the structural funds can be seen as both an instrument for achieving European integration and as a tool for cutting across the hegemony of nation states by establishing a direct link between the EC and the regions (Hallin 2000, 28). This appears to be enforced by the unique institutional constitution of the CSD that fits none of the normal categories of the EU (Zonneveld 2000, 267). Such developments are symptomatic of what the Danish political scientist Ove K. Pedersen has called the double tendency of the "explosion and implosion" of politics in contemporary Western liberal democracy (Pedersen, ed. 1994). Thus, politics and planning explode out of representative organizations (e.g., national parliaments) and implode into semipublic and closed institutional settings outside the realm of democratic control.

Another interesting institutional feature of the EU spatial planning discourse and activities is the attempt to create an EU-wide expert infrastructure to facilitate the further development of the ESDP, perhaps with a view of legitimizing the process and providing it with an aura of scientific knowledge. Dubbed the European Spatial Planning Observatory Network (ESPON), this institution was proposed as a networking think tank to underpin and qualify the discourse. So far, anticipating its establishment, only a two-year study program (1998–1999) has been launched (SPESP 2000).

The ESDP Rationales

The entire reason for creating the ESDP document was to express a "shared vision of the European territory" (CSD 1998, 3). This chapter will not delve into the founding rationale of the Schumann declaration of 1950, but the ideal of European peace through collaboration is at the heart of these visions (Williams 1996). It appears, however, that the postwar objectives of peace and reconstruction no longer carry the same weight (Dutch National Spatial Planning Agency 2000, 49). The rationale of the ESDP is to be an intervention in a development characterized by competition among regions and cities to secure a better balance between competition and cooperation, the aim being that of achieving an "optimum level of competitiveness" (CSD 1998, 2). Thus the document advocates a new scale of spatial planning and as such a new vision of the EU's territory. The ESDP can be interpreted as an attempt to address the dual process of internal European diversification and external pressure of competition from the two other parts of the Triad: the U.S. and Japan. The ESDP's notion of balanced development, however, is primarily driven by the discourse of economic competitiveness.

The above analysis concentrated mainly on the rhetoric of the ESDP policy document. One of the functions of this rhetoric is to generate new concepts, new knowledge forms and a specific rational for European spatial development. In the words of Faludi (2001b), the success of the ESDP must be measured by its ability to "shape the minds" of social agents. This puts the reproduction of the discourse at the center of the investigation. As the emerging discourse becomes institutionalized in new practices, including those of spatial analysis, the construction of new fields of knowledge results in boundaries being established between valid and invalid, as well as reasonable and unreasonable forms of knowledge. Such boundaries are vital in institutionalizing European spatial planning as a rational, science-based policy field. At the same time they act as powerful instruments in the process of excluding other forms of knowledge (e.g., radical environmental considerations or indicators of social equality). The recently approved Study Program on European Spatial Planning (SPESP 2000) serves as an example of this knowledge policy at work. Apart from stressing a need for more comparable data and more solid knowledge of the spatial development of the European territory, the document also introduces the concept of infography.

In the end, the ESDP relates to the ambiguous rhetorical device that one finds in the policy triangle of growth-ecology-equity, termed the *magic triangle* by Eser (1997, 18). Since the ESDP vision is biased toward the growth side of this triangle, it can be seen as an expression of the basic economic rationale that lies behind European cooperation as an "economic club" (Krätke 2001, 109). Such a rationale, however, is contradicted by the political integration philosophy based on the ideology of a common European culture and society. This not only contradicts the growing emphasis on competition among cities and regions, but also addresses the implicit rationale of the ESDP. Thus, beneath the discussion about growth, ecology and equity lies the question of how to imagine a territorially based European identity and unity. Even though the explicit rationales of the discourses underlying the ESDP might be seen as mutually incompatible, here the discourse is interpreted as one of building a European identity. More than anything else, however, the idea is that of a "Europe of difference." Thus, speaking about building identity does not necessarily mean cultural homogenization. Rather there is a built-in tension between imagining Europe as a homogenous cultural denominator on one hand and acknowledging "identity as diversity" on the other (Dutch National Spatial Planning Agency 2000, 7). This process leads the ESDP discourse into yet another terrain of tension and conflict.

NorVISION: A Short Exploration of a Followup Vision

As an example of the fast-growing number of projects under development in the slipstream of the ESDP, the chapter now focuses on the Interreg IIC North Sea Region (NSR) program's spatial vision called NorVISION. Geographically, the NSR consists of regions from the U.K., The Netherlands, Sweden, Denmark, Norway and Germany bordering the North Sea (Figure 2). In line with the ESDP, any Interreg program must articulate a spatial vision. Thus the individual projects should fit within the knowledge frame set out in the Potsdam document (CEC 1999a).

FIGURE **2**
Representing the North Sea Region

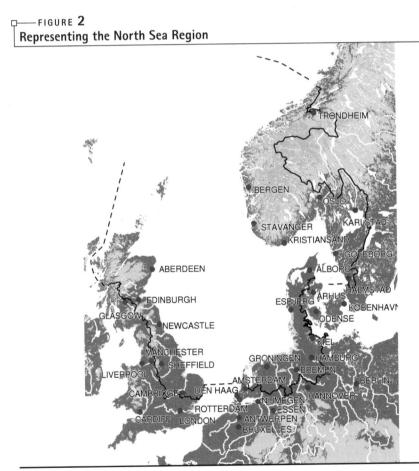

Source: VWG (2000b, 2)

See insert Figure A18 for a color version of this map.

Language/Articulation: The NorVISION Document

The NorVISION document deals with the strategic role and position of this transnational region in the new Europe and gives an assessment of its strategic strengths and weaknesses (VWG 2000b). Thus, the document is within the same genre as other spatial development perspectives such as the ESDP (CEC 1999a) and Visions and Strategies around the Baltic Sea (VASAB) 2010 (Ministers for Spatial Planning and Development 1994).

The NorVISION document begins with the message that the NSR should be seen as a specific example of ESDP thinking (VWG 2000b, 1). Thus the NSR presents itself as one of the potential new dynamic global economic integration zones launched in the ESDP (CEC 1999a, 20). A gap identified at the transnational level is to be bridged by Interreg projects. Even though the Vision Working Group (VWG) characterizes the ESDP as more metropolitan and agglomeration-oriented than NorVISION, and thus not as polycentric as it might appear, NorVISION sees its region in much the same way as the ESDP imagines the European territory (polycentric here means balanced (see Chapter 4). In an increasingly globalized world, themes such as information technology, the knowledge society, increased mobility, changing life styles, environmental degradation and growing conflicts between short- and long-term goals within politics are key (VWG 2000b, 3).

Social Practices: NorVISION Institutions, Agents and Events

A meeting in Aalborg, Denmark in March 2000, involving partners in the North Sea Region Interreg IIC project, had the explicit goal of refining the NorVISION document. This section looks into who the agents are and what institutional links they represent. By taking a specific event as a point of departure, the practice side of the discourse analysis is thus explored.

Among the several agents and institutions represented at the Aalborg meeting were the North Sea Region Spatial Vision Working Group (VWG); the national and regional planning authorities of Denmark, Germany, The Netherlands, Sweden, the U.K. and Norway (buying herself into Interreg, since she is not an EU member); the head of the Interreg IIC NSR secretariat in Viborg (Denmark); and a German consultant were present. Also included were representatives from academia, as well as from neighboring Interreg IIC visions—the Northwest Metropolitan Area and the Baltic Sea Region—for a total of 39 participants.

The participants gathered in four working groups to discuss themes of transport and information technology; environmental protection and energy; rural development and tourism; and urban development and participation (the only theme dealt with here). In the plenary session, one of the main issues discussed was the relationship between rural and urban areas (VWG 2000a, 1). Two issues dominated the proceedings: the conceptual framework that leaves the impression of a rigid split between rural and urban areas; and the debate on the status of rural areas. As in many ESDP discussions, the issue was urban hegemony over rural peripherality. Another theme central to the agenda was the question of competition. Several workshops reported that their themes needed to be seen in the light of increasing competition among cities and regions. In accordance with the ESDP, however, the question of competitiveness is articulated within the vocabulary of balanced competitiveness and competition within cooperation (VWG 2000a, 2)

Studying the process and methods used at this meeting, it becomes clear that the practice of transnational policy formulation has as much to do with network building as with the more specific wording of documents. The workshop activities give an indication of the character of the whole exercise as one of building a common language. This form of collaborative spatial vision making is an attempt to construct a vocabulary about spatial issues and problems. In this case the connection to the ESDP was clear, giving another important function to this "mother document," namely, to facilitate such transnational discussions all over the EU using an adequate vocabulary and within the right frame of mind. Furthermore, the working process and the discussions around NorVISION cannot be described as anything but elite-oriented and without much transparency, which also conforms to the ESDP process.

The NorVISION Rationales

How the basic rationale of this vision links up with the power theme can be seen by the document's primary capacity to promote the emergence of links, networks and communication among planners from different countries. Thus, a vital part of its rationale is to encourage transnational exchanges among the national territories nested within the larger territory of the EU—and beyond this limit with the participation of Norway. Thus, breaking with spatial thinking oriented around nation states appears to be one of the prime targets of NorVISION. This can be seen as a rationale embedded within a discourse of European unity that is part of the implicit rationale of reimagining European identity. It appears crucial to acknowledge that such a framing exercise is by no means a neutral affair. The conflict between rural peripherality and urban centrality finds its way into this vision, and one finds tension and contradiction between competing rationales.

Similar to other processes of European spatial vision making, the rationale is articulated with the vocabulary of balanced competitiveness and polycentrism. Furthermore, there are good reasons to view the ESDP as a rhetorical and funding device that seeks to optimize areas of urban growth. This does not appear to be the case with NorVISION, at least not quite to the same extent. Like the ESDP, NorVISION relates to the ambiguous rhetorical device of the policy triangle of growth-ecology-equity (Eser 1997, 18). The relationship here, however, is not as clear-cut as within the ESDP, perhaps because there is a more realistic scope for this vision to be framed outside the urban-agglomeration logic. Thus, the spatial context for NorVISION differs from that of the ESDP, making a vision based on a rationale less biased toward urban agglomeration a more realistic option.

In reimagining European identity, NorVISION appears to point in two directions. One is the continuation and support of the ESDP discourse that has been identified as one of articulating European identity. The other bears on the idea of nested discourses of identity. NorVISION often draws from the shared history and "imagined community" of Scandinavia (Anderson 1991). Things get confused, however, with the inclusion of the U.K. Thus, NorVISION is more of a prolongation than a break with the ESDP "master narrative" of reimagining European identity. Along with this conclusion is an ex ante evaluation of the next generation of Interreg programs for the North Sea area (IR IIIB) stating that networking within the Interreg program is the "principal form of European integration promoted by Interreg" (Kokkonen and Mariussen 2001, 27).

Excavating the Rationales

New discourses on European space and territory carry within them three explicit rationales and one implicit one. Here, the main features of such nested rationales are drawn out.

First, the three explicit rationales are identified as economic growth through global urban competition, environmental sustainability and finally social cohesion (spatial justice). These are not only clearly articulated as the basic values; they are also mutually incompatible in that none of them can be attained without damaging the others. This can be seen in the bias toward economic growth and global urban competition. In Hajer's words, this is a spatial representation primarily in the "Europe of flows" (Hajer 2000, 135). In a policy discourse of a Europe of flows, regions and cities will increasingly present their visions as repositioned and connected to the spatiality of flows. Ascribing hegemony to the Europe of flows by representing European spatiality in the vocabulary of flows is an act of naturalizing the growing urge to be a principal player in global competition. Such a notion clearly contradicts the idea of infrastructures for a more balanced form of development. There appears to be support for a reading of the ESDP as a "winner's story" in a globalizing world (Newman 2000, 901), or in words of Zonneveld (2000, 278): "Now, the ESDP officially recognizes the economically better-off 'locomotives' of the European Economy as official policy categories."

Second, there is the implicit rationale of reimagining European identity. The question of representing European identity and territory together with the rationales of growth, ecology and equity can be seen as part of a general theme of rescaling that cuts across EU policies:

> [R]escaling processes are intensifying in the 1990s as various powers of central state institutions are re-articulated upwards towards supranational regulatory regimes such as the European Union, and devolved downwards towards subnational scales of governance such as regional, local, and municipal state institutions or newly constructed urban and regional levels of governance (Brenner 1998, 476).

The EU discourse could be said to express a certain way of framing knowledge and reality. Such notions of space and knowledge are being installed as the natural way of seeing European space. One of the most illustrative examples of the scope of this new spatial logic is the plan to let the ESDP be the backbone for a new geography textbook for secondary schools (Ministers Responsible for Spatial Planning and Urban/Regional Policy 1999, 6). This is a clear expression of how this discourse attempts to frame the minds of social agents by creating a specific European spatial identity thinking. Furthermore, it is an example of the microprocesses within which such discursive powers operate. The ESDP might be thought of as a new geographic imagination facilitating the construction of a European identity, thus complementing the other new symbols of EU unity: the flag, the hymn, the passports and so forth (Hedetoft 1997, 152–153; Kohli 2000, 121). In this sense the underlying discourse of European identity is akin to building an "imagined community" (Anderson 1991).

A consensus exists among a number of analysts about viewing the question of European identity as something that could be constructed, but not in opposition to national and subnational identities. According to such thinking European identity cannot take its cues from national identity. Rather, what is needed is a "new hybrid" (Kohli 2000, 114). Thus, European identity is not opposed to national identity, since identity should be understood as multilayered (Kohli 2000, 126) and implying a shared loyalty toward more than the (so far) hegemonic nation state level (Castells 1998, 333; Weiler 1999, 346).

In analyzing these new discourses of nested European territories, the importance of the identity building process should not be underestimated, even though the question of cultural identity is less prominent in the ESDP (Dutch National Spatial Planning Agency 2000, 70). Furthermore, this question will gain even more weight with the enlargement of the EU. Here this sort of thinking could work as a stimulus to the new real or imagined geographies of Europe. In this process, such representations of space and their accompanying transnational institution and network building might function as a vehicle for further European integration. Although the explicit discourses underlying the ESDP are at odds with each other, this analysis suggests an interpretation of the general discourse as one of building European identity. This takes place, however, in the form of identity as diversity. Thus, one can see adding a layer of community building to the notions of identification with the "European idea" or "constitutional patriotism," in Habermas' words (1996, 507).

The point is that these new spatial visions complement this loyalty to the idea with an attempt to articulate a loyalty to the territory. The question remaining is whether this opens the political agenda to use documents like the ESDP and NorVISION in an act of identity construction coined around openness and a "progressive sense of place" (Massey 1993) or whether the effect is rather the opposite. Here the question of enlargement can easily put a stick in the wheel and thus obstruct the vision of an enlarged imagined community. In the end, one can say there is a new agenda for European planners and policy makers, an agenda that is born out of a new societal context for planning, or a new era.

The age when urban developers and planners could simply concern themselves with one spatial, geographical reality—and could produce planning or design proposals for them in a logical sequence of operations—seems to have come to an end. Instead, they have to take account of several spatial domains—fixed places, physical and virtual networks—and several notions of space and time: the sequential clock time and the timeless time of telematics networks with their temporal 'loops' and their yearning for immediacy. (Dutch National Spatial Planning Agency 2000, 124)

Concluding Remarks

The ESDP and NorVISION are based on a process of reimagining European territorial identity. The resulting visions are more than rhetorical devices, however, because they establish frameworks that direct EU measures toward a coordinated set of objectives. These new transnational processes are characterized by their dimensions of second-order governance, informal procedures, networking and low transparency of the infranational level of governance. Thus, the institutional and practice-oriented side of the discourse analysis makes the problem of democracy-as-transparency explicit. It is legitimate to voice concerns here for the democratic perspectives of such new forms of planning. Furthermore, both the ESDP and NorVISION process are examples of a new form of transnational planning, where planners develop new capacities for networking and collaboration: creating new vocabularies for dealing with spatial issues and establishing such notions of space and knowledge as the natural way of perceiving European space.

The discourses underlying the ESDP (and NorVISION), however, represent an incoherent composite of rationales. Perhaps most visible is the tension between competition and cohesion. This is not a regrettable omission but an illustration of the political pragmatism governing these new spatial visions. Such pragmatism leaves room for power struggles over how the European territory should be represented in global urban competition, environmental sustainability, social equity (spatial justice) and territorial identity. Here the aim has been to identify the emerging complex representation of Europe's territory. On one hand, this explicitly relates to the quest for economic growth, environmentally sound development and social cohesion, and on the other, it carries within it the underlying message of reimagining European identity.

What this new spatial discourse could mean for planners and policy makers in the U.S. is difficult to predict. For one thing, regional economic differences are much more outspoken within the European territory than in the U.S. Furthermore, there is a more homogenous culture, self-perception and identity in the North American context, at least at the national level. But the plural cultural identities throughout the U.S. might call for some cross-border exercises that could find a similar expression by imagining new distinct regional identities and forms of collaboration. Furthermore, the European experiment can be studied by North American planners and politicians with an eye toward building capacities and links across state borders. To the best of this author's knowledge, this is not standard procedure in the U.S. The problem of balancing growth, sustainability and equity is not an exclusively European issue. There is room for mutual learning across the Atlantic. The most reasonable scope for utilizing these new European experiences in the U.S. might be in seeing them as an opportunity to study the difference between the U.S. and the EU.

Visions and Visioning in European Spatial Planning

Vincent Nadin

Cooperation on spatial planning in Europe has given rise to a new planning instrument: the transnational spatial vision. Four principal examples of such visions have been produced covering large parts of the European territory. This chapter examines the process and product of these transnational visioning exercises and reflects on their significance in the context of European integration. It compares the objectives, scope and process of the four examples and then turns to a more detailed examination of one example: A Spatial Vision for Northwest Europe (NWMA Spatial Vision Group 2000). Finally, tentative conclusions are offered on the value of the visioning process in transnational spatial planning and on its significance for the process of European integration.

Transnational Spatial Visions in Europe

The roots of transnational spatial visioning can be found among the national and transnational regional planning strategies prepared by governments of the smaller countries of Northwest Europe, such as the Dutch spatial planning strategy (VROM 2001) and the Benelux structure plan (UEB 1997). Chapter 3 explains how these and other experiments raised awareness of transnational spatial development trends and the potential of planning responses at the same scale. The first transnational vision document, Vision and Strategies around the Baltic Sea Region (VASAB) 2010 (Committee on Spatial Development of the Baltic Sea Region 1995) and had significant influence on the European Commission's support for transnational visions that followed under the European Community initiative Interreg IIC. There are other examples of international regional planning on the grand scale, such as the Third Regional Plan for the New York–New Jersey–Connecticut metropolitan area (Regional Plan Association 1996), that show some similarities with what is happening in Europe. The added dimension of spatial vision exercises is the challenge of cross-sectoral work across national borders.

Chapter 1 explains how the Interreg IIC initiative was created to promote transnational cooperation on spatial planning among the EU member states, in parallel with the later stages of the preparation of the European Spatial Development Perspective (ESDP) (CEC 1999a). Seven transnational regions were defined in which spatial planning projects involving partners from a number of member states would benefit from co-financing from the EU. The transnational regions defined under the earlier Europe 2000 reports were the starting point for defining the Interreg regions, although significant changes were negotiated (see Chapter 3). Figure 1 shows the agreed transnational areas for Interreg IIC that later went on to prepare spatial visions.

Each Interreg IIC program co-financed numerous cooperative projects on spatial planning, but the EC guidelines also called for each transnational regional partnership to prepare "a vision" for its region: an overarching transnational planning strategy or framework. The proposed visions were to provide a statement of shared goals for the transnational spatial structure and a focus for drawing together findings from numerous rather small and independent

FIGURE **1**
The Four Transnational Regions that Produced Vision Documents

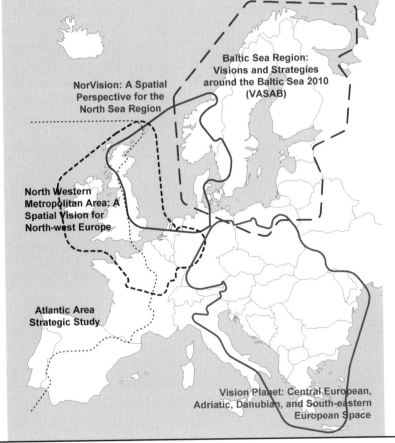

Courtesy of Vincent Nadin

projects. Another intention was that each vision should provide a bridge between the ESDP and national and regional plans through a more detailed examination of spatial development trends within the transnational region in question. Though the thinking behind the visions has not been made explicit, the implicit argument is that they add value to national and regional planning processes in three ways: measuring the territorial impacts of sectoral policies at this scale; identifying and managing conflicts among territorial demands; and revealing opportunities for synergy among the actions of member states and regions (Schindegger 2000). Thus, the long-term horizon of the visions, looking ahead 30 years or more, was intended to complement priorities set out in detailed operational programs for each transnational region that governed the selection of transnational projects over a much shorter time.

To date, only four of the seven Interreg regions have produced a vision document (see Table 1).[1] In two transnational regions, cooperation through a visioning process was motivated by the rapid changes in economic and political geography of the transition in the former communist states. VASAB 2010 was published in 1995 by the Baltic Sea region states and predates the Interreg IIC initiative. VASAB was advanced through a second document, From Vision to Action, published in 1997, and in 1999 work began on an updating and extension of the strategy. The CADSES region involves 12 countries across both eastern and western Europe, around the Danube and Adriatic areas, and work began on its vision document in 1997, resulting in the report, Vision Planet (Vision Planet Project Panel 2000).[2] Both VASAB and Vision Planet emphasize establishing effective spatial planning within the newly democratic states and encouraging effective liaison between them and the EU states.

The North Sea Region began work on a spatial vision in 1998 and its final document was NorVISION (VWG 2000b). The Northwestern Metropolitan Area (NWMA) was the last to begin work on visioning with its discussion document, A Spatial Vision for Northwest Europe, published in late 2000. A more detailed account of the process and product of the vision for Northwest Europe is presented in the second part of this chapter. The Atlantic Area also published a strategic study in 2000, which in many respects is similar to the other four documents, but it is not considered in detail here.

---

[1] The vision documents and further details are available as follows: the Baltic Sea Region's VASAB 2010; CADSES' Vision Planet: the North Sea Region's NorVISION *(www.mem.dk/lpa/landsplan/ international/norvision.htm)*; and the Northwestern Metropolitan Area's Spatial Vision for Northwest Europe *(www.uwe.ac.uk/fbe/vision)*. The Atlantic Area program has also produced a Strategic Study on Interregional Cooperation in the Atlantic Area. This has many similarities with the vision exercises, although it focuses more explicitly on forming a strategy for the implementation of Interreg III over the subsequent six years. Of the other Interreg IIC transnational regions, the Atlantic Area secretariat reported that a similar process had been undertaken in preparing the operational program for Interreg IIC and its successor the program for Interreg IIIB. None of the Article 10 pilot action regions produced a vision document.

[2] Cooperation within the CADSES region is closely linked to another transnational cooperation area around the Black Sea: European Space and Territorial Integration Alternatives (ESTIA). Six countries in Southeast Europe are cooperating on transnational spatial planning through ESTIA but this project lies outside the Interreg Initiative discussed here. There is also a spatial planning cooperation program in the Black Sea Region, and a joint concept has been prepared.

TABLE 1

Summary of the Vision Partners and Processes

The Baltic Sea Region States	VASAB 2010	11 countries EU: Denmark, Sweden, Finland, Germany (Schleswig-Holstein, Hamburg, Mecklenburg-Vorpommern, Berlin, Brandenburg) Non-EU: Norway, Russia (Murmansk oblast, Karelia, St. Petersburg, Leningrad oblast, Novogorod oblast, Pskov oblast, Kaliningrad oblast), Estonia, Latvia, Lithuania, Belarus, Poland	The process began in 1992 with a ministerial conference, followed by publication of Vision and Strategies around the Baltic Sea: Towards a Framework for Spatial Development in the Baltic Sea Region in 1995. A document From Vision to Action was published in 1997. An updating and extension of the strategy was started in 1999 to be completed by 2001.
CADSES	Vision Planet	12 countries EU: parts of Austria, Germany, Italy Non-EU: Bulgaria, Croatia, Czech Republic, Hungary, Romania, Slovak Republic, Slovenia, Yugoslavia, parts of Poland Note that the CADSES region also covers Albania, Bosnia-Herzegovina, Macedonia, Moldova and parts of the Ukraine (but the Vision Planet document only covers the 12 above) There is also close cooperation with the ESTIA zone involving Greece, Albania, Bulgaria, Romania, Macedonia, Yugoslavia	In 1997 Austria and Germany initiated the Interreg IIC project: Vision Planet (note that the non-EU partners were not able to access Interreg IIC funds). The vision document was published in 2000.
North Sea	NorVISION	7 countries, including one external partner subregions from: southwestern Norway, western Sweden, Danish Jutland (excluding its eastern parts with Århus), northern/northwestern Germany, northern Netherlands, northern and eastern U.K., including major parts of Scotland	In 1998 work started, and phase one and two reports were published for consultation in 1999. The final NorVISION document was published in July 2000.
Northwestern Metropolitan Area	A Spatial Vision for Northwest Europe	7 countries, all EU: the U.K., Ireland, Belgium and Luxembourg; northern France, the southern Netherlands, the western part of Germany	The project began early in 1999 and a conference was held at the end of that year. Consultation undertaken in spring 2000 with publication of a first vision statement in July 2000.

European Integration and the Emergence of Transnational Spatial Visions in Europe

The expansion of transnational cooperation on spatial planning is associated with the spatial development consequences of the growing economic interdependence of nations. Aspects of spatial development are effectively being globalized and made independent of nation states, a process strongly reinforced in the EU by the creation of the Single Market. Borders are far less important as physical, economic or social barriers, and there is much more inter-EU trade as a result. Firms and individuals are more locationally independent, and there is increasing competition among regions for inward investment. In the transition countries of Central and Eastern Europe, the changes have been even more dramatic.

The impacts of these forces on patterns of spatial development are widely recognized. Of particular note in the European context are increased spatial concentration of economic activity and the increasingly dominant position of global and some regional cities. Intensified competition exists among cities across national boundaries, with corresponding polarization of economic prosperity and negative environmental consequences (Sassen 1995; CEC 2000d). Locally such trends are experienced through, for example, changing patterns of cross-border commuting for work, shopping and leisure; more intense development pressures on favored locations; increased congestion around transnational transport axes; and development pressures around transport nodes of international significance. Other longstanding environmental problems, while not arising from the integration process, have nevertheless been given more prominence, notably river management and flooding in catchments that cross borders, and environmental pollution passed from one country to another along coasts, waterways or in the air.

Transnational cooperation on spatial planning offers an opportunity to address the growing transboundary spatial development issues and local problems that result from increasing interdependence. But the growth of transnational cooperation on planning is by no means an automatic response to increasing interdependence. Globalization and European integration challenge the sovereignty and autonomy of nation states and it is often resisted. In spatial planning, as in other policy fields, there has been an unwillingness by some national and regional governments to cede competencies to transnational institutions or in some cases to see them devolved to lower-level jurisdictions. What does the transnational spatial vision process tell us about European integration? Most importantly, what is the significance of the vision process? Do the vision strategies, alongside the ESDP, signal a further fundamental step in European integration through cooperation on spatial planning?

Among the numerous theoretical perspectives on European integration, there are two general and distinctive positions explained further by Faludi (see Chapters 1 and 10), and these provide useful benchmarks for considering the role and significance of spatial visions. The *intergovernmental position* emphasizes integration through cooperation among national (and in some cases regional) governments in pursuit of their individual political and economic interests. Intergovernmentalists have argued that national governments engage in cooperation for reasons of self-interest only. Governments do cede competence for specific functions to transnational organizations, but they retain ultimate control and could, if it were in their interest, regain these competencies. Integration proceeds largely by way of bargaining among the member states. Deals are struck, often involving concessions to ensure that the national interest or sovereignty is not compromised on issues of significant national concern. The result of negotiation among strong member states is that outcomes are limited to lowest common denominator solutions, and costs and benefits are generally spread evenly. Thus, a good deal of compromise exists, rather than true integration, where a more uneven distribution of advantage may be necessary. The emphasis on the nation state also applies to the role of interest groups, which continue to be organized predominantly along national lines.

The *functionalist or neofunctionalist position* emphasizes actors above and below national governments in the process of integration. EU-wide institutions and interest groups and regional governments play the dominant role in the extent and direction of change. Integration is said to have an internal logic: integration gives rise to further integration through a process of spillover. Thus, one set of common actions creates "a situation in which the original goal can be assured only be taking further actions, which in turn create a further condition and a need for more action, and so forth" (Lindberg 1963, 153). The case for transnational cooperation on spatial planning is sometimes thus argued as a necessary antidote to contradictory effects of regional policy and other uncoordinated EC actions. Linked to this is the notion of "creeping competence." This concept refers to situations where the EC takes an action, which is difficult to justify with reference to treaty obligations (such as the first round of environmental legislation), except in that it tackles the consequences of or is needed to complement other actions that are. Another aspect of the internal logic of integration is the redefinition of interests, as actors and groups who originally represent their own narrow interests recognize the benefits of and align themselves with common interests.

Aside from the driving forces of integration there is little argument that the powers of nation states have weakened (although from the position of the intergovernmentalists, national governments could still reverse the integration process). The multilevel or multijurisdictional nature of governance has intensified. The notion of a transnational region for spatial planning adds a further tier of jurisdiction to that usually discussed in this context. An important precondition for integration (and many others not discussed here), however, is the need for some common identity or shared sense of community. The existence of shared identities varies, but its general weakness in the EU—especially in comparison with the strong shared sense of identity of the U.S.—is a challenge to the notion of functional integration.

These two theoretical positions (albeit presented briefly here) provide a means of explaining and testing the significance of the transnational spatial visions.

The following sections briefly explain the objectives, content and procedure of four vision statements, then explore one vision process in more detail.

A Comparison of Four Transnational Spatial Visions

The word vision generally refers to a visualization of a predicted future state of affairs, perhaps to a desired outcome in the long term, and increasingly in its modern use in recognition of past failures to predict, to a vision of the future that can be "invented" (Shipley 2000). This interpretation comes from American experience where the visioning process has been used to enable a community to "determine what it wants to become and begin organizing to achieve it" (Solop 2001, 51; Oregon APA 1993, quoted in Shipley 2000). These general ideas of visioning are as relevant to the transnational as to the local level, though there will be considerable variations in practice at both levels.

A useful starting point for describing various models of visioning is provided by Shipley and Newkirk (1999) who identify four substantive forms of planning vision:[3]

□ The *vision as master plan* suggests a product providing a view of what the region covered should be like in *x* years time.

□ The *vision as the truth* is a forecast of what the region will be like in *x* years time.

□ The *vision as utopia or dystopia* will also be used to promote action by presenting a possible perfect situation or the worst horrors.

□ The *vision as mission statement* does not show a picture of the future, but instead sets down fundamental principles that should govern actions for the long-term good.

Shipley and Newkirk also suggest a number of functions of the visioning process: to identify the priority issues or an agenda for future cooperation; to generate solutions, alternative options and pathways; to generate commitment and build consensus around a common purpose; and to enable participation or manipulate opinion through debating long-term goals.

To some extent all four purposes of visioning suggested by Shipley and Newkirk are found in each example, but the model that comes through most strongly in all cases is the vision as mission statement. The visions have provided a forum where a mix of interests, predominantly those of national and regional governments, have been able to agree on a set of common principles to guide spatial planning in the future. The mission statement includes both substantive goal statements about spatial development patterns and principles about ways of doing planning that are conducive to taking into account long-term and transnational issues. The substantive objectives of the visions are similar. All have an environmental, economic and social dimension, and they seek an integrated strategy for the sustainable development of the region.

---

[3] Shipley and Newkirk (1999) present numerous meanings of vision, and this discussion only addresses those considered to be particularly useful in understanding visioning in spatial planning.

They take their cue from the fundamental objectives of the EU—economic competitiveness, sustainable development and social cohesion—and from the aims of the ESDP, primarily more balanced development and accessibility. Each speaks of the need to reconcile competing demands. The objectives of VASAB and Vision Planet emphasize social considerations and the promotion of the basic values of democracy and equality that reflect the particular situation in parts of these regions.

There is little evidence of the vision as utopia, and indeed the visions are not at all visionary in the utopian sense. The vision as the truth is evident in all, although with mostly general statements of damage that may be caused in the long term by current trends if action is not taken.[4] The vision as a master plan is only evident in general statements, for example, about the need for a more balanced settlement pattern. There are few specific proposals. A more accurate characterization of the main purpose of these examples is perhaps the vision as the current state. While this may appear to oppose what the word vision suggests, clearly a primary role of the European vision processes so far has been to exchange positions and understandings and reach some agreement about what is rather than what will be. The documents suggest that progress needs to be made, and indeed has been made, in developing a shared understanding and common language about the nature of spatial development and the possibilities of cooperation.

The principal purpose of the process has been to identify priority issues and set agendas for future cooperation, and to build some consensus around that agenda, but it is no more than an agenda of issues at this stage. There is much less attention given to generating solutions or enabling participation. All the visions are heavily government-inspired and led predominantly by central government planning bodies, although regional representatives have played a part in most cases. All the visions have been subject to some consultation, but this has been primarily among other government departments and agencies, and there is little evidence of wider ownership, especially among development interests. Political scrutiny and adoption of the visions has been limited, but perhaps less so for VASAB and NorVISION where a political tier of cooperation has been established. All of the visions recognize, however, that their long-term viability rests on generating a wider involvement and ownership of the vision objectives. As to methods, the visions have adopted a fairly standard, top-down and technocratic survey-analysis-plan approach. The result is that the visions have compiled a considerable amount of data, although comparability across national boundaries remains a significant barrier to analysis.[5]

In sum, the visions have contributed to a better understanding of spatial development patterns and trends in the transnational regions, but they are far from being visionary in the generally accepted sense of the term. Two prin-

---

[4] Most of the Europe 2000 transnational regional documents contained visions of the truth—explanations of spatial development trends and their wider implications that generally gave a negative picture for example, by describing increasing polarization of development and peripherality.

[5] The Programme on European Spatial Planning (Nordregio 2000b), a European Commission–sponsored study, details the categories of territorial analysis but this came too late to influence the current vision documents.

cipal factors have to be considered here. First, the visions are transnational, cutting across national and regional planning systems, policies, languages and cultures. Second, the visions, like the ESDP, promote a spatial planning approach, which for most places is a considerable departure from traditional land use planning.

The Transnational and Spatial Planning Dimensions of the Visions

The novelty of the visioning process creates considerable challenges, not least because of the scale and extent of transnational cooperation. There is only weak institutional apparatus at this level, both in technical expertise and a political platform, although there is considerable variation among the regions. Thus, there are questions about the leadership of the vision exercise, consultation and participation, and the issue of political scrutiny and adoption of the vision outcomes. (Leadership may be less of a problem where the transnational regions have a stronger institutional base, notably in the Baltic region). For technical analysis there are problems of data availability and compatibility, and about the conceptual understanding that drives data collection and analysis.

Underpinning these issues is the question of subsidiarity: what planning issues have to be addressed at the transnational level? The subsidiarity principle is widely used in European law and political debate, and it means that competencies should be located at the most appropriate jurisdictional level and should not be located at a higher level than is necessary. The transnational vision process signals that there are important competencies that lie above the member state or region and below the European Community level. In deciding what these are, the EU applies two rules: there must be a need to intervene at the higher level (that is, effective action is not possible at the lower level) and the intervention must bring some benefit to the parties involved (Nadin and Shaw 1999).

How these criteria might be applied to spatial development can be illustrated with a distinction between two extremes. At one extreme are spatial development issues that cut across national borders, where two or more countries must cooperate to adopt or apply a policy successfully, as in the case of a major cross-border road or railway. This is an interpretation of transnational in its most narrow sense, and it is evident here that transnational cooperation is both necessary and beneficial. At the other extreme are policies that can be adopted and implemented within one country or region, yet have no significant effect outside that country. Most local planning issues fall within this category, and it would be difficult to demonstrate either need or benefit. It can be argued, however, that there are benefits in addressing some issues at the transnational level to promote more consistency in policy and action, for example, policies tackling urban sprawl or access to urban services in rural areas. Including these issues means adopting a much wider interpretation of *transnational*.

Most spatial development issues fall between these two extremes, and in the end it is a political question. To what extent are national and regional governments prepared to allow a transnational intergovernmental approach to issues that otherwise are in their own jurisdiction? This is the ongoing debate in the spatial vision exercises. Across most of Europe there is limited understanding and few agreements about what the appropriate agenda is for planning at the transnational scale, or what institutional apparatus is required to deliver it. Although there is little explicit discussion of the concepts of transnationality and subsidiarity in the visions, the whole process of visioning has so far been centered on identifying the issues that can be addressed justifiably at the transnational level and the mechanisms for further cooperation at this level. Although not the normal use of the term, this is visionary.

Another factor that explains the apparent lack of vision is the spatial planning approach, used extensively here and in other chapters, but its meaning needs clarification. Spatial planning should not be confused with systems of physical–land use–city and regional planning in a country or region. In the EU context the term means coordinating the spatial or territorial dimension of sectoral policies (Nadin 2000; Nadin and Shaw 1999). The EC has described spatial planning as a method of securing "convergence and coordination between various sectoral policies" (CEC 1999b; Bastrup-Birk and Doucet 1997). This task is addressed to some extent by all planning systems with greater or lesser success, but generally planning does this from a position as one sector of government activity (and generally a weak sector). In European planning discourse there is a sense of the need for a spatial planning approach that transcends sectoral divisions, one that should act as an umbrella of policy as a territorially based strategy shared by each sector. This sense has grown in response to the criticism of the poor coordination of the sectoral activities of the EC (although this might apply equally in many member states).

Each vision states its objective on this broader spatial planning approach, but this is an ambitious aim, one that will diminish the potential for a visionary statement. First, one needs to understand the relationships among sectoral policies and their spatial development impacts, and the vision processes are only beginning to explore what the notion of spatial planning means in practice. The vision documents lean more toward the traditional land use and regional planning approach as to who is involved and consulted, and what policy options are proposed. Perhaps this is too critical; the visions are only a first step toward a spatial planning approach. In his review of VASAB, Groth (1999, 69) suggests that it presents the potential or an argument for "the further development of the concept of spatial planning as a cross-sectoral discipline."

The challenges of transnational spatial planning are reflected well in the use, or lack of use, of visualization in the spatial visions. Visualization can be an important tool in drawing attention to spatial development trends at the transnational scale, in managing the vision process and in defining the key spatial planning issues of transnational significance (Dühr 2001). Visualization through strong metaphors, in either verbal or visual forms, might be particularly effective in a context where different languages and planning cultures are brought together, but there are few examples in the vision documents produced so far. Most illustrations reflect the idea of the vision as what is: for example, the existing state of the economy, regional disparities, infrastructure networks; and this reflects the immature stage of the vision processes. Having identified the general problem, the visions are generally only at the stage of reaching agreement on purpose and method.

A Spatial Vision for Northwest Europe

The points made here can be further illustrated with a more detailed reference to one example of the transnational vision process (in which this author was involved): A Spatial Vision for Northwest Europe, and the subsequent consultation response to that document (NWMA Spatial Vision Group 2000).[6]

Northwest Europe is perhaps the most complex zone of urban development and communication links in the world. The Interreg region covered seven countries, a population of 143 million, numerous cities and cultural assets of international rank, the world's greatest concentration of global economic command functions and a major share of the world's international trade and communications gateways. The high and growing level of interdependencies across the region is undisputed. Intense industrial and commercial activity together with extensive mobility has produced a complex web of physical, economic and social interaction. As a result, cooperation on spatial planning has increased, especially at the cross-border level as shown in Figure 2. Although there have been previous studies, interdependencies in spatial development are not well understood.

The main part of the vision for Northwest Europe is an agenda for further cooperation, and thus it takes the form of a mission statement. Six priority challenges set out the long-term unsustainable trends requiring action:

- To enhance the global role of Northwest Europe's metropolitan areas;
- To ensure more fairness in the distribution of prosperity throughout Northwest Europe;
- To reduce the global environmental impact of Northwest Europe;
- To protect or manage the cultural and natural resources of Northwest Europe;
- To maintain a high level of access to and from Northwest Europe;
- To improve internal access and mobility in a sustainable way.

The challenges are intended to provide a foundation of shared goals and principles for future action, no more. The obvious interconnections and incompatibilities among the various aspirations have not been addressed. An agenda for discussion sets out the principal threats and opportunities for transnational spatial development. A diagram visualizes some of the priority issues, and it is here that the vision is most visionary (see Figure 3). There was considerable difficulty reaching agreement about the vision diagram, but it has

---

[6] A Spatial Vision for Northwest Europe was the outcome of the Interreg IIC vision project for the Northwestern Metropolitan Area Program (NWMA Spatial Vision Group 2000). For further details, see Chapter 3. The document is accompanied by a supplementary report on the consulting exercise.

FIGURE **2**
Areas of Cross-Border and Transnational Cooperation in Northwest Europe

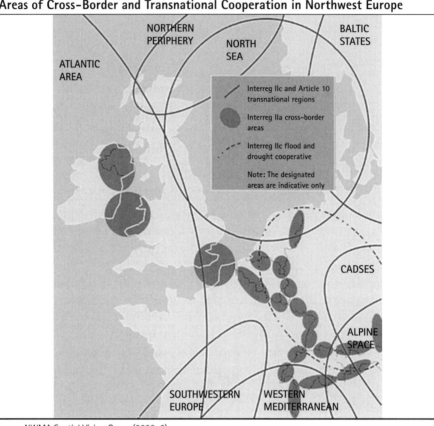

Source: NWMA Spatial Vision Group (2000, 6)
See insert Figure A17 for a color version of this map.

provoked discussion among relevant interests, beginning a process of establishing a common spatial development identity for Northwest Europe. The main agenda items of the diagram are:

☐ Four transnational cooperation zones defined according to common problems requiring further cooperation at the transnational level. The agendas for each zone may provide a starting point for considering the need for new transnational cooperation projects.

☐ Transnational transport axes and development corridors, identifying existing transport axes that may become development corridors; alternative transport axes that have the potential to bypass congested areas, and new and improved connections that are needed with other parts of Europe and the world.

☐ International gateways and investment zones, developing the ESDP principle of more balanced development of urban regions and promoting the idea of alternative economic zones with global economic, trade and communications functions. The vision argues that some networks of cities are well positioned to become 'counterweight global gateways' for Northwest Europe.

FIGURE **3**

A Vision for Northwest Europe: Spatial Vision Diagram

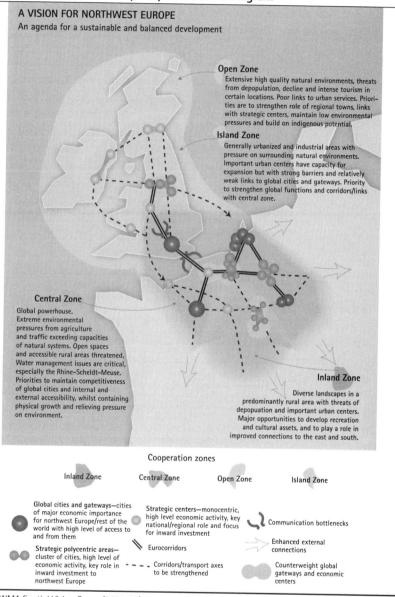

A VISION FOR NORTHWEST EUROPE
An agenda for a sustainable and balanced development

Open Zone
Extensive high quality natural environments, threats from depopulation, decline and intense tourism in certain locations. Poor links to urban services. Priorities are to strengthen role of regional towns, links with strategic centers, maintain low environmental pressures and build on indigenous potential.

Island Zone
Generally urbanized and industrial areas with pressure on surrounding natural environments. Important urban centers have capacity for expansion but with strong barriers and relatively weak links to global cities and gateways. Priority to strengthen global functions and corridors/links with central zone.

Central Zone
Global powerhouse. Extreme environmental pressures from agriculture and traffic exceeding capacities of natural systems. Open spaces and accessible rural areas threatened. Water management issues are critical, especially the Rhine-Scheldt-Meuse. Priorities to maintain competitiveness of global cities and internal and external accessibility, whilst containing physical growth and relieving pressure on environment.

Inland Zone
Diverse landscapes in a predominantly rural area with threats of depopuation and important urban centers. Major opportunities to develop recreation and cultural assets, and to play a role in improved connections to the east and south.

Cooperation zones

Inland Zone   Central Zone   Open Zone   Island Zone

Global cities and gateways—cities of major economic importance for northwest Europe/rest of the world with high level of access to and from them

Strategic centers—monocentric, high level economic activity, key national/regional role and focus for inward investment

Communication bottlenecks

Strategic polycentric areas—cluster of cities, high level of economic activity, key role in inward investment to northwest Europe

Eurocorridors

Enhanced external connections

- - - Corridors/transport axes to be strengthened

Counterweight global gateways and economic centers

Source: NWMA Spatial Vision Group (2000, 30)
See insert Figure A21 for a color version of this map.

The response to consultation has supported the agenda-setting purpose of the visioning exercise, although there has been some criticism of individual items that certain groups perceive as damaging to their interests. Generally the vision agenda has succeeded in stimulating thinking at different levels of government about the transnational positioning of cities and regions, and in shaping ideas about the need for more specific transnational cooperation projects. But there is also wide support for using the vision process more purposefully to guide strategic investments from the EU, member states and the private sector, and to assist in selecting priority areas for regional policy support.

The process by which this agenda has been reached has been entirely government sponsored and controlled. A Spatial Vision Group was formed of officials representing the national and regional levels of government in the seven member states, and a multinational consulting team provided technical assistance. They used an analysis of spatial characteristics and dynamics (based on previous studies) and an evaluation of existing national and regional planning policies. The group engaged in a political process of debate, negotiation and consensus building on the critical issues and long-term development goals for the region. The whole process has taken place within the technical sphere, and politicians have only been involved in launching the documents. Two conferences were held primarily for those involved in the Interreg IIC projects in this region, and a few specific transnational projects made important contributions to the process.[7] Consultation on the document was carefully controlled by the vision group members in their own countries, in part because of questions raised about the competence of the vision group as a whole to consult in the countries. The consultation exercise was conducted almost entirely within government circles, primarily with planning authorities.

The process has found support, but has also received considerable criticism concerning the top-down nature of the vision exercise, and the failure to engage the regions, service providers and the private sector. Questions have also been raised about the perceived weaknesses in the technical underpinning of the vision document and its urban bias. Some national and regional governments have suggested that the vision process should pay more attention to existing national and regional planning strategies as a starting point. Little support exists for the creation of major new institutional arrangements to support the vision process, but rather encouragement to continue the informal intergovernmental cooperation. There is recognition that if the vision process is to play a more significant role in relation to directing investments, however, proposals must be discussed and agreed upon at the political level. This would also go some way toward addressing the widespread uncertainty about the status of the vision discussion document.

The challenge presented by the transnational dimension is enormous. Such cooperation among so many planning jurisdictions would be difficult enough, but it is compounded by the fragmentation of physical geography (with extensive coastline borders); the political and cultural geography of many national and regional borders; and numerous official languages. Consultation feedback also made reference to the limited capacity of national and regional institutions and instruments to address these challenges effectively.

The vision group engaged in extensive debates about the meaning and significance of certain spatial development trends and planning approaches,

---

[7] For example, the North European Trade Axis project *(www.netaproject.org.uk)* seeks to develop the potential for a new east-west trade axis; and Sustainable Open Space *(www.sosnwma.org)* examines the distribution and conservation of natural resources; and Gemaca II on strengthening the complementarity of metropolitan regions.

not least of all the very purpose and form of the vision itself. The scope of the vision process was also a contentious issue and the outcome was to seek to limit the vision agenda issues to those with a strong need to cooperate. The balance of opinion in the consultation response, however, was strongly in favor of widening the scope of the vision process, thus adopting a wider definition of transnationality to foster more cooperation on issues of shared concern, such as urban growth management. Other pressures on the vision group worked in the opposite direction. The vision has been developed and co-financed within the EU structural fund regime, which emphasizes generating concrete benefits and demonstrating added value in the short term. An understandably defensive attitude exists among vision partners, who are perhaps reticent to fully engage in a transnational enterprise and are more concerned about the implications of any strategy for their home countries and regions.

Like the other vision documents, A Spatial Vision for Northwest Europe asserts the importance of a horizontal, cross-sectoral and integrated approach. In practice, however, the product is still largely organized around sectoral policies rather than integrated strategies. Some compartmentalization is inevitable; but the challenge is to provide an integrated evaluation framework for proposed sectoral policies and actions at the transnational scale. Here, the vision still has some distance to go. The limited involvement of representatives of other sectoral policy areas in the vision process and consulting exercise (a choice of the vision group) is one indication of the limited progress that has been made in moving from a land use planning to a spatial planning approach.

The vision diagram demonstrates where most progress has been made in integration and it has had considerable impact, at least in provoking comment. The diagram has successfully challenged respondents to consider their transnational position to the rest of Northwest Europe and to challenge the agenda given (and their own). Numerous comments, however, seek only to safeguard or promote the status of particular countries, regions and cities through their designation on the vision diagram. Other comments point to the different interpretations of key concepts and symbols in different regions.

Conclusion: European Integration and the Spatial Visions

The European transnational visions are an ambitious experiment in spatial planning. While there is variation in the depth of experience, in all cases the visioning process is in its infancy and expectations of its value should be judged with this in mind.

At this stage the visions could hardly be described as visionary. For the most part they tread a well-worn path of reasoning and offer no radical insights. Vision is perhaps a misnomer. In the main they are much more pragmatic documents, serving up a mission statement or a political agenda about where there is a need for cooperative action on spatial development at the transnational level. Thus, they reflect the complex transnational situation they seek to address. Each recognizes and illustrates the considerable effort that is needed to arrive at a shared understanding and definition of the issues among partners with different planning traditions. They also concentrate largely on immediate problems, rather than anticipating future states in the long term.

The mission statements provide an agenda for action in the next stages (for those vision processes that continue), but they are not convincing on the spatial planning approach. Their aspirations are stated, but in practice the vision processes are typical top-down and rather technocratic planning processes, so far led by planners for planners. Many of the issues are discussed predominantly in land use planning terms. This is not to undermine the value of these visions, but rather to hint at how the next stages may be handled differently.

This experience of the visioning process reflects the tension between the intergovernmental and functionalist views of European integration. The intergovernmentalists might point to the heavy hand of national governments that have carefully defended their interests. Their pragmatic response is reflected in the lack of visionary content. The involvement of other nongovernmental interests has been limited, and where they are represented they are largely nationally or regionally based. The emphasis on national interests has led the visions to be inward-looking, concentrating on relations among the constituent countries and regions while giving only passing reference to external relations. The outcomes reflect a process of bargaining among interests, or indeed, a collection of different interests, rather than a definition of a shared interest. A truly visionary vision would require clear position on the shared interest.

The functionalists might point to the influence of the European institutions. Despite the high level of interdependence, much of this cooperation would not exist without the EC and the support it has received on spatial planning from other European institutions and governments. Certain member states have also played a determining role. Functionalists might also cite spillover because the visions address the contradictions and consequences of other interventions. It could be argued, however, that spillover has been more important as a justification for the EC to act, rather than itself leading to further integration. While most of the vision debates appear to be about protecting existing interests, there is some evidence of a redefinition of interests around common concerns. This comes out clearly in the consultation on the vision for Northwest Europe, which has prompted national and regional governments to look afresh at their interests in the light of the analysis presented in the vision documents, and in some cases, national and regional policy is being reviewed with this in mind. Thus, the next round of visioning may see more, quite different inputs from some interests.

Whether a wider range of interests becomes involved in future development of the spatial visions will depend on the institutional arrangements through which they are prepared. National governments generally will continue to resist establishing strong spatial planning organizations at the transnational level. Although institutional capacity is being strengthened at the transnational level, for example, in relation to the management of EC programs, spatial planning could, only in its broadest and most limited sense, be described as a contribution to multilevel governance. This process could be accelerated, however, particularly since competency over some areas of strategic planning, as a rather inconsequential area of public intervention in the minds of many national politicians, could be traded off against other more pressing demands. It is difficult to generalize about the actions of governments; their responses on transnational spatial planning have varied considerably. In general, the smaller countries such as The Netherlands, where interdependence with neighboring countries has been a fact of life for many years, have been the strongest supporters. But for other reasons, some large countries such as France, or regions within a country such as Italy, have also been in the vanguard of promoting more transnational cooperation on planning.

The significance of the vision process for European integration is not so much with the creation of new transnational planning agencies and instruments, although some will be concerned about that. Rather, the visions, and the Interreg process generally, are helping shape an identity for the transnational regions and helping break down existing barriers to identifying and tackling spatial cross-border development problems. Networks are being established and the capacity of planning organization in transnational planning strengthened through joint working on planning issues. Above all the vision processes have begun the task of uncovering and sharing different understandings of spatial development and planning—something that has probably been underestimated. Rarely does this joint work lead to concrete outputs, but the gradual shifting of attitudes, the reshaping of definitions and identity, and the gradual effect of this on changing priorities may be more important in the midterm. In this way the vision processes contribute to satisfying a fundamental precondition for further European integration.

The most likely next step for a more differentiated vision exercise involves a process of consensus about a shared and perhaps radical vision for the long term; a more focused process to identify a program of key decisions, investment priorities and evaluation criteria, but concentrating on a narrow range of strongly transnational issues; and a wider process of discussion and debate to tease out a shared understanding (or to recognize different understandings) of a much wider range of spatial planning issues. In any event, the visions will remain nonbinding and reliant on persuasion to exert influence. The effectiveness of the visions as mission statements depends on the extent to which other powerful public and private interests can be encouraged to adopt the same principles. Much more attention needs to be paid to involving other interests in the process and to communicating the outcomes more widely and effectively.

How to Reduce the Burden of Coordination in European Spatial Planning

Arthur Benz

The European Spatial Planning Perspective (ESDP) signifies the emergence of a new policy field of the EU. Although the status and future role of the program are not yet clear, the ESDP intends to provide a basis for planning and coordinating European policies, and for guiding spatial planning at the national, regional and local levels. To fulfill these functions the ESDP has to be a coordinated process that cuts across levels and includes several sector policies. This coordination has to rely on communication and negotiations for the time being, since the EU has no formal spatial planning powers and the ESDP merely represents an informal accord of the member states' governments. Few instruments are available for inducing national, regional and local actors to take the ESDP into account in their own planning.

Since it is impossible to achieve agreement among all relevant actors affected by the program if the ESDP relies merely on persuasion, spatial planning is doomed to become a symbolic policy. At the same time, coordination by negotiation also carries risks. In particular, it raises the transaction costs. It is difficult to detect all interests affected by planning and it is even more difficult to come to an agreement among relevant actors. Transaction costs increase with the number of actors involved, but even more so with the actors' commitment to the government or constituency they represent. To prevent spatial planning from becoming inflexible and from being doomed to deadlock, it is necessary to find ways of reducing the costs of negotiations. Coordination has to focus on core aspects of spatial planning, and it has to be based on procedures that allow decisions in spite of the multitude of actors and organizations involved and the divergent interests to be considered.

This chapter discusses strategies of selective coordination that maintain far-reaching autonomy in policy making at the national and regional levels. In particular, it considers forms of issue-specific positive coordination (simultaneous decision on different policies); negative coordination (a single policy is examined regarding its negative external effects); coordination by focused (i.e., decision-oriented) discourses and ideas; and the use of incentives and benchmarking. The intention here is to show how cross-sectoral and cross-level coordination is feasible in a system of multilevel governance.

The Quest for Coordination in European Spatial Planning

Coordination is a fundamental task of planning in general and spatial or territorial planning in particular. Planning can be defined as the systematic coordination of various policies and activities aimed at influencing future developments. This includes the cognitive task of analyzing developments, searching for realistic goals and elaborating perspectives for the future, as well as the political task of overcoming conflicts of interest and integrating divergent policies. Cognitive and political aspects of planning are interrelated. Political conflicts are influenced by the quality of the analysis and the scenarios, the availability of convincing information and the formulation of goals. How knowledge is interpreted and goals are formulated, however, are determined by the political process. Moreover, when it comes to the application of a program, cognitive limits of planning turn into political conflicts in the coordination process. Leaving aside the more technical aspects of planning, the following sections deal with this political dimension of the formulation and application of the ESDP.

The need for coordination in spatial planning at the European level is not self-evident. While it is widely accepted that the European Commission should consider spatial development in its policies, whether and to what extent the EU should deal with regional development in member states is under debate. Indeed, some of the most relevant factors influencing the territorial allocation of resources that are amenable to government control are determined at the local and regional level. Thus, economists have suggested regionalizing policies designed to promote spatial development. Moreover, conflicts over the use of space by public and private investors that ignore ecological, social or cultural concerns usually arise in national and subnational territorial settings. They can be better managed at decentralized levels of government.

Even if these strong arguments for decentralization in spatial planning are acknowledged, it must be realized that in the integrated Single Market of Europe, development in the regions is now much more interdependent than in the past. The particular spatial structures of member states and their regions are to a considerable degree influenced by decisions beyond the reach of the authorities responsible for spatial planning. These decisions are made partly by private organizations operating in the market and partly by political and administrative authorities of the EU and the member states.

As to the repercussions on the economic sector, the creation of the Single Market has deeply affected the macrostructures of European space, by a real-location of economic resources. The free flow of people, goods, services and capital has extended and intensified European-wide competition among private firms as well as among localities. Beyond the consequences for intraregional development, the Single Market has brought about several changes for European spatial structures.

First, a new functional division of labor between regions is evolving. European regions with particular economic advantages and excellent infrastructure attract investors from their former locations that were considered optimal in a national setting. The reallocation of investments in the larger European context is driven by the opportunities to reduce costs by adequately combining private and public activities in production clusters and networks. This leads to a concentration of highly specialized economic functions in a few regions. At the same time, other investments are more dispersed over the larger European territory, thus increasing transport volumes. The specialization of regions and the dispersion of private investments throughout Europe increase the need for an integrated European network of transport and communication infrastructure.

Second, in the larger city regions, the need for central locations for specialized activities causes increasing pressure for land use in the whole agglomeration. From a European point of view, these regions have to fulfill their function in a territorial division of labor. From a regional point of view, the same structural changes can provoke conflicts among economic, social and ecological concerns, or between competing interests in the use of attractive locations. If these regions are unable to deal with these conflicts and fail to implement a sustainable development strategy, they cannot adequately fulfill their functions in the European setting.

Finally, regions that profited from the protective effects of national boundaries have lost in the competition among regions in Europe. At the same time, European regional policy has to avoid the decline of these regions because an unbalanced territorial structure can have negative consequences for the future cohesion of the Single Market.

Beyond these reasons relating to the economic dynamics of the Single Market, the need for coordination of national and regional spatial planning at the European level can be justified by pointing to the political consequences of European integration. The Europeanization of particular policies has led to the formation of coalitions of administrations at various levels. The political system of the EU is characterized by interlocking politics linking executives from the European Commission and from national ministries. By using the advantage of closed policy networks, they are able to shield their sectoral policies against external influences. Departments of national or regional government can take positions on external constraints when it comes to coordination processes inside their administration. For this reason, it must be assumed that the intensity of vertical linkages in Europeanized sectoral policies goes beyond what is reasonable in functional terms. This vertical fusion of power among special administrations reduces the effectiveness of horizontal coordination in member states and their regions. Spatial planning is the most important among policies negatively affected by deficient horizontal coordination. For these reasons, political decisions relevant to the territorial development of Europe have to be guided by a European spatial planning perspective and should be coordinated on this basis.

Problems of Coordination in Multilevel Governance

The ESDP does not aim at integrated planning covering all policies relevant to the shaping of territorial development. According to the standard definition of the EU, spatial planning is a policy designed to support the development of regions according to set principles and guidelines (ARL 1996, 4). Among these principles, sustainable development stands at the top and from the EU's point of view the ESDP should constitute an element of a strategy to implement this principle (Faludi and Zonneveld 1997, 263; Martin and Ten Velden 1997). Accordingly, the ESDP is focused on selected policy fields that are of particular importance for the development of macrostructures of European space (CEC 1999a).

Nevertheless, the ESDP itself recognizes that European spatial development policy affects different policies at different levels. On one hand, the program should be taken into consideration in the sector policies of the EU. *Territory* is defined as "a new dimension of European policies" (CEC 1999a, 7). Without a legal basis for spatial planning in the treaties, the EC and the informal meetings of the ministers of spatial planning are limited to making recommendations. The ESDP has been declared a nonbinding framework that has no immediate repercussions for the allocation of financial resources of the EU (CEC 1999a, 11). The goal of coordinating sectoral policies, however, is explicitly stated as a task of European spatial policy.

On the other hand, even if the ESDP does not set binding norms and goals, it should have consequences for planning in member states and regions. The relationship between European and national or regional spatial policies is guided by the subsidiarity principle, but what this means for the practice of coordination is not entirely clear. In 1994 the informal Council of Ministers of Spatial Planning at its meeting in Leipzig agreed to achieve better coordination of national and regional spatial planning by intergovernmental coordination among member states. The ESDP, the informal council concluded, has no binding effects for member states and the compliance of the relevant national or regional institutions with its goals will be voluntary only. By agreeing to the program, however, each member state government has accepted the obligation to take it into account in its own planning and policy making. This self-binding effect influences coordination in spatial policy at the levels of national and regional governments. Moreover, the ESDP is supposed to guide relevant cross-border cooperation among responsible authorities of member states. Through this cooperation, regional and local governments are affected in their planning. This is the reason why the German Länder and the EU Committee of the Regions demanded participation of regional and local governments in the elaboration of the ESDP (Kunzmann 1998, 107).

Like national spatial planning systems, the ESDP is directed to three dimensions of coordination:

1. Coordination among European sector policies affecting territorial development;

2. Coordination of activities in different European regions that should be achieved by cooperation among member state governments (or the institutions responsible for regional planning in member states);
3. Coordination among spatial planning at different levels, i.e. European, national and regional planning (CEC 1999a, 38).

How coordination among policies and governments at different levels is to be realized, however, and how the different parts of EU multilevel governance should interact in the application of the program are currently not clear (David 1998, 48). One reason for this is the problematic legal basis of the ESDP. The other reason is that, given the high costs of decision making, simultaneous coordination along all dimensions is hardly a feasible proposition. Moreover the institutional framework of multilevel governance generates additional problems that impede coordination.

The competency issue and practical reasons both prevent the EU from resorting to unilateral control, or from setting binding goals for public or private actors. At the same time, member states and regions cannot be expected to act on their own to voluntarily adjust their spatial policies. Therefore, coordination in European spatial policy has to be accomplished through the processes of negotiation and cooperation. Thus, both the elaboration and the application of the ESDP is burdened by all the problems of intergovernmental cooperation that are well known from national intergovernmental policy making and from public administration generally (Benz 1994; Scharpf 1992; Scharpf 1997, 116–150).

The basic problems of negotiation can be analyzed by referring to a simple—but for analytical purposes helpful—model drawn from game theory (Benz 1994; Scharpf 1992). Actors like governments or special-purpose agencies are generally interested in joint policy making around issues that cannot be dealt with in the context of their jurisdiction. This is often the case in spatial planning. These actors, however, also pursue their own interests. Although they engage in a search for joint solutions to problems, they also favor decisions that maximize the advantages of their own policies. Hence, negotiations are burdened by a collective choice dilemma: even if all actors are willing to agree on a joint policy, negotiations may fail due to distributive bargaining strategies of some or all participants.

In game theory this negotiation can be called a "prisoner's dilemma game" (see Table 1). By remaining firm and letting other parties make concessions,

TABLE 1
The Negotiator's Dilemma

		Negotiator A	
		Concedes	Does not concede
Negotiator B	Concedes	3 3	4 1
	Does not concede	1 4	2 2

actors can maximize their interests. Therefore, it is not attractive for them to take the first step in giving up the original bargaining position. Moreover, making concessions not only means that they abandon their best alternative (here indicated by the rank 4) but also that they risk being exploited by a firm negotiation partner and end up with the worst possible outcome (1). If both negotiators stand firm, however, they are unable to find an agreement, and negotiations fail. The outcome (2/2) for both actors is inferior to a joint decision (3/3).

The prisoner's dilemma game can easily be solved if actors communicate about their behavior. This is not possible, however, for a negotiator's strategy, which only makes sense if it is concealed from the other party. To overcome the negotiator's dilemma (Lax and Sebenius 1986), actors have to adopt cooperative strategies and evaluate issues not only from their individual point of view but also from a "collective perspective" (Scharpf 1997, 124). They have to reflect on their interests in the light of the consequences for the general issues at stake. This is usually what actors do in practice, and they are able to coordinate their negotiation strategies by mutually making incremental concessions.

The willingness of actors to cooperate and their ability to come to an agreement in negotiations depends on the type of policies (regulative, distributive or redistributive) and the kind of interests involved. In redistributive conflicts, negotiated decisions are feasible only if actors resort to "arguing" (providing arguments to defend one's claims) on norms of distributive justice, instead of trying to maximize their profit by strategies of "bargaining" (using power and tactics to maximize individual interest) (see Benz 1994, 118–127; Saretzki 1996). Moreover, differences between short- and long-term policies of participants and the commitment of actors to the special interest groups they represent reduce the possible range of acceptable solutions.

Both reasons for an increase in coordination costs apply to spatial planning. Here, policies concern the provision or preservation of common goods. The implementation of such policies yields joint benefits for all actors involved, but it also implies asymmetric distribution of costs and benefits. (In terms of game theory, the structure of the problem resembles the battle of the sexes[1]). While joint profits usually are realized in the long run, costs affect short-term interests of specific groups. To overcome these distributive conflicts, actors

---

[1] In these games, actors can realize joint benefits if they concur on one solution (be it solution 1 or 2), while disagreement leaves them both with the status quo they want to improve. The distributive outcome of both solutions differs, however. Negotiator A prefers solution 1 to 2, and negotiator B prefers solution 2 to 1. These antagonistic interests can impede an agreement as long as there is no accepted norm of distributive justice or another criterion that supports one solution against the other.

		Negotiator A	
		Solution 1	Solution 2
Negotiator B	Solution 1	2 3	1 1
	Solution 2	1 1	3 2

must trust the success of cooperative behavior, while strategies emphasizing individual interests end up in stalemate.

Experienced politicians and administrative experts can be expected to understand the dilemmas of negotiation processes. Empirical studies of negotiations in the public sector reveal that actors do not pursue pure bargaining strategies but shift between bargaining and arguing (Benz 1994, 118–127). The behavior of negotiators, however, is influenced by the institutional setting in which negotiations take place. The specific framework of European multilevel governance causes additional difficulties for negotiations and cooperative policy making.

When speaking about intergovernmental cooperation in the EU, different languages and different administrative cultures in member states may impede the understanding of the negotiating actors, but should not be overestimated. Experiences in transborder cooperation among regions reveal that intercultural communication is not a serious obstacle for policy making in Europe. According to sociological studies, European integration has generated a "transnational administrative elite" (Bach 1992, 26) consisting of actors who are used to communicating and negotiating in different languages and between different national cultures. During the long process of elaborating the ESDP, a network of professional planners has emerged from national and regional administrations and from the scientific community. This policy community helps reduce the difficulties of understanding.

The more important obstacles to coordination through negotiation in European spatial planning are caused by the structural conditions of multilevel governance. The notion of multilevel governance is used to describe an institutional setting characterized by intergovernmental or interorganizational policy making with no center of accumulated authority and the sharing of power between several units (Hooghe and Marks 2001). This is an adequate concept for understanding the structural conditions relevant for the application of the ESDP as it focuses analysis on institutional aspects. The consequences of this framework for coordination in spatial planning are summarized in Table 2 and discussed below.

TABLE 2
Problems of Coordination in European Multilevel Governance

Structures of Multilevel Governance	Consequences for Negotiation and Coordination Processes
1. Many actors	High transaction costs
2. Control of parliaments	Egoistic orientations of actors and bargaining strategies
3. Complexity of planning at all levels	Time-consuming process of coordination
4. Interlocking politics in sectoral planning	Powerful coalitions of special administrations
5. Different institutional frameworks in member states	Disagreements on concepts and tasks; different powers of participants
6. Varying structures of European policies	High complexity of processes

1. The larger the number of actors involved and the more issues at stake, the more likely it is that negotiations will fail. Both factors influence the transaction costs, i.e., the effort required to find a common ground for a compromise or a package deal. Because it cuts across sectors and levels of government, spatial planning necessarily involves a great number of actors and issues.

2. The negotiator's dilemma is usually rendered manageable in policy communities of experts. They have emerged in the European system of "fused bureaucracies" (Bach 1992, 24) that exist in all of the EU's policy sectors. These bureaucracies are effective, however, because they create nearly closed networks. The autonomy of policy networks increases the chance for coordination, but it turns political decisions into technocratic administration. Since spatial planning concerns fundamental interests of European citizens and basic policies of national, regional and local governments, it should be open to the participation of elected representatives. The latter should at least have the opportunity to scrutinize decisions of experts and their governments. Participation of national and regional parliaments is thought necessary in order to avoid uncontrollable interlocking politics between administrations of the different levels (Siedentopf 1994, 226).

   If negotiators are subject to control by external institutions, however, they tend to rely on bargaining instead of arguing, and they fight harder for their constituency than for a joint policy, as revealed by negotiation studies in general (summarized in Benz 1994, 187–192). If they are accountable to parliaments, then the dilemma facing the negotiating governments and administrations worsens. In parliamentary democracies in all member states of the EU, government is usually supported by a majority party or by a coalition of parties. The loyalty of the majority in parliament generally gives the executive sufficient leeway to balance national interests with European concerns. Nevertheless, government and the majority factions in parliament must also take into account possible reactions of their electorate. In the parliamentary arena, majority and opposition parties compete for the support of voters, thus influencing government behavior. Even if the majority parties agree with their government on accepting a European policy, the opposition parties may blame the government for giving up essential national objectives, forcing the government into a rivalry on who is the better representative of the people. Party competition for votes in elections induces governments and administrations to adopt a bargaining strategy in EU negotiations, and the loyalty of majority parties in parliament is not enough of an antidote. For this reason, the dilemma of joint policy making worsens (Benz 1998; Lehmbruch 2000). This dilemma exists even if parliaments have only the right to issue nonbinding statements. The voices of parliaments influence action orientations of the members of government subject to public scrutiny. Thus, negotiations between member states in the EU are generally jeopardized by the joint decision trap (Scharpf 1988).

3. Beyond this basic dilemma of multilevel governance, coordination in the application of the ESDP may reduce the flexibility of planning. The quest for coordination among sector policies and among levels of government

affects single decisions as well as policy concepts and planning schemes of governments and administrations. These are by themselves the result of coordination processes. If the application of the ESDP requires an adjustment of these plans, the breakdown of an agreement inside a specific sector can occur. This is not what the ESDP intends; if the ESDP wants to gain relevance, however, this has to be taken into account in the development of national or regional concepts for territorial planning. The reformulation of plans and policies can require a rather time-consuming process and ignite new conflicts. In the system of linked levels of spatial planning in the EU, the mutual influences of planning at different levels can instigate learning processes. If the costs of decision making get too high, the whole adjustment process may be deadlocked.

4. Special departments interlocking at different levels increase the risk of deadlock even further. More often than not, planning in sectoral policies like economic development, road construction, railways or other infrastructure facilities constitutes a closed system linking various levels of government together. In spatial planning these coordinated plans or policy concepts are on the whole not open to discussion and have to be taken as given. The leeway for those responsible for spatial planning is thus considerably reduced. The application of a program can fail due to constraints set by sector policy decisions.

5. Additional problems for coordinating spatial planning at the European level are caused by the different institutional frameworks in member states where national planning systems vary considerably. Procedures, definitions of the tasks and planning practices are not compatible. National negotiation and policy making styles also have negative consequences brought about by the divergence of national laws. This may cause disagreements on fundamental issues such as planning concepts and the functions of spatial planning (ARL/DATAR 1994; Kistenmacher, Marcou and Clev 1994; see also Chapter 1, this volume).

6. Coordination among policies at the European level is further burdened with the structures of European policies, which show large variance. This is true even if the focus is on those policies particularly relevant for implementing the ESDP. The EU structural policy designed to reduce regional disparities and to assist regions in need is implemented in cooperation between the EC and the responsible national or regional administrations of individual member states. The resources are allocated on the basis of development plans that have to be elaborated by the regions concerned and have to be adjusted to the program of the European Commission (Community support framework). European coordination of highways, railways and communication systems, or trans-European networks (TENs) is still done in intergovernmental settings between member states. By contrast, agricultural policy is more Europeanized. The policy networks among European and national experts that have emerged in this context have gained a high degree of autonomy (Bomberg 1998). All this makes coordination rather complicated.

Thus, it is hardly possible to comprehensively coordinate planning at all levels, among all regions and all relevant policies. This is why the German approach to spatial planning has not become influential in European spatial policy. It is based on the idea of effectively adjusting territorial and sector policies at all levels of government. Legally binding plans guarantee this adjustment. Such a comprehensive integrated system of planning (see Chapter 1) reaches its limits when applied at a higher level than a region (Kunzmann 1998, 118). The policy approach of the ESDP mainly follows the model of spatial development planning practiced in France (Fürst 1997, 48). Member state governments, however, have not been able to agree on what spatial planning is about and how it can be rendered effectively. Rather, the ESDP demonstrates the incompatibilities of European planning systems, which are the inevitable result of unresolved conflicts in negotiations on the formulation of the program. When it comes to the application of the ESDP, these incompatibilities, as well as the other structural problems mentioned above, will continue to burden the coordination processes.

A Coordination-Reducing Policy Design for Spatial Planning

Spatial planning in Europe is faced with the dilemma of an institutional structure that could lead to a "joint decision trap" (Scharpf 1988). This term describes a situation in which actors profiting from the status quo can block reforms or policy changes simply by refusing to cooperate. The trap occurs where decisions require agreement among a multitude of actors from different institutional settings found in multilateral negotiations. As a consequence, decision-making deadlocks are likely to occur. With the structure of policy making itself the result of agreements among actors, one cannot expect the system to change in any fundamental way. Institutional reform of European spatial policy will be incremental at best. Member state governments are hardly willing to give up competencies and therefore the EU has to live with the situation. The formulation as well as the application of any spatial planning scheme in member states and their regions will have to rely on negotiations and cooperation.

To avoid the joint decision trap in European multilevel governance, decision costs must be reduced, and coordination limited to what is necessary and feasible. From a normative point of view, this suggestion follows from the subsidiarity principle, which implies a restriction of European planning competence. In this way the number of actors and issues involved can be reduced, if only to a certain degree. The subsidiarity principle, however, provides no guidelines for coordination among levels of government and sector policies to carry out the necessary functions of European spatial planning. After considering possible consequences of the subsidiarity principle, therefore, this chapter proposes a policy design for the ESDP that reduces the problems of coordination.

Implication of the Subsidiarity Principle: Selective Planning and Division of Functions

In general, planning at the EU-level should focus on genuine transnational concerns and as far as possible maintain the autonomy of national and regional authorities. By applying this principle, the need for coordination among levels and policies can be significantly reduced.

An allocation of competencies among levels, that maximizes autonomy and reduces coordination costs, can be derived from the normative theory of federalism (Oates 1972; on spatial planning, see Biehl 2001; Eser 1996). It states that each level should in principle fulfill its responsibilities without interference by another authority. Tasks should be decentralized to the lowest level on which no external effects are produced. For spatial planning this would require a clear separation of functions among the EU, the member state governments and the regions. The ESDP should focus on aspects with a clear European dimension (Eser 1996; Karl 1996). In the field of spatial policy, however, an unqualified separation of levels of planning is impractical. The development of the macrostructures of the European territory and the spatial development of states and regions are interdependent. For this reason, the principles of the normative theory of federalism, developed for the delivery of public services and infrastructure, do not apply to spatial planning. This is a policy field in which external effects at all levels are the norm and not the exception, and which has to deal with typical problems of preserving a collective good.

Nevertheless, ways of dividing competencies and a planning system guided by the subsidiarity principle are feasible. Planning at the higher levels should be limited to specific issues with priority from a central perspective. The ESDP does not cover all policies of the EU, nor of the member states, but instead focuses on particular issues that require transnational coordination. These include the development of large networks of cities and regions, the European metropolitan regions, the problems of peripheral areas of Europe and the TENs of communication and transport. Moreover, the general principles of sustainable development and the preservation of natural and cultural resources are explicitly mentioned in the program.

The ESDP concerns certain types of regions and draws conclusions from the interdependence among regions; thus the need for coordination of national and regional planning and policy making is irrefutable. The goals chosen for particular regions can have considerable repercussions for policy making in those regions. In addition, better coordination is essential among sector policies of the EU affecting spatial development (CEC 1999b). Therefore, the fact that the ESDP is limited in its substance does not help avoid the burden of coordination. It is reduced to particular policies and includes only specific regions, but the problems of multilevel coordination still persist.

A second way of dividing responsibilities is by distinguishing specific functions of spatial planning. Indeed, the ESDP is designed to fulfill a limited set of functions. While this is a consequence of the lack of competence of the EU, the vice can be turned into a virtue. European spatial policy then has to concentrate on the following functions.

First, it should coordinate all policies of the EU territorial development. In particular the ESDP should guide the allocation of funds supporting regional development (ERDF, cohesion fund, Community Initiatives like URBAN, Interreg and Phare programs). Moreover, the development of TENs should follow the propositions of the ESDP. All European institutions, in particular the EC itself, should abide by the ESDP in their decisions. Yet, binding planning schemes that determine land use should be left to central and regional governments of the member states, which is exactly the intention behind European spatial policy.

A second function of European spatial policy could be to support territorial planning in transborder regions in which the EU is already actively involved through regional cooperation by grants from its Interreg programs. In addition, it could contribute to improving transborder regional planning by setting standards for coordination among responsible authorities in neighboring member states, by mediating among the relevant regions in cases of severe conflicts, or by assisting with specific projects that implement joint spatial planning.

Although this functional division of powers among the European, national and regional levels reduces the burden of coordination by limiting the number of actors and issues to be considered, European spatial policy still remains a multilevel process. Coordination of the sectoral policies of the EU—particularly those on regional development—affects the interests of member states that are represented on the Council of Ministers. Transborder cooperation in regional planning or in the implementation of joint projects requires the agreement of the responsible authorities of the member states or regions. By focusing on selected issues and on special functions, the burden of coordination in European spatial policy is reduced, but the traps of multilevel governance still jeopardize policy making, and should be avoided.

Loose Coupling of Arenas in Multilevel Governance: Modes of Coordination

A second, more important way to reduce the problems of coordination in EU spatial planning relates to the linkages of arenas in multilevel governance (Benz 2000; Benz and Eberlein 1999). As outlined above, due to the inflexibility of actors participating in coordination processes, negotiations are likely to end in the negotiator's dilemma. This inflexibility is caused by institutional settings that link actors to particular arenas, like parliamentary governments, networks of specialized administrations or national, regional or sector planning systems. Inflexible actors are unable to engage in effective negotiations because they cannot give up or modify their positions. Thus, they can easily impede coordination or at least drastically raise its costs. If these actors cannot be excluded from policy making, those responsible for coordination must find other strategies to increase flexibility.

From a theoretical point of view, avoiding strict coupling of arenas increases flexibility. So any system of multilevel spatial planning should constitute a setting of loosely coupled arenas. The term *loose coupling* signifies that decisions in one arena do not completely determine decisions in other arenas but have only partial influence on particular aspects (Weick 1985, 163–165). In practice, this can be achieved if politics in different institutions or organizations are linked by communication and information rather than by binding decisions, and if participants in negotiations pursue flexible goals of the organization they represent instead of narrowly defined mandates (Czada 1997). If so, then decisions in one arena do not constrain others, rather they set frameworks for coordinating the policies in that particular arena. Coordination has to be mediated by independent actors formulating agendas and proposals (and who, in so doing often become more important than those who have the formal mandate to make decisions or apply veto powers). Loose coupling is realized by a shift in the logic of interaction among actors at different levels or in different institutional arenas. The emphasis of this interaction is not on control or decision making, but on information exchange and persuasion.

European policies that cut across levels regularly constitute loosely coupled structures of multilevel governance (on EU structural policy, see Benz 2000; Benz and Eberlein 1999). Loose coupling, however, is jeopardized by multilevel governance tending either toward an increased fusion of powers of a great number of actors or institutions (strict coupling) or toward a separation of policies (decoupling). The fusion of powers is caused by the logic of an incremental evolution of EU policies. As a rule, the EU achieves its powers based on compromises among transnational and national or regional interests. As a result of the Europeanization of policies, these compromises imply that lower level governments lose some or all of their powers, for which they have to be compensated, by giving them the right to participate in decision making. Moreover, when policy making has been transferred to European negotiation systems, parliaments also have demanded the right to control their executives. In part they have succeeded in reinforcing their positions (Kamann 1997; Weber-Panariello 1995).

In the horizontal dimension, sector departments tend to shield their programs against external influences and reinforce their sector policy networks by forming tightly coupled alliances. Normative theories dominating the discussion on institutional policies, like parliamentary democracy (participation of parliaments), federalism or regionalism (participation of lower level governments) or pluralism (diversity of the public sector) justify the respective strategies. This dynamic, however, increases the costs of decision making and renders coordination difficult, and is particularly problematic for spatial planning.

Thus, modes of coordination have to be found that stabilize loosely coupled multilevel governance in spatial planning. As far as possible, they have to maintain the autonomy of national and regional authorities and those of special departments, but at the same time guarantee that the decisions of these organizations conform to the goals of the ESDP. Coordination has to find a balance between the principles of autonomy and community (Scharpf 1994).

The following three modes of coordination conform to the requirements of loosely coupled governance. The first is already applied in the practice of spatial planning of the EU; the other two should be used to increase the prospects for the application of the ESDP.

Coordination by discourse and ideas

The ESDP summarizes the suggestions of EU member states and the EC about spatial planning perspectives. At the same time it presents scenarios for potential developments in European regions and the macrostructures of the European territory. Furthermore, the ESDP aims at creating a cognitive framework, distributing ideas on methods of problem solving and inducing discussion on the spatial development of Europe (Fischler 1998, 3). The program was elaborated in intensive discussions among experts on spatial planning both from the public administrations of member states and from academia (Faludi 1997; 2001b). The ESDP was later debated in a series of conferences on specific issues. These discussions spread information on the ESDP to the relevant institutions in member states (including those of the accession states).

The relevance of discussions for European policy making and for the coordination of national and European policies has been emphasized in several case studies (for regulatory policies, see Jörges and Neyer 1997; for research and development policy, see Kohler-Koch and Edler 1998; for environmental policy, see Héritier 1997; for spatial planning, see Chapter 5, this volume). As a rule, experts cooperating on committees or in stable policy networks dominate these discourses. Lacking any formal powers, they nevertheless can successfully influence policy making at all levels by providing new information and by developing innovative ideas (Kohler-Koch and Edler 1998). Ideas and information from experts offer theories about the realities of a policy field, and they propose policy concepts and experiences on the potential effects of instruments. In general, "they stabilize expectations regarding strategies to solve problems, and they provide convincing reasons for these strategies, their advantages and their prospect" (Kohler-Koch and Edler 1998, 178, translation by the author). Through a network of communication channels, these ideas spread to all levels and arenas.

Ideas influence governments and administrations in member states to argue on their behalf in discussions with parliaments and the public. General policy principles and knowledge provided by independent communities of experts can hardly be refuted by power arguments in bargaining processes. More often than not, they become accepted standards for evaluating decisions. Thus, they guide the activities of autonomous governments and administrations at all levels.

Such discussions can also help frame interactions in coordination processes about specific issues of spatial planning, thus focusing on particular problems and the application of ESDP principles at national or regional levels. Rather than pursuing their own interests, actors can be motivated to consider more carefully the joint benefits of spatial planning. Since the typical negotiations about implementation of spatial planning combine distributive conflicts and the achievement of a common good and include actors with both individualist (egoistic) and cooperative orientations, the framework of a discussion can influence negotiation behavior in ways that make agreements more likely.

Coordination by incentives and competition

Discourses and ideas are important modes of coordination in multilevel governance, although they are only weak instruments for influencing the behavior of actors. Where spatial planning affects fundamental interests of regions or powerful societal groups advocating sector policies, it is doomed to fail. Thus, coordination has to be supported by stronger modes of governance. Even where this is not the case, the effects of discussions and ideas can be improved by giving actors incentives in exchange for abiding by the goals of spatial planning. Financial incentives and competition among regions or sector departments are devices that can influence the policies of national or regional governments and administrations without evoking their resistance or provoking parliamentary vetoes. Those subject to coordination are motivated to voluntarily adjust their decisions to spatial planning goals, but they are left wide discretion as to how to do so. Therefore, both modes safeguard the autonomy of lower-level governments and administrations.

Governing by means of financial incentives to regions is an important potential instrument for implementing the ESDP. There are tendencies for the European Commission to use its Interreg funds to gain influence on territorial planning in member states (Graute 2001; see also Chapter 3, this volume). Moreover, the grants to regions in need provided from the European Regional Development Fund (ERDF) have obvious repercussions on territorial development. For this reason, the Commission should effectively coordinate spatial planning and the ESDP. The structural policy of the EU constitutes an intelligent, well-established instrument for influencing regional development policies at the member state level (Allen 2000; Heinelt and Smith 1996; Hooghe 1996; Marks 1993). It avoids the typical problem of special grants that usually lead to a de facto centralization of power if conditions for support are narrowly defined by a central institution (Karl 1996, 73–74).

While the European Council and the European Parliament define the general goals and rules for funding, coordination among European and regional policies is achieved through bilateral negotiations between the Commission and lower-level governments. Under EU funding rules, subsidies to specific regions are given on the basis of regional development programs formulated at the national or regional level. These programs are then coordinated via negotiations with the Commission's policies. Following the theory of endogenous regional development, the Commission expects regions to develop their programs in cooperation with economic and social partners. Moreover, the structural policy of the EU is intended to reduce regional disparities as well as to support sustainable regional development. Thus, it could be used for coordination by incentives that follows the principle of loose coupling in multilevel governance.

In the loosely coupled multilevel structure of EU regional policy, a level of competition among regional governments about best practices further increases the quality of policy making. The rules of EU funding merely determine whether a region is eligible or not. According to the logic of the system (although not in practice), the amount of grant money to individual regions depends on the quality of programs and the effectiveness of coordination among the regional partners and between regional programs and the Commission.[2] In addition, a certain level of competition exists among regional public-private partnerships trying to present themselves as innovative and effective. Thus, one finds promoters from the private sector (e.g., representatives of chambers of industry and commerce) stimulating regional governments and administrations to adopt new ideas for and approaches to regional development. This competition not only affects scarce resources but also the quality of regional policies and innovative solutions to problems. A policy designed to support best practices also could be used to foster the implementation of spatial planning goals. Some first steps in this direction have already been taken. For several years, the EU has invited regions to compete on the basis of best practices and used the approach of benchmarking to implement standards of good regional planning although, up to now, this has not been done in a systematic way.

Combining positive and negative coordination

To further strengthen the power of coordination, the ESDP could be made a binding spatial planning framework for member states and regions (in particular for the allocation of grants from the EFRE) on condition, however, that member states and regions do not register complaints. This rule would reinforce the political and normative weight of European spatial planning without severely restricting the autonomy of member state governments. In administrative studies, such a practice is labeled *negative coordination* (Scharpf 1973, 85–89). Here, considerations are restricted to negative external effects, rather than considering the whole range of policy, in contrast to *positive coordination*. Those affected have the chance to cast a suspending veto. In this case the conflicting parties (here, the European institution responsible for the ESDP and the national or regional authority that is negatively affected) enter into bilateral negotiations. The negotiations are designed to find a compromise on the specific issue at stake.

Thus, a limited number of actors engage in positive coordination on a limited range of issues only. These procedures are embedded in a structure of intergovernmental relations loosely linked by negative coordination (Scharpf 1997, 146). Hence, a veto does not obstruct planning and coordination but leads to an improvement of the coordination process. It introduces additional information and forces the responsible authorities at different levels to consider their mutual interests. If a lower-level authority does not present convincing reasons for its veto, it can be voted down. The purpose of combining positive coordination between openly conflicting programs and policies and negative coordination between the many actors who are potentially affected by European spatial planning goals is to induce innovations and learning processes in the whole European planning system.

Such a proposal is not intended to turn the ESDP into a kind of regulatory policy. Rather than being concealed by the informality of the ESDP, it is based

---

[2] With the Agenda 2000 passed in 1999, the regional policy scheme was reformed. Now a moderate amount of the ERDP is used to support best practices in regions.

on the idea that conflicts among European and national or regional spatial planning goals should be brought into the open. These conflicts should not be resolved by resorting to hierarchical directives, but by means of communication and negotiations among the actors concerned. As a result, the ESDP has to be seen more as a starting point for a continual process of European spatial planning, in cooperation with national and regional authorities, rather than as a crowning document after nearly a decade of intergovernmental policy making. To become a conditionally binding framework, however, the EU has to be formally empowered with a competence for spatial policy.

Conclusion

The ESDP is currently a weak instrument for coordinating European, national and regional policies on the development of spatial structures in Europe. By invoking intelligent modes of policy coordination in multilevel governance, however, it could gain in importance. These modes already exist; they only have to be used in a more systematic and elaborated way. Coordination does not inevitably make spatial planning unmanageable. On the contrary, it can contribute to more flexible and innovative planning at all levels.

An effective system of spatial policy in European multilevel governance requires a division of functions rather than a separation of powers among different levels of planning. Each level should focus on specific tasks. The EU has to deal with issues concerning the macrostructures of the European territory selectively. At each level, policies most important for influencing the development of territories should be linked by processes of positive coordination. Other policies that may affect the implementation of spatial planning should be included in procedures of negative coordination. In addition, mechanisms of coordination that safeguard the discretion of autonomous governments and administrations, like discussions and the diffusion of ideas as well as incentives and procedures fostering competition between best practices, should be used more effectively.

Coordination that overburdens spatial planning is not a necessary outcome. The integration of policies of governments on different levels, of different states and regions, and of different sectors of government and administration can be achieved in a dynamic process of ongoing mutual adjustment. Indeed, the ESDP may represent the end of a long cooperation process among national governments, revealing all the characteristics of a compromise on the level of the lowest common denominator. There is evidence that relevant actors are frustrated, in particular in the face of the bleak prospects for the application of the program. The ESDP, however, may signify the start of an evolution of a new quality of multilevel governance in spatial policy, integrating European, national and regional policies into a learning system.

Section III

The Future of European Spatial Planning

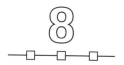

The European Union and Its Frontiers

Toward New Cooperation Areas for Spatial Planning

Jean-François Drevet

When the European Community was established in 1957, there were limited expectations for its expansion. Its six member states were challenged by a European free trade area (EFTA) of seven members led by the U.K., which was then a major commercial power. On their eastern and southern borders, these European nations were surrounded by nondemocratic countries very unlikely to join.

During the following 30 years, however, the Common Market, as the European Community was then called, was able to attract a number of EFTA members, which have been integrated into the Community, somewhat reluctantly, from 1973 (U.K., Ireland and Denmark) to 1995 (Austria, Sweden and Finland). Only Iceland, Switzerland (the Swiss application has been frozen since 1992) and Norway (after two unsuccessful attempts) remained outside. This expansion brought together countries with comparable levels of income and advanced levels of democracy.

A turning point came in the 1980s, with the integration of Greece, Spain and Portugal, which had income levels significantly below the Community average and were recently restored democracies. Contrary to expectations, these three Mediterranean countries caught up quite well; their democracies have strengthened and they have proved their ability to participate in the Single Market (1986–1993) and to comply with the criteria for joining the Monetary Union. Thanks to the intervention of Community structural funds, the gap between their income and the Community average has decreased significantly.

Since the opening of the Berlin Wall, the challenge, represented in Figure 1, has taken on an altogether different dimension (Draus 2000). To some extent most former communist countries are now oriented toward the West, where they see a better future for themselves by integrating into the EU sooner than later. But their situation cannot be compared to that of previous candidates.

This chapter expresses the author's personal views only. See the extended version, "Where to with the Enlargement of the EU," being translated from the French (Drevet 2001).

FIGURE **1**
Future EU Enlargements

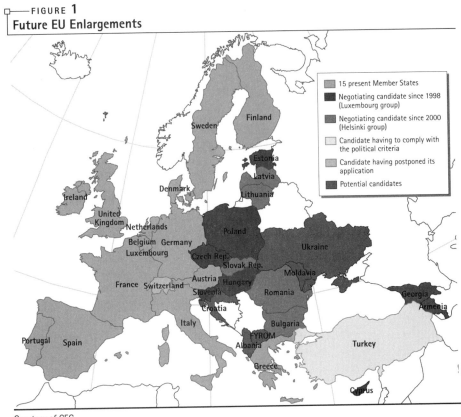

Courtesy of CEC
See insert Figure A3 for a color version of this map.

Democracy in those countries is even more fragile than in post-Franco Spain
or post-Salazar Portugal. And their level of income, even after a decade of economic transitions, is quite low: globally one-third or less than the EU average.
Integrating 100 to 200 million of these new Europeans cannot be compared
to the previous operations, which involved a maximum of 50 millions citizens
at one time.

In geographical terms, therefore, Europe faces an unprecedented problem,
comparable to the expansion of the U.S. in the nineteenth century (Meining
1998).

First, Europe confronts the reshaping of a continent, which was artificially
divided for more than 45 years. It must decide how to shift from the management of what has been its western seaboard (the aggregation of the insular and
peninsular states of maritime Europe) to a transcontinental dimension, without
any clear eastern border. This calls for the recomposition of a vast territory that
has long been fragmented. Second, Europe faces the management of a moving
frontier (Turner 1996), from the heartland of Germany to somewhere on the
Russian plains, during a period of three or four decades. Since the collapse of
the Iron Curtain, Europe's external border is moving eastward. Beyond Germany, it is now within Central Europe to accomplish reunification. When the

frontier goes beyond the Polish–ex-USSR border, the integration process will bring together Europe as a whole. The EU needs to master its new geography, allowing the border to move at the pace of efficient integration and at the same time combat the negative consequences of this evolution.

Both of these problems should be addressed with improved Community policies. The future of spatial planning at the European level as well as cross-border and transnational cooperation will have to be assessed within this framework. Since the ministerial meeting at Nantes in November 1989 (right after the opening of the Berlin Wall), the EU has developed a policy aimed at increasing the efficiency of spatial planning in Europe. Originally designed for a Community of 12 member states, this policy has been extended to the new countries that joined in 1995, benefiting from their wide experience with national spatial planning as well as their achievements in transnational cooperation within the Nordic Council (for Sweden and Finland).

The 12 current candidates will add more than one million square kilometers (see Figure 1), and they suffer from a number of problems, including soil and water pollution, lack of modern infrastructure, lack of communication among countries isolated for many years, low levels of income and limited budgetary resources (Bachtler 2000). Their integration into the EU, therefore, has a major territorial dimension that requires an intensification of EU structural funds interventions. Candidate countries must reinforce their administrative capacities to address these problems and make efficient use of Community funding. Spatial planning will likely play an increasing role in contributing to the territorial coherence in the implementation of Community policies (transport, environment and structural policies, among others). A strategic contribution is therefore expected from an extension of the ESDP to new member states forming a compact territorial grouping in the core of greater Europe. A first contribution on this subject was made by the ministerial meeting in June 1999 at Potsdam that approved the ESDP.

In keeping with a commitment made in 1963, the Berlin summit accepted Turkey as the thirteenth applicant to be considered on the same footing as the others as soon as it meets the political criteria. A poor country of over 65 million inhabitants with strong demographic growth, Turkey is therefore destined to join the long line knocking impatiently at the EU's door.

Extending the EU from 15 to 27 or 28 member states will not be the end of the operation. The Balkan countries, already considered potential members, some former Soviet republics, and countries of the south and eastern Mediterranean are prospective applicants for membership; they are simply waiting for the right moment to submit their official applications (Brzezinski 1997).

Of the current 12 official candidates, 10 are former communist countries. In the previous enlargements, seven of the nine countries were members of EFTA, which functioned as the EU's antechamber, a role that the now-defunct COMECON could hardly be said to fulfill. While the previous applicant countries had to adjust to the *acquis communautaire*, the current challenge is of a different order. The reforms demanded of Spain and Portugal cannot be compared to the constraints that the introduction of private property, a labor market, and supply and demand mechanisms will impose on the countries of Central and Eastern Europe.

Many of these countries have just regained their independence or had never been independent. This grouping includes two former British colonies (Malta and Cyprus, part of the latter occupied by a foreign army), old nations long subject to others (Poland, the Czech Republic, Hungary, Romania, Bulgaria), countries that slipped in and out of independence (the Baltic states), and countries that were never independent before (Slovenia and Slovakia, which applied for membership a few months after gaining international recognition).

The countries lined up behind these are even more complex: a former empire now in the shape of Turkey, and countries that did not necessarily ask for existence, such as Moldova or the former Yugoslav republics. Countries even more distant, whose very existence or independence is still a point of discussion (Ukraine, Georgia and Armenia), are also lined up.

All of these countries are engaged in a European transformation that has only one watchword: "no western borders." Twenty or more nations are moving inexorably toward the only entity—the EU—that offers them prospects of integration and some compensation for a painful return to a market economy. For the moment, accession itself constitutes their goal.

Are they capable of joining a system that requires a certain ability to share sovereignty in essential areas (Siedentop 2000)? Will they have both the economic flexibility seen now in the EU after two decades of sharper competition and administrative systems equal to the sophisticated game plan of the Single Market (Drevet 1997)? Will the applicant countries achieve in a decade what it took the member states, with their considerable financial and administrative resources, 30 years to achieve? If not, how long will the process take and what will it take for them to achieve their goals?

Europe's continuous expansion thus has a strong territorial dimension to it. Its borders are shifting without real knowledge of where the final limits of the EU will be. What role will borders have within the enlarged EU to differentiate it from other Eurasian entities? In this state of flux, how can cross-border and international cooperation help to balance and enhance the regions?

This chapter deals first with the process of enlargement, then with the EU's developing borders. Next it summarizes the basic data on cooperation efforts undertaken with Community funding and identifies the main problems with these measures, focusing on issues related to spatial planning.

The Domino Scenario

Wherever they might be located, the countries of Central and Eastern Europe no longer want a barrier with the West that cuts them off from the most advanced part of the continent. In 1989 Hungary opened its borders with Austria. Other countries followed, the Berlin Wall came down and the USSR dissolved.

In the older and newer member states, concerns for external security have been replaced by a desire to establish and maintain friendly relations. Each wants to contribute to the stability of its eastern neighbors. France adopted this approach toward Germany in 1954, and today Germany adopts the same approach toward Poland, which seeks the eventual accession of Ukraine. Austria encourages Hungary's membership, while Hungary wants Romania to join, which in turn encourages Moldova to move along the same path. The Nordic countries have made the Baltic states their priority. Only Greece has too many problems with Turkey to feel safe about its membership.

Should this march toward the east, which moved from the Elbe in 1990 after German unification, has temporarily halted along the Oder-Neisse line but appears to have no clear end, be limited? Once the EU formulates its position on each application for membership from this vast area covering the Balkans, the former Soviet republics to the west of Russia and certain Mediterranean countries, it will not have a known geographical framework to refer to. The only criteria it will have are those established in Copenhagen in 1993.

The Role of the Copenhagen Criteria

The European Council identified the following accession criteria in its Copenhagen meeting in 1993. EU membership requires that candidate countries have:
☐ achieved stability of institutions guaranteeing democracy, the rule of law, human rights and respect for and protection of minorities;
☐ a functioning market economy as well as the capacity to cope with competitive pressures and market forces within the EU; and
☐ the ability to take on the obligations of membership, including adhering to the aims of political, economic and monetary union.

These criteria make stiff demands that have required significant efforts on the part of the current 12 applicants, which they have not yet fully met. The economies of the former communist countries are fragile and their democratic systems still embryonic, which increases the obstacles to accession and even to applicant status.

Turkey is an example of a country whose application has been blocked indefinitely because of a failure to comply with the political criteria. The other potential applicants around the Black Sea or Mediterranean are also handicapped for the same reason: as long as the former Soviet states are incapable of restarting their economies, it is unlikely that their relations with the EU will move forward. Not one potential applicant country currently complies with the criteria.

The current situation, however, will inevitably change. All countries concerned are developing market economies. Within a decade they should have established or reestablished fundamental market mechanisms and be open to trade. Their situation at this moment is no worse than that of Romania or Bulgaria when they were accepted as applicants in 1997. From a political viewpoint, one can hope that the move toward democracy will continue. It is estimated that some of the countries concerned will have become democratic by 2010, their situation being similar to that of the current Central and Eastern

European applicants. There is, therefore, no reason to refuse to a new group of countries what has already been accepted for the 10 applicant countries from Central and Eastern Europe and for Turkey.

By using the term *potential applicants* for the Balkan states, the EU has opened the way for later applications for membership from Croatia, Macedonia and the other countries, once the opportunity arises. While the stability and association agreements do not explicitly provide for this eventuality, they are preparing these states for it.

Once Turkey begins its accession negotiations, several countries around the Black Sea and Mediterranean will be encouraged to apply as well. This will certainly be true of Moldova and the Ukraine, and perhaps of Georgia. A rejection of Armenia would be tantamount to saying that it is less European than Turkey. Similarly, some Mediterranean countries will also adopt this line of approach. Europe cannot indefinitely tell the countries of the Maghreb (Morocco, Algeria and Tunisia)—as Morocco was told in 1985—that they are not part of Europe because the Straits of Gibraltar are just slightly wider than the Bosporus. The Lebanese may also ask why they are not entitled to the same future in Europe now being offered to the Kurds of Turkey.

A Europe of Concentric Circles

Let us assume that all or most of the 12 current applicants for EU membership become members by 2010. A new line of applicants will have formed in the meantime. Some of these will be on the opposite shore of the Mediterranean, in Asia or in Africa. How should the EU react when faced with these new applications and a growing pressure from them to be treated like earlier ones?

Current relations have developed through preferential agreements between the EU and most of the countries on its southern or eastern borders. These were arranged first with Greece and Turkey (1963), then with the countries of the southern and eastern Mediterranean (SEM) in the 1970s and, since the 1990s, with the countries of Central and Eastern Europe and the other former Soviet republics.

These agreements, with numerous political and trading provisions and accompanied by financial aid, offer many prospects for a rapprochement through strengthened trade and commercial links. They also contain political terms and conditions that allow the agreements to be suspended should their move toward democracy falter or go into reverse.

The agreements fall into several categories, ranging from simple partnerships offering free trade to the Europe Agreements, in which accession is mentioned as a goal, and with it the transposition into national law of the entire acquis communautaire. Between these two extremes fall stability and association agreements, which offer closer relations without mentioning accession as a prospect, and which have been created for countries in difficult political or economical circumstances that wish to move closer to the Community. This is currently the case of Albania and the former Yugoslav republics, and will be the case of Moldova and the countries of the Caucasus.

Adapting the agreements or changing from one category to another can produce a gradual rapprochement, whereby those countries with the capacity to do so can achieve a status close to membership. This is a logical development for those countries close to the EU and who trade mostly with it rather than with other blocks or states.

Through the integration of the 12 current applicants, plus an unspecified number of newcomers, therefore, Jacques Delors's "Europe of concentric circles" may expand from 15 to 36 member states in about 15 years. The remaining countries (TACIS and MEDA states) will benefit to varying degrees from evolving association or partnership agreements but will not be candidates for membership.

The above scenario may appear unlikely, or overly optimistic or restrictive where some countries are concerned. Its sole aim is to project current developments to their logical conclusion. Many variations are possible, depending on the country concerned. The course steered may accelerate or slow down, depending on the applicants' performances and the EU's capacity to incorporate them.

The alternative would be a temporary or sustained block in the process under way since the 1990s, leading to a distancing of states that are not members of the EU. This would be a new trend, one never previously encountered, but not entirely improbable.

By expanding ever further from its point of origin to absorb increasingly dissimilar and distant countries, the EU will reach fragile areas, where its powers of integration will not necessarily be as great as they are in a Europe recently liberated from Soviet domination. Leaving aside the individual destinies of the countries concerned, rising tensions along the EU's southern and eastern borders could produce three major reversals that would halt the developments described above and weaken the EU's influence: resurgent Russian expansionism, a reorientation of Turkey toward the East and fundamentalist Islamic regimes or similar governments of the southern and eastern Mediterranean countries.

Shifting Borders

An obvious consequence of current developments is the frequent shift in the EU's external borders and their evolving role as the status of the countries concerned changes.

The "Canal Lock" Effect

Almost completely closed for four decades, the borders will now play a pivotal role in the economic and regional management of the changes under way. Because of the many political divisions, the border regions of the applicant countries are relatively twice the size of those of the EU (58 percent versus 25 percent), with 61 million inhabitants compared to the EU's 93 million.

Based on the average of a future EU of 27 member states, the main problem is the succession of income gradients:

☐ EU regions bordering the applicant countries are close to the average figure of the EU as presently constituted (115 percent versus 116 percent)

☐ The drop in income is severe once crossing into the applicant countries, although the regions bordering the EU are none-the-less more highly developed than the average (53 percent compared to 44 percent of the EU average for 27 states);

☐ The border regions between the applicant countries are less developed than those with the EU (42 percent versus 53 percent), but more developed than their border regions with third countries (TACIS and the Balkans) where GDP per person is even lower.

Incomes decline the further one goes east—a constant feature of European history that has worsened in the twentieth century, particularly during the communist period. This income gradient is reflected especially in the level of infrastructure provision, roads and motorways.

The borders in the enlarged Community will act as canal locks, offering points at which current disparities can be managed and where efforts will be made to level them out. Increased trade should add to the osmosis effect, raising living standards on the eastern side of the border. This way, development will spread like a wave, gradually smoothing out discontinuities in Europe. This is how the "frontier system" is expected to operate in an enlarged Europe, contributing to the spread of development further into Eastern Europe.

EU Border Policies

Through a mixture of deregulation, new rules and subsidies, the EU is now tackling this important policy challenge.

Deregulation is the instrument of choice at the internal frontiers. Since the completion of the Single Market, the Community has been striving to transform the old political borders into simple administrative boundaries. The expansion of the Schengen area is the most visible manifestation of this process. The current borders among the applicant countries and between them and the EU will share a similar fate. In their case, however, the process will be less rapid because the barrier effect of these borders is far more pronounced than it is in Western Europe. The need for numerous transition periods will probably result in the retention of border controls for several years after accession.

The abolition of internal border controls is inextricably linked to the introduction of common rules at the external borders. Compliance both with the standards of the Single Market and the Community's visa policy rely on this. The logic of Schengen will require more systematic controls along the eastern borders of Poland and Romania than are currently in place. Both sides of the border dread the brickwall effect of these controls. Since the collapse of the USSR, Ukrainians and Belarussians have not needed a visa. Poland wants to open its borders to develop trade and contribute to the stability of its eastern neighbors. Poland does not intend to give up this crucial aspect of its *Ostpolitik* and refuses to become a long-term frontier state, defending Europe's *limes* (the Roman Empire's fortified borders along the Rhine and Danube) against the new barbarians (for a typology of border areas in Central Europe see Figure 2).

Interreg and Similar Initiatives

At the start of the 1990s the EU introduced a system to support cross-border cooperation under the Interreg program. Established when the EU had a membership of 12, its primary objective was to overcome the difficulties that would arise when the internal borders would be abolished as part of the Single Market.

The Community's external borders (Figure 2) were eligible for Interreg support in 1988. While eligibility was initially intended to help them combat isolation (the border between the two German states, Greece's land and sea

□——FIGURE **2**
Typology of Border Areas in Central Europe

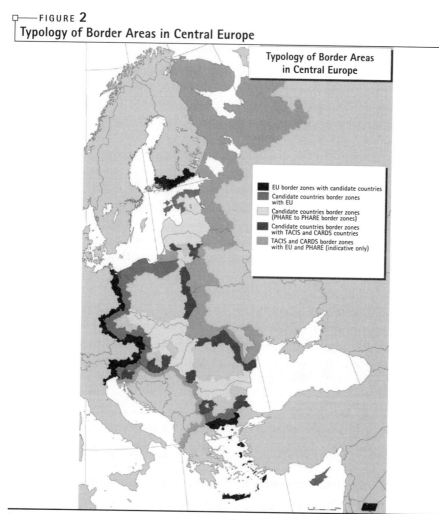

Courtesy of CEC

See insert Figure A16 for a color version of this map.

borders), its usefulness became evident several months later when the Iron Curtain fell. From that moment, the Interreg initiative funded early measures to establish friendlier relations across the Oder-Neisse line and among Greece, Bulgaria and Albania.

Interreg A

Since the 1999 European Council in Berlin, the EU's border regions with the applicant countries have been particularly noticed, and the areas concerned have received a considerable increase in funding. Deciding to spend 73 percent of its Interreg allocation in its border areas with the applicant countries, Germany will provide them with 16 Euro per person per year between 2000 and 2006. In Austria, which has longer borders but less funding, the amount will be 4 Euro per person per year, much more than what had been spent in the previous period (1.5 Euro per person per year between 1995 and 1999).

These are not mere symbolic amounts—they have a real catalytic effect. They help speed the provision of facilities at border posts, create new ones and stimulate economic activities such as tourism. They encourage the development of joint measures and make the local populace aware of the value of cooperation. For these reasons the programs are strongly supported by the elected representatives of the regions concerned, notwithstanding the management problems encountered.

Phare CBC

Since 1994 funding has been extended to the other side of the border through creation of a special Phare budget line (Phare is a cross-border cooperation program with accession states from Central and Eastern Europe) to fund measures in the applicant countries (Figure 2). The funding initially concentrated on the border zone with the EU but was subsequently extended to include the border zones among applicant countries (Phare with Phare), and later with their TACIS neighbors, Russia, Belarus, Ukraine and Moldova.

The funding allocated by Phare to this type of cooperation between 1994 and 1998 was quite substantial—9 Euro per person per year—almost equivalent to the 7 Euro per person per year Interreg had allocated on the other side of the border. Unfortunately, the Phare payments arrived much later than those for Interreg, while the latter already lagged behind the other structural programs.

Phare-CBC suffered from administrative problems and problems particular to international cross-border cooperation. Its generous budget was more than the regions could absorb. In the absence of genuinely cross-border projects, the authorities involved used the initiative for regional development or industrial conversion measures that had failed to find funding elsewhere since, until recently the applicant countries had no access to integrated regional development programs like those of Objective 1. These programs were sometimes severely criticized by the Court of Auditors or by the MEPs (members of the European Parliament) who had promoted them. Nonetheless, they played an important role for those in the border regions as demonstration projects.

Credo–TACIS

In 1995 Phare established the Credo program to develop cross-border cooperation among the countries then eligible for Phare (the 10 applicant countries,
plus Albania and Macedonia) and their neighbors in the TACIS program
(Figure 2). This program, with an initial budget of 102 million Euro, proved
to be overly ambitious; 458 projects were put forward, with a total volume of
39 million Euro. About 100 were selected and 7 million Euro was spent.

In the case of the countries eligible for TACIS most of the appropriations for
cross-border initiatives served as matching funding for the Interreg community
initiative along the Finno-Russian border. Some projects, notably to establish
border posts, were funded along the borders with the applicant countries.

Transnational Cooperation

Over the next two decades the geographical makeup of Europe will fluctu-
ate and has to be managed accordingly. Cross-border cooperation will figure
largely among the instruments needed to achieve this end. Given the shift in
the EU's borders and the change in status of the countries that will accede,
cross-border cooperation will be needed even more than in Western Europe.
After all, this type of cooperation is more able than others to take account of
the territorial dimension of the current and planned changes. This cooperation
should involve three categories of countries: the member states, the applicant
countries and others, whether prospective applicants for membership or not,
in coherent geographical areas (see Table 1 and Figure 3).

This has already happened around the Baltic Sea community, a grouping that comprises member states (the three Nordic members of the EU plus
Germany as presently constituted with its newly acquired Baltic seaboard),
applicants (Poland and the three Baltic States) and others, such as Norway
and Russia.

Other groupings have already come into being in the Alps and around the
Black Sea. Similar needs will be met through the creation of new international
areas, including the Danube basin, the Adriatic and perhaps the Balkans and
the Mediterranean.

Nordic Cooperation

The new Nordic member states, particularly Finland, have been encouraging
the EU to develop its Nordic dimension by enhancing cooperation with countries sharing an Arctic coastline, particularly Russia. To the east, the future
accession of the Baltic states and the inclusion of Belarus in Baltic cooperation
will stabilize the new regional model that has resulted from the breakup of
the USSR. The Nordic countries have chosen to intensify regional cooperation
around two primary natural zones: the Arctic and the Barents Sea on one hand
and the Baltic basin on the other.

TABLE 1
Prospects for Transnational Cooperation

Area	Member States	Applicant Countries Currently in Negotiations	Other European Countries
Barents Sea	Sweden, Finland, Denmark		Norway, Iceland, Russia
Baltic Sea	Germany, Denmark, Sweden, Finland	Estonia, Latvia, Lithuania, Poland	Russia, Norway, Belarus
Alps	France, Germany, Italy, Austria	Slovenia	Switzerland
Danube Basin	Germany, Austria, Italy	Hungary, Czech Republic, Slovak Republic, Romania, Bulgaria, Slovenia	Croatia, Bosnia-Herzegovina, Serbia-Montenegro, Moldova, Ukraine
Adriatic and Ionian Seas	Italy, Greece	Slovenia	Croatia, Bosnia-Herzegovina, Serbia-Montenegro, Albania.
Balkans	Greece	Bulgaria, Romania, Turkey	Serbia/Montenegro, Albania.
Black Sea	Greece	Bulgaria, Romania, Turkey	Moldova, Ukraine, Russia, Georgia, Armenia, Azerbaijan, Albania

Relaunched Cooperation in the Arctic and Barents Sea

Because of their strategic importance, the arctic regions (Lapland, the islands of the north Atlantic and the Barents Sea) have long benefited from a concentration of military expenditure and resources that have helped support economic activity and maintain local populations, but at serious cost to the environment.

North of the Arctic Circle, cooperation has taken the form of a Barents Council comprising the five Nordic countries and Russia. The participating countries want to take advantage of the new, more open Russia, so that a new way of managing the Arctic regions can be established. Their first aim is to eliminate major environmental risk factors brought by the processing of mining and nuclear waste that are abundant in Russian territory and in the Arctic Ocean. Each area will then be opened up by filling in the missing links between east and west (opening of border crossing points, new roads and a rail link, modernization of port infrastructure, new telephone lines).

Arctic cooperation is aimed in particular at Russia. Of the 19 million people currently living above the 60th parallel in the northern hemisphere, 10.6 million (56 percent) live in the Nordic countries. Only 560,000 (3 percent) live in North America (Canada, Alaska, Greenland). The others (7.85 million, although the number is falling fast) live in the far north of European Russia and in Siberia, with a living standard roughly one-third of that available to the other two population groups.

Transnational Cooperation Areas with Partners Outside the EU

Courtesy of CEC
See insert Figure A15 for a color version of this map.

Previously fearing for their security, the Nordic countries now fear the adverse effects of the current restructuring taking place in Russia's vast Arctic territory. Norway and Finland are anxious about the fallout from difficult adjustments along a border stretching over 1700 km. They also worry about the knock-on effects of chaotic administration in the neighboring regions of Karelia and the Kola Peninsula, where areas damaged by mining and military activity are common.

The Baltic Basin

During the Cold War, the Baltic Sea was a place of confrontation and its ports doubled as naval bases. However, since 1990 Europe's second inland sea has rediscovered its commercial and economic potential.

Sustainable regional management must first deal with the state of the sea basin since the waters of the Baltic are particularly sensitive. More than others, this sea has suffered from pollution dumped by communist economies: the exploitation of bitumen deposits in Estonia; the pumping of waste waters into the Gulf of Riga; effluents from the Oder and the Vistula; and radioactive leaks from nuclear power plants. At the beginning of the 1990s the work to clean up the Baltic had an estimated price tag of 18 billion Euro over 20 years. In 1992, a Baltic program for the environment was launched in Helsinki. All of the countries concerned, however, are short of funds and those in the east have only a few alternatives for their industrial development or energy production.

In March 1992, through a German-Danish initiative, a Baltic Cooperation Council was established with a broad agenda, including economic and technological cooperation, environmental protection, development of transport, tourism and culture. In December 1994 the countries surrounding the Baltic drew up and had their respective ministries approve a spatial plan for the Baltic (Committee on Spatial Development of the Baltic Sea Region 1995) representing an initial attempt at developing international management of the basin beyond environmental protection alone.

The EU agreed to fund Baltic cooperation under the Interreg IIC initiative on transnational planning and is pursuing its efforts under the Interreg IIIB strand. Approved in October 2001, this first transnational program under Interreg IIIB provides EU structural funds support of 97 million Euro to promote transnational cooperation among Denmark, Northeast Germany, Sweden, Finland, Norway, Estonia, Latvia, Lithuania, Poland, Russia and Belarus (Table 2). According to Commission estimates, European funding will attract a further 85 million Euro in investments from the public sector and 4 million Euro from the private sector. In addition, 32 million Euro will come from other sources (mainly from the Phare program) and from Norwegian national contributions, creating total resources of 218 million Euro for the period 2000–2006.

Alpine Cooperation

Since the accession of Austria in 1995, Switzerland is now entirely surrounded by four EU member states. While officially an applicant, Switzerland does not now want to become a member. Because of the Alpine arc's geographic location, its environment is particularly threatened by the unchecked development of road traffic through the mountains. The efforts made by Switzerland and Austria to check this traffic have come up against Community rules on free movement, which prevent the EU's alpine valleys from taking the restrictive measures needed to preserve their environment and protect tourism. Only Switzerland is in full control of its mountain areas, but must spend a great deal on developing an integrated transport network, something that has been

---

TABLE **2**

Overview of Baltic Cooperation under Interreg IIIB

Priorities of the Program	Contents	EU Funding
Spatial development	Promotion of spatial development concepts	29 million Euro
	Tourism development	
	Development of coastal zones	
Sustainable development	Strategies for Pan–Baltic intermodal transport	48.7 million Euro
	Development of green networks, management of water resources	
Transnational institution building	Spatial development activities across borders relying on local and regional networks	13.9 million Euro

made clear by the accident in and subsequent closure of the St. Gothard Tunnel. Since a previous accident in the Mont Blanc Tunnel, and its closure, France and Italy are also engaged in a similar operation. Nowhere else in Europe is the need for an international spatial planning policy to harmonize each country's efforts, reduce costs and maximize the benefits as obvious as here.

The European Community is a contracting party on this issue to the Convention on the Protection of the Alps (known as the Alpine Convention) adopted and signed in 1991. It covers the entire Alpine range (191,000 km) with a population of some 13 million inhabitants in the eight countries concerned, including four member states (Germany, Austria, Italy and France), as well as Switzerland, Liechtenstein, Slovenia and Monaco. Through the implementation of its various protocols (nature protection, mountain agriculture, land planning and sustainable development, tourism, forests, soil protection, energy and transport), the Alpine Convention should eventually be in full coordination with the Community's environment policies on the preservation of the atmosphere, soil, water, biodiversity and biotopes.

The Danube Basin

The Danube basin covers more than 800,000 kilometers in 14 countries, two of which are EU members and seven are applicants.

Since the end of the Austro-Hungarian Empire, which covered most of the Danube area, numerous cooperative efforts have been made in the region, which is seen as a natural geographical unit. The projects for a Danube federation and for a free trade area failed, however. Since the fall of the Iron Curtain, which put most of the former empire (with the exception of its capital) in Europe's eastern sector, these opportunities have been proposed once more in the context of better bilateral relations.

The EU's external border is temporarily fixed to the east of Vienna, pending accession of the first applicant countries in this region. While 17 percent of the area of the Danube basin is now part of the EU, this proportion will reach 74 percent once the countries of Central and Eastern Europe join. The programs of international and cross-border cooperation will thus be an important factor in their integration. The EU's new external borders will then touch Ukraine and Moldova.

Yet, international cooperation is marking time. Despite the many needs in common to improve the environment and transportation, or to develop the river and its tributaries, no cooperative structure for the Danube basin had been put in place before a September 2001 joint initiative from Austria and Romania.

The Adriatic Area

While the larger Yugoslavia existed, cooperation in the Adriatic was a bilateral question, to be managed between Rome and Belgrade. Albania at the time was closed in to itself.

The breakup of the Yugoslav federation and the resulting chaos have changed the nature of the problem. For Italy, the effects have been particularly negative, including increased illegal immigration and trafficking of all kinds and marine pollution from the dumping at sea of bombs not dropped during the Kosovo campaign.

Italy wishes to stabilize the region by obtaining projects of good conduct from the countries concerned. Since they will not be EU members for years to come, it is important to cooperate actively with them. For this reason, Rome took the step of inviting these countries (plus Greece) to Ancona in May 2000. A declaration on international cooperation among the countries of the region was adopted by Italy and Greece, on one hand, and Slovenia, Croatia, Bosnia and Albania on the other, based on the following points: the control and prevention of illegal activities; maritime security; and culture and the environment.

Vast opportunities are now in the offing with the Council's adoption of the Community Action for Reconstruction, Development and Stabilisation (CARDS) program, with a budget for regional cooperation of 460 million Euro, some of which will be devoted to trans-Adriatic cooperation.

The Balkans

The EU has been a Balkan power since 1981, but Greece remained completely isolated in the south of the peninsula until the fall of the Iron Curtain. Some months later, the breakup of Yugoslavia increased its isolation. Unlike Central Europe, the enlargement process here has not had the same beneficial effects on relations among neighboring states.

The uncertain future of the countries of the western Balkans (those of the former Yugoslavia with the exception of Slovenia and Albania) make international cooperation in the region a hit-and-miss affair. New hopes and prospects have arisen, however, with the end of sanctions against Serbia, which occupies a place of prime geopolitical importance on the peninsula. Since NATO's intervention in Bosnia and Kosovo, and the involvement of the U.S., the region looks toward a better future.

Cooperation is thus beginning to take off. Through Interreg and Phare cooperation programs, Greece has shown the way to Bulgaria, an applicant country, and Albania and Macedonia. In 1999, after the Phare regulation on cross-border cooperation was revised, Romania and Bulgaria launched a cooperation program across the Danube. With the adoption of the CARDS initiative and its joint intervention with Phare, other programs will gradually include other new and old borders.

Beyond the geographically limited field of cross-border cooperation, international cooperation should also be developed along lines of common interest such as water management and transportation. There are still a number of hurdles to cross before this cooperation takes shape.

The Black Sea Economic Community

The Black Sea basin once played a pivotal role in international affairs (e.g., the Crimean War). The Cold War standoff, however, turned the region into a backwater. Turkey found itself alone, under pressure from the USSR and its two satellites, and pursuing the region's classic model of confrontation that had prevailed since the eighteenth century.

Links between the two zones were reduced to a minimum, including little international traffic by air or sea; land borders also were completely closed (between Turkey and the USSR) or barely open (Romania and the USSR). Despite a fragile sea basin almost totally enclosed, environmental protection was not considered. Marine pollution and pollutants from the Danube and Soviet rivers placed the Black Sea in an almost hopeless situation.

Few regions of the world have more to gain from the recent changes. Not only have Romania and Bulgaria rediscovered their freedom to act, the break-up of the USSR has also created a new political order around the Black Sea. The disappearance of the Warsaw Pact and the decline of the Black Sea fleet have ended military friction, alone an event without precedent.

Turkey has launched the Black Sea Economic Community (BSEC), a vast group of 11 countries surrounding the sea or concerned with its development, six of them with a Black Sea coastline (Turkey, Bulgaria, Romania, Ukraine, Russia, Georgia), and five neighboring countries (Greece, Albania, Moldova, Armenia, Azerbaijan). While the initial objective is to develop trade in a region where the Turkish economy enjoys a comparative advantage, the BSEC may become a forum where sometimes opposing countries can deal jointly with issues such as improvements to the environment, passenger and goods transport networks and energy grids.

Unlike the Baltic, the EU's access to the Black Sea is still in the future. The only member state currently involved is Greece. While not with an actual Black Sea coastline, it is linked to the sea for historical reasons dating back to antiquity. By taking in more than 300,000 Russian Pontics, Greece realized that it still had a stake in that part of the world, yet it does little in the way of trade there. Most of the Greek trade is with its Balkan neighbors, carried on in a context not specifically related to the Black Sea.

With the likely accession of Romania and Bulgaria, two new member states will have direct access to the Black Sea, although it is not clear whether this will be of particular importance. Even more than Athens, Sofia and Bucharest have their sights fixed firmly westward. Turkey alone has realized the value of cooperation around the Black Sea. Its products are well suited to economies in transition. Its geopolitical position makes it easy for the country to export its products either through official channels or though trafficking known as *suitcase trade*, which proliferates with the countries of the former USSR. Increased trade relies in part on the development of transportation routes (construction of new infrastructure, opening of border posts and new air and sea routes), which is in turn linked to greater cooperation among the members of the BSEC.

The current structures of the BSEC are not up to the job. Although motivated, Turkey lacks the expertise and resources to go beyond a small intergovernmental secretariat, and the other countries are too impoverished or have other priorities. The EU alone is in a position to vest this cooperation with the structures and resources it needs, but it is not yet sure it should do so. Furthermore, developing a program of cooperation with the BSEC would mean involving numerous Community financial instruments, all with differ-ent operating rules, including the structural funds (Greece), Phare (Romania, Bulgaria, Albania), TACIS (the former Soviet republics), MEDA and ad hoc funds (in Turkey).

As in the Baltic, the development of a structured system of multilateral cooperation would also help facilitate the treatment of many regional problems. The development of new networks for the transportation of passengers and goods, energy grids and information networks has many points in common. The same is true of environmental protection and of large-scale spatial plan-ning issues.

The Forgotten Mediterranean?

Further to the south, efforts made to develop cooperation in the Mediterranean basin have suffered from a persistent mismatch between stated intentions and real action. With a number of well-intentioned documents and increased aid to the countries of the southern and eastern Mediterranean accomplished, the actual implementation of Community policy is facing various obstacles. Europe thus continues to be slow in finding ways and means of engaging in a stable management of its southern borders.

The countries along the southern coastline already belong to other group-ings such as the Arab League and the Organization of African Unity (OAU). Unlike Turkey, which has always had a foothold in Europe, the three Maghreb countries (Morocco, Algeria and Tunisia) are considered non-European. None are members of pan-European cooperation bodies such as the Council of Europe or the OECD, even though the geographical area of such organizations has been broadly defined. Despite the links forged in colonial times, there are no strong institutional relations.

The association agreements do not have a territorial dimension. There is a risk, therefore, that for some time the trans-Mediterranean cooperation will not get past the talking stage. This despite the fact that action is particularly warranted, given the threats to the development of these places posed by water shortages, pollution, unchecked urban sprawl, vulnerability to natural disasters, erosion and so forth.

Conclusions: Possible Consolidation Measures

Transnational cooperation is one of the building blocks of the EU's expansion, and it meets objective needs of shared activities, most notably on the environ-ment and transportation (spatial planning in other words). There is still much to be done, however, before this cooperation becomes as active a factor for development in the areas described as it is in the Baltic.

As for Community measures, which have a catalytic effect on this type of cooperation, three elements need development:

☐ Establishment of political forums in these cooperation areas;
☐ Preparation of a reference framework for programing the measures;

☐ Better coordination among the financial instruments, especially when they involve the Community budget.

The Political Forum

Numerous ministerial meetings have taken place over the past 10 years, that identified a large number of new cooperation areas and other short-lived Euro-regions, often, however, with nothing more to show for them than some sightseeing on the part of well-meaning civil servants.

International cooperation is impossible without a political body to exert pressure on administrations that do not have the spontaneous reflex to work in concert. As in the Baltic, the other cooperation areas must, if they so wish and along appropriate geographical lines, establish operating structures supported by those in political power.

The Reference Framework

As this policy priority has been established here, it is now necessary to formulate clear common priorities and present them in a reference document that will serve as the framework for cooperation. The Baltic countries have been using just such a document since the early 1990s: Visions and Strategies around the Baltic Sea (VASAB). A wide range of shared priorities can be included in this framework document and subsequently serve as a basis for cooperation.

Since 1993 member states have been working on a European Spatial Development Perspective (ESDP), on which political agreement was reached at the Potsdam ministerial meeting in 1999. One way the ESDP might be applied would be to develop regional cooperation plans for member states, applicant countries and any third countries wishing to take part, strengthening the regional groupings mentioned above.

The extension of ESDP to the 12 applicant countries in various phases of accession negotiations, possibly including Turkey (which has been working on similar lines with the Council of Europe), would be a major step forward.

The Financial Instruments

The usefulness of this cooperation lies in getting countries categorized differently but almost all of which have access to a Community fund (structural funds for member states, Phare, TACIS, MEDA and others for nonmember countries) to work together.

Using the structural funds and Interreg in particular as a model, the countries of Central and Eastern Europe have developed various forms of cross-border and (to a lesser extent) transnational cooperation. While Community funds are involved in almost all cases, the administrations concerned find it hard to coordinate their assistance because of differing legal systems and management arrangements. In many cases the most significant mismatches occur between the structural funds and the external cooperation instruments, but they occur between outside instruments as well.

It is paradoxical that the very financial instruments designed to encourage cooperation among the countries concerned should find it so hard to cooperate with each other. Without going into detail, this paradox could be overcome by devoting adequate resources to the problem, for example, through the creation of ad hoc budget lines, as the Nordic states did for Baltic cooperation.

The creation of integrated financial instruments for cooperation would be one of the most useful ways of tackling the shift in borders and changes in a country's status. These financial instruments would also encourage countries in different categories to cooperate with each other, especially in the border areas that will be pivotally important to the Europe of variable geography that all will be forced to live in for the next several decades.

Spatial Planning in the European Union

A Vision of 2010

John Zetter

> We imagine the past and remember the future.
>
> —*Sir Lewis Napier*

After nearly a decade of much-reduced mutual interest in transatlantic political relations, the visit of President Hillary Clinton to Brussels in October 2010 made headline news. Heralding a new period of closer cooperation, she looked forward to "a prolonged period of peace and prosperity in which global competition was used in a positive way to enhance the development of the whole world." In light of this momentous event, the twenty-first meeting of European ministers responsible for spatial development, held in Nicosia at the invitation of the Cypriot Presidency of the EU, went totally unnoticed by the world's media.

The local press, however, was ecstatic. It quoted with approval the statement of the Lithuanian deputy commissioner for regional affairs that "more attention needed to be given to the developmental needs of the smaller EU member states." He made the statement backed by the eight-member strong Nordic group. Increasingly frustrated by the policies of the larger, long-standing EU member states, these northern countries considered setting up their own, independent grouping outside of the EU. They were particularly concerned at the continued rampant growth of the London-Paris-Milan-Munich-Hamburg pentagon.

During the 2000s the European Spatial Development Strategy (ESDS, formerly ESDP) came of age. The mood at the end of 2010 was remarkably buoyant, considering that at the start of the new millennium the ESDP, as it was still known, had been in the doldrums. The lack of a firm statistical basis and the sheer number of policy options—60 in total—had been identified as major weaknesses. After the considerable effort involved in producing the document in the first place, the major protagonists mostly had retired from the scene to take a well-earned rest.

The future of the Committee on Spatial Development (CSD) also looked bleak. The European Commission had partially seized control from the member states in a botched power-sharing deal involving two committees when one would have served. Even the location, let alone the program and working arrangements, of the European Spatial Planning Observatory Network (ESPON) had proved contentious. The German and French governments had fought to a virtual standstill over securing this prize. Geographically situated between the two, Luxembourg emerged as an acceptable compromise, suggested as might be expected by the British. The interests of the pentagon had been maintained at all costs.

Nevertheless, if the factors that would influence the future of the ESDS could have been successfully identified in 2002, its increased status at the end of the decade could have been foreseen with some accuracy. The Second Report on Economic and Social Cohesion (CEC 2001), for example, made the link between this major area of EU policy and the ESDP. Furthermore, the report effectively disposed of the competency argument that had proved so troublesome during the preparation of the ESDP. Finally, the guidelines for Interreg III were in place. At last, a major, well-financed program could be launched to implement a European spatial planning policy.

The comitology issue had been solved by placing the ESDP technically under the wing of the powerful Committee on Development and Conversion of Regions (CDCR). In fact, the committee, later to be retitled, had far larger fish to fry in running the structural funds. For a decade it was to pay scant attention to its new charge. This allowed the spatial planners a fairly free hand. Success fed on itself, as European spatial planning activity accelerated by dint both of increasing finance and data.

The status of a number of important factors was crucial to the way in which the ESDS, which was in effect an exercise in strategic planning, developed during the first decade of the new millennium. No such activity is free from the institutional framework in which it is carried out. That tends to shape its ethos and purpose. The legal framework is also important because, making allowances for interpretation, it defines the broad scope of what can and cannot be done. Additionally, strategic planning is undertaken in a variety of different circumstances and by a variety of different actors. Thus the ESDS was not immune to influences from other strategic planning exercises, both within Europe and beyond. From this analysis, and with the benefit of hindsight, six factors were important to the trajectory taken by European spatial planning in the 2000s, including the state of (1) the European Union; (2) the European treaties; (3) the European Commission; (4) the ESDP/S institutions; (5) spatial planning; and (6) the world.

The State of the European Union

Despite the best efforts of all policy makers within a reformed European Commission, economic, social and environmental differences within the EU had widened between 2000 and 2010 because of enlargement rather than EU policies of various sorts. While regional and cohesion funding had made the position better than it might otherwise have been, it was the actual situation that mattered in policy-making circles. The European Parliament, with more statutory power but more diversity of views as well, found reaching consensus on most matters elusive. The democratic deficit at the heart of the European institutions had not been significantly reduced.

In the European Council, where the larger countries were now strongly outnumbered in voices if not votes, deals became increasingly difficult to broker. Views became more and more polarized among the larger number of member states, and regional blocs began to emerge. This became particularly significant for spatial planning policies. The imminent accession of Turkey would rebalance the situation somewhat in favor of the larger countries but also away from the "investor" countries. Nevertheless, as was to be expected, inviting the Turkish government to the Nicosia ministerial meeting as an observer had not been without significant controversy.

Cohesion in the EU, however, was seen slightly differently. Diversity became more valued in a Europe becoming more alike. For example, the French had successful argued for a French language version of the Presidency's conclusions, alongside the Greek, Turkish and English texts. The Cypriots were anxious to please and show that they could host such a meeting with diplomatic aplomb. This was a small reversal, however, on the general path to the predominance of English for the conduct of EU business, boosted by the accession to the EU in 2004 of two former British colonies.

Furthermore, GDP was fast loosing ground as the be-all and end-all of EU regional and cohesion policies. A more-refined measure of quality of life, pioneered in the ESDS in 2004, was being worked on in the European Commission in Brussels, which had antecedents at the start of the decade. The results of the pilot phase of the European Urban Audit in 2001 had looked at a wide range of social factors, including the proportion of EU nationals in urban populations, single-parent households, employment and unemployment, and female employment rates. Comparative crime, housing and health statistics had also been included. Finally, education and training, as well as environmental factors and cultural and recreational facilities, had been measured and compared as further ingredients in establishing an index for the quality of life.

No one stopped to compare the results with the much simpler and better founded analysis that would have been possible based on GDP. From a political perspective, distressed regions were easier to distribute more evenly among member states than gross measures of wealth. It would have been necessary to set the ceiling for wealth at too high a level to include any regions in the 15 original EU member states.

The fourth and fifth enlargements of the EU had led to fierce debate on cohesion during the 2000s. In previous periods, three countries per decade had been the norm, with Denmark, Ireland and the U.K. in the 1970s; Greece, Portugal and Spain in the 1980s; and Austria, Finland and Sweden in the 1990s. Quadrupling that rate in the 2000s was a megachange. Possibly only superstition had prevented the list of new members in the first decade of the twenty-first century from rising to 13. Clearly a policy of equating economic and other aspects of performance across the whole of the EU was no longer, if it had ever been, a realistic policy objective. With flexibility of movement, the accent was on providing a diversity of lifestyles in the different parts of the EU. Enlargement policy, as it had always been destined to be, became a question of political necessity rather than technical criteria.

Spatial planning was seen as a valuable way of portraying, if not achieving, diversity. It concentrated on identifying what gave places their character; the measures needed, depending on political choice, to maintain or develop that character; and measuring the impact of new sectoral policies and development proposals on that character.

Sustainable development, enshrined in the Treaty on European Union, was still the watchword, although *technological fix* was coming up fast on the rails. Scientific advances had made even greater strides in this decade than that preceding it. Social, economic and environmental factors could be more accurately measured, but how they were traded off remained intensely political, despite a new range of technical instruments for doing so. These went under the umbrella term of *kinetic omnibus factoring* (KOF).

Monetary policy, after several hiccups at the start of the single European currency, had also been seen as a major plank of cohesion policy. Even the initially reluctant countries had at long last joined the Euro, albeit with a list of special transitional arrangements needed to convince just over 50 percent of their populations to vote "yes" in the referenda on membership. The beneficial effects of a single European economic space, as it was argued initially, could be held back by the rigidities of a spatial development strategy.

The increasing use of economic instruments in spatial planning within the member states, however, convinced the doubters that the Euro and the ESDS need not necessarily conflict. The strategy could at least identify those areas that would benefit from agglomeration economies, without incurring excessive congestion costs. Influential economists were arguing that continuing structural change in the European economy was likely to outweigh the Euro effect by a margin of three to one. Although, they pointed out, the extension of the Euro zone would itself accentuate structural change.

The State of the European Treaties

After the major changes made in the 1990s preparing for EU enlargement, there was little stomach for further amendments to the European treaties on the EU and the economic communities in the 2000s. The intergovernmental conference in 2004, held on an aircraft carrier among scenes of unprecedented security, illustrated this point. In contrast, the golden jubilee of the EU in 2007 had been celebrated in style (see Table 1), with the accent on direct involvement by the people. Slices of a new European cake had been served to schoolchildren throughout the EU. (Unable to break the habit of a lifetime, the recipe was kept

TABLE 1
Major Events in European Spatial Planning, 2000–2010

Date	Event
2000	INTERREG III introduced
2001	ESPON established in Luxembourg
2002	Work on revised ESDP started
2003	Greek and Irish Presidencies skip hosting planning ministerial meetings
2004	ESDS agreed at Maastricht under Dutch Presidency
2005	Thirtieth anniversary celebrations of the structural funds
2006	Structural funds review; new Regional Policy Council set up
2007	Treaty of Rome golden jubilee celebrations
2008	Fourth cohesion report published
2009	ESDS II agreed at Nantes
2010	Cypriot Presidency hosts twenty-first planning ministerial meeting

secret by the European Commission.) The year was used to mark the second, larger stage of enlargement in the decade. Periods of widening and deepening had tended to follow rather than coincide throughout the history of the EU. With an ever-growing number of countries, it became increasingly difficult to negotiate major treaty changes without opening a Pandora's box of smaller issues promoted by only four or five countries. Thus, those who had been in favor of a treaty change at the beginning of the decade, to recognize spatial planning as an EU competency, quietly dropped their campaign.

In 2000 the Treaty of Nice had amended the reference to town and country planning in the Treaty of Amsterdam, making it no longer subject to unanimity. Even before, however, this had been increasingly seen in a negative light. Spatial planning was developing more of an identity of its own. The link of planning solely to environmental policies in the treaty, as it stood even after being amended at Nice, was regarded as too limiting.

The issue was viewed as less important, however, once spatial development itself was seen as a new approach to implementing both regional and cohesion policies. These were both firmly embedded in the European treaties alongside sustainable development. Planning was just a technique that could be used in conjunction with any policy for which the EU had competence. This also put the final nail in the coffin of the intergovernmental approach to the preparation of the original ESDP. The chair of the Committee for the Development and Conversion of Regions (CDRC) (as it was still called before 2006) from DG Regio (as it was still called after 2007) could scarcely conceal her delight at the collapse of the no competency case in 2003.

Likewise, the debate about subsidiarity, which had fizzled during the preparation of the ESDP, did not resurface. Clearly, if spatial planning at the European scale was to be done by anyone, it was the EU. Fifteen countries acting together to prepare the ESDP might have just been possible, though difficult. Once the figure rose above 20 it was never considered again, particularly as the European Commission was no longer willing to pick up the tab. All of the member states, old and new, had experience of the "general principles" formulated by the former Council of Europe in 2000. In the view of some, this had proved to be an uninfluential damp squib. These principles were not linked to any other Council of Europe policy agenda. Most Council of Europe members were now in the EU. The financial resources to back up the principles were meager. Even the term itself sounded strange to a new generation brought up on political spin as much as policy substance.

Whether a strategy was necessary to deal with spatial development policy issues remained a more valid issue. Surely member states with shared spatial development opportunities or problems could cooperate in threes and fours, without involving the whole EU membership. But administrative advantages were seen in wrapping up all these issues, many of which were in any case similar, in the same policy framework. The growth in cross-border, interregional and transnational cooperation on spatial planning, stimulated in the early part of the decade by Interreg III, made the case for an overarching European strategy more rather than less convincing.

Again, a pragmatic approach proved more effective at the end of the day than a principle enshrined in a legal document. The case stopped short, however, of arguing for a Global Spatial Development Perspective (GSDP) in the face of strong opposition from the U.S. It was pointed out that experience showed that it was apparently too easy to turn a perspective into a strategy. Europeans could not be trusted not to try to pull the same trick twice.

The State of the European Commission

The 2000s were not a good decade for the European Commission, but was it not ever thus? Enlargement involved the absorption of numerous staff from the new member states. Expectations differed more greatly than ever before. Even what constituted a day's work, or an acceptable standard of submission to a commissioner, varied. Early retirement packages for existing staff, young and old, were generous in these turbulent times, and considerable experience was lost. Budgets became overstretched. Many of the same people were reemployed as consultants at even higher salaries than they had previously enjoyed. Newer and more stringent anticorruption measures made it difficult to take action quickly. The workload increased as more and more member states requested information and meetings and had to be consulted over policy. The translation services reached the breaking point. The Finnish version of the ESDP had been difficult enough to follow in 2000. The Hungarian version of the ESDS in 2006 was virtually incomprehensible even to native Hungarian speakers, based as it was on the Finnish translation of the English version of the Dutch original.

Fortunately for those who held the ESDS dear, European regional policy was still seen as a priority. The common agricultural policy (CAP) had faded, although the unimportance of traditional agriculture to the new economy had been only slowly realized. The symbolic level of the CAP, accounting for less than 50 percent of EU expenditure, had been passed. The food-related health scares at the turn of the millennium also had devalued this area of policy. Those involved in genetically modified organisms might have wished to have access to EU finance, but they were much more interested in deregulation than subsidy. How much longer would regional policy be in the ascendancy? None of the older and larger member states were significant beneficiaries of old style regional assistance. Most were not beneficiaries at all.

A Robin Hood approach (transferring resources from rich to poor regions) was no longer the predominant regional policy paradigm. Nevertheless, the poorer and newer member states did not quite see it that way. Self-help and endogenous development were the continuing buzzwords. Every region was said to have economic and/or social and/or environmental attributes that could be used to secure an improved quality of life sometime in the future. But, it could be argued, they probably did need some funding to realize these assets. So mainstream structural fund money continued to flow, but eastward rather than southward. Concern about water resources maintained the former southward orientation. It was fairly evident in 2010 that water policy would soon replace traditional transportation policy in European level interest and expenditure. A similar change in EU policy priorities had happened earlier when the EU's Agricultural Council was abolished to be replaced by a Health Council.

The change to regional policy had figured strongly in the review of the structural funds in 2006. The Irish "miracle" at the beginning of the decade had been followed by the Spanish, Italian and Portuguese "miracles." How much this was due to structural change in the economy and careful macroeconomic management by the European Bank, as opposed to regional and cohesion assistance, was not deeply questioned. A cutoff point at 80 percent of average EU GDP, raised from 75 percent as much to exclude (for different reasons) some regions in the east of Germany as well as southern Italy, left the existing member states high and dry.

At first glance this could have whittled away interest in the ESDS. But the existing member states saw European spatial development policy as giving them some degree of control over how their money was being spent. Furthermore, as the silver jubilee of the establishment of the structural funds had been overlooked at the time by the emphasis given to the misplaced millennium celebrations in 2000, the thirtieth anniversary in 2005 became a major EU event. To tone down support for the new ESDS at such a time was considered to be politically inept.

Interregs III (2000) and IV (2006) had contributed significantly to the success of ESDS. These programs of cooperative funding, mainly across borders and among adjoining regions, had given rise to a large and vociferous spatial planning lobby. Moreover, it depended on European funding. Importantly, these interests were not so much among member state governments as regional governments. The rise of power at the regional level, at the expense of the nation state (with the ironic outcome of preserving the nation state), had given this level of government considerable political clout at the European and national levels. Enjoying the best of both worlds, the funding for Interreg IV, announced in 2006, was just beginning to have an impact on the ground by 2010. Seen largely as a way of implementing the ESDS, the tenfold increase in Interreg funding, at a time when deflation had replaced inflation, catapulted the ESDS into the spotlight in the middle of the decade.

The State of the ESDP/S Institutions

The ESDP was originally produced in an unorthodox (some would argue illegal) manner, at least as far as comitology was concerned. The Committee on Spatial Development (CSD) was chaired by the presidency, not the European Commission that provided the secretariat, interpretation, meeting rooms and so forth. However, since the CSD itself had no legal standing the Commission had no obligation (some would say right) to spend resources in this way.

The CSD reported to an informal Council of Spatial Planning Ministers. All councils are established by treaty, and use of the words *formal* and *informal* here is a tautology. The terms formal or informal council denote the status of a particular meeting, not the status of the council itself. For spatial planning, the ministerial meetings were even more curious. Not only were they not legally speaking councils, they were usually concerned with regional policy as well. This is a well-established and well-financed aspect of EU policy. Not having a separate council of its own for regional policy was strange indeed, but this was rectified by establishing the Regional Policy Council as part of the 2006 review of the structural funds.

At the beginning of the decade the Committee on Spatial Development had been, to all intents and purposes, absorbed into the CDCR, now called the Committee on Regional Policy (CRP). Chaired by the commission, this committee administered the structural funds. Now with a council of its own, the ESDS, as part of the delivery mechanism for regional funding, had at last an officially recognized, formal home. Although not the purpose of the reform, this had the effect, linked to the earlier promotion of the ESDS as an instrument of cohesion policy, of further enhancing the strategy. The ESDS had effortlessly become part of the mainstream of EU activities, far less easy to marginalize than when its ministerial and committee support and legality were subject to question.

At the beginning of the decade another change was afoot that delivered increased prominence to the ESDS. One of the weaknesses of the original ESDP was the lack of comparative statistical data among the 15 member states. With a larger EU, the need to build a database on spatial development trends became imperative, if this area of policy was to be meaningfully pursued. Starting a mechanism to give technical support to spatial planning work at the European level proved extremely difficult, however, because: (1) funding was small scale; (2) agreement could not be reached about the location of this work; and (3) the EC believed that since it provided the funding it should have more say in how the work program was decided and implemented.

Thus, ESPRIN (European Spatial Planning Research/Information Network) became ESPON (European Spatial Planning Observatory Network) at the start of the decade. But, despite the name, it was founded with the emphasis on observation without a strong network, which presented more opportunity to let data-gathering exercises take place by competitive tender rather than with reliance on "tame" national institutes in the majority of member states. This was particularly so since the national level was increasingly squeezed by international and regional level interests.

While the mechanisms proved controversial, however, the data to be collected proved easy. Cohesion had never been measured before. Thus, the way ahead was seen through regularly taken, standardized, structured, sample surveys of views and opinions about various aspects of Europe, the EU and the commission. Although not cheap, these opinion polls proved far less expensive than attempts to standardize disparate national data. This decision fortunately had to be made before the nearly disastrous experience, recorded later, of asking for the general public's view of the ESDS.

The State of Spatial Planning

Planning at any level is a political activity. This quality intensifies geometrically, however, as the spatial scale increases arithmetically. Despite this, the nature of the ESDS, as revised before the review of the structural funds in 2006, reflected changes in planning theory and practice almost as much as changes on the political scene. Planning by objectives had been discredited. Targets were either missed or expressed so vaguely that whether they were achieved or not overshadowed the merits of the strategy itself. Likewise, the majority of visions had been written in the most glowing terms, not least in the ESDP. A generation of plans, which did not appear to recognize that we live in an imperfect world, lay discredited.

In their place, coping with uncertainty became the main planning order of the day. In this way awkward questions about the future could be shelved. Mathematicians and modelers and their universal statistical language took over from the babble of different European planning languages. Risk assessment replaced public participation as well as grand visions for the future. The setting of objectives, which usually changed before they were anywhere near being reached, faded into obscurity. The more flexible planning systems in the European family became the basis for innovation and invention. The 2000s were a technocratic decade in which planning again became respectable. National and regional populations, facing an increasingly uncertain future, sought reassurance from a process that—possibly because they were no longer part of or understood it—they trusted more than the failed, previous participatory approach.

A "knight in shining armor" appeared in the form of the Sustainable Impact Assessment Method (SIAM), itself a replacement for an earlier, failed attempt at Territorial Impact Assessment (TIA). The new acronym also appealed more to an EC bureaucracy still keen on that aspect of its responsibilities. Work on TIA was a valuable exercise in itself because it helped to clarify the nature of spatial planning. It also had the advantage of reducing the European attention given to Environmental Impact Assessment (EIA), now seen as far too limited for the sustainable development age. Trying to measure the degree and direction of likely change in the location of activities and people, hence the future character of places, via SIAM, proved difficult though not impossible. But the purists eventually won the day by proving that planning was a means rather than an end in itself.

As sustainable development still held sway as one of the predominant European Treaty policy aims, it needed to be reflected when formulating the contents of the ESDS. This was helped throughout the 2000s by the increased devolution of power from national to regional and local governments. While sustainable development was a global concept, internationally agreed action (e.g., the Kyoto protocol) had failed dramatically. Greenhouse gas emissions had not even been controlled between 2000 and 2010. Thus the emphasis shifted to regional action where specific effects were easier to perceive, especially in the case of water.

The five-meter contour became a global red line, as far as insurance companies were concerned. Land use planning became land and water use planning. Increased precipitation in northern Europe led to regular and long-lasting flooding of many coastal and low-lying inland areas. The malaria-carrying mosquito also moved its habitat northward with the water and the warmth. By contrast, drought in southern Europe raised the possibility of desertification. The ESDS was pressed into service as a framework for the reallocation of water resources from north to south via a massive network of new canals and pipelines. These initiatives became the major focus of the Trans-European Networks (TENs) program. The water engineer gradually emerged as the hero in a growing number of popular television dramas.

In the first half of the decade public participation was still seen as a valid part of the planning process. The largely failed attempts for meaningful public debate about the ESDP in the late 1990s was replaced by a website approach in the mid-2000s. The number of hits broke all-time European records and nearly led to the collapse of the ESDS process. Experts were hurriedly assembled in Brussels in October 2004 for a specially convened meeting of the Committee on Regional Policy (CRP). The decision to take a 1 percent structured sample as representative of the whole response to the draft ESDS, proposed by the Greek delegate, was greeted as one of truly Socratic wisdom.

The topics of interest to spatial planners had also changed dramatically over the decade. With the further decline of EU support for traditional agriculture and the rapid rate of urban growth in countries with formerly substantial rural populations, urban-rural relationships had been played down when the ESDS replaced the ESDP. The European Parliament, always a powerful lobby for urban affairs, continued in that role. Polycentric urban development had become a European mantra as part of the "compact city" sustainable development ethic. Whether it should be applied at the European level, involving reduction of the pentagon, or just at the level of individual city regions however dominant, was left unstated. Emphasis was placed on the creation of new communities, both in and out of town. Only in this way could more adaptable new housing be provided, equipped with modern amenities and energy-saving devices. In certain urban areas this housing was affordable to the new urban migrants, while in others, built to a far higher specification, it proved attractive to increasingly rich urban elites.

Peripherality had also been abandoned as a focus of planning interest at the European level. Massive investments in new and improved transportation links had had little effect. The obvious point that transport was a two-way street was increasingly recognized at the time that the ESDS replaced the ESDP. Investment in transport infrastructure might lower the costs of exports from an area, but it also did the same for those exporting to it. Similarly, it might be easier for tourists and other visitors to travel to the periphery, but it was also easier for those already there to go elsewhere. Physical movement had become subservient to electronic communications for a generation more adept at using the new technology to good effect for both business and leisure.

Furthermore, peripheral areas provided well for alternative lifestyles. With more freedom about work and home locations, supported by enhanced investment in ICTs, few places could be regarded as inaccessible to the European or even the global economic and cultural mainstreams. The policy of parity of access to infrastructure, enshrined in the 1999 ESDP, was seen with hindsight to have been far-sighted. Similarly, wise management of the natural and cultural heritage (also a main plank of the ESDP) helped unspoiled areas retain and enhance their status. The core-periphery model of Europe, which to a certain extent had inspired the ESDP, was finally laid to rest in the ESDS.

The State of the World

Many of the factors already considered were brought about by real-world changes. These are worth considering separately, however, to identify their direct effect on the ESDS.

Globalization continued its headlong rush in the first decade of the millennium. But there was a stronger public mood to at least try to shape its impact on places and spaces. Despite earlier roots they may have had in one country or continent, multinational companies began to take a wider view of their international responsibilities. With interests in so many countries, "beggar thy neighbor" policies could damage a particular company as much as it might its competitors. Gains in one place or one sector could easily be canceled out by losses elsewhere within the same conglomerate. Some measure of security for existing investment and safeguard for future investment, in the form of the ESDS, were advocated by enlightened private sector interests.

Globalization also assisted the growth of regionalism evident at the beginning of the decade. Identifying competitive advantage needed much more fine-tuning than could be done at the national level, certainly in the larger countries. Similarly, the value of human resources, in comparison with land and capital, emphasized the local delivery of education and health policies. The growth of Interreg IV funding at the expense of mainline regional development assistance accelerated this trend, particularly as far as Europe was concerned. Innovation in one sphere tends to lead to and reinforce innovation in another sphere. Spatial development policies, therefore, increasingly found their natural expression at the regional scale.

The end of history had been declared in the 1990s and the supposed end of geography was announced in the early 2000s. Was this the end of spatial planning as well? While economic and social activities in an increasingly wired-up continent could be located almost anywhere, they did have to be somewhere. Spatial development studies at least made it easier to compare locations and to identify benefits and disadvantages of locating new investment in one region rather than another.

This situation, however, was inherently unstable. Human resources were much more mobile with mass immigration taking place, much of it illegal, from outside as well as within the EU. Taking work, particularly Internet and telephone-based work, to the workers was also an increasing trend. It was too soon to predict which tendency would predominate. Certainly, the immigration that did occur in Europe in the 2000s, was to urban areas. The need to provide a framework for this, as well as a basis for more rational choices about expensive new infrastructure investments, provided a further justification in the minds of many to retain the ESDS.

Conclusions

One of the most difficult anti-ESDS arguments to refute has always been that if North America could successfully do without such a plan, surely Europe could as well. After the far-from-soft landing of the U.S. economy in the first half of the decade, however, this sentiment was less expressed. As the quality rather than the quantity of life became increasingly more important to Europeans, the "third-way" became the predominant political belief. The EU continued its efforts to meld European social equity concepts with American equality of opportunity ideas. This allowed for a degree of strategic planning to embody the provision of social goods. The ESDS was seen as a reasonable way to fit that bill at the continental scale.

Strangely, by 2010 the factors that mainly provide the context in which the ESDS is seen were pulling in the same favorable direction. For different reasons, the member states in the enlarged, less homogeneous EU saw benefit in it. The ESDS provided a framework for giving and receiving regional assistance. It could be targeted to the resurgent, politically more powerful regional level of government. Fortunately, this appeared to be the level at which entrepreneurial talent could be unleashed, and where differences based on history, geography and natural endowment could be fostered in a "Europe of the regions."

Advances in planning methodology, generally as well as specifically at the continental scale, also helped convince skeptics that the second ESDS was now on a firmer statistical and substantive basis than the 1999 and 2004 versions. Legal wrangling over the legitimacy of the exercise was in the past, and the institutional frameworks for making political decisions on spatial development were in better shape than ever. The EU, always in search of a practical purpose, identified spatial planning as a policy area where it had a cutting edge. To support this was a skill base for the exercise in the graduates of European spatial development courses, which were spreading from the small base established at the start of the decade.

Finally, the interpretations of the effects of the major trends in the world—globalization, regionalization, spread of ICT and mass immigration—were still ambiguous. Would they cancel each other out? Against this backdrop, it would be better not to drop the ESDS. It might be needed before the obituaries for geography could be written. Hence, the importance of place and space to development could not yet be discounted.

The celebration of the tenth anniversary of the ESDP, on 11 May 2009 during the French Presidency of the EU (again in Nantes, where the process had started in 1989), had been somewhat overdone. The decade had been a good one for European spatial planning. Planning systems in Europe had converged to such a degree that one of the original spurs to the preparation of the ESDP had largely passed. Although hope springs eternal in the planner's breast, to continue for another 10 years at such a peak was unlikely. Still, vast quantities of the local Loire-Atlantique specialty—veal escalop—were consumed, washed down by copious amounts of the local muscadet. The 1999 vintage had been a good one and had kept well.

Section IV

Conclusion

10

Spatial Planning and European Integration

Andreas Faludi

The contributors to this book have shown that European spatial planning touches a sensitive nerve, the ability of member states and their regions, already affected by European integration, to exercise control over their territory. Is this threat real? The answer hinges on how one views European integration.[1]

To date, attempts to interpret spatial planning and/or the ESDP—in the light of the extensive literature about integration—have been sporadic. To do so may turn out to be a fool's errand since the literature in question is complex and much is about grand issues. A growing body of midrange theories based on empirical research into European policy processes, however, invokes concepts familiar from the planning literature, like networks, discourses and governance. As will become evident, these theories hold the most promise for coming to grips with the position of planning.

The book, *Government and Politics of the European Union* (Nugent 1999), gives a comprehensive overview and will serve as a guide. Rather than taking a firm stand, this work examines conceptual and theoretical perspectives on integration around several clusters of concepts. Likewise, the purpose here is not so much to argue the case for European spatial planning as to explore the conceptual issues underlying it.

Nugent's first cluster of theories relates to the very nature of the EU; the second to concepts from constitutional theory; and the third to "grand theories" explaining European integration. Each will be discussed, pointing out its significance for interpreting the ESDP process. The focus will then switch to midrange theories. The chapter also draws conclusions on the future of European spatial planning—a future crucially dependent on whether and how planners can address the challenges in the wake of the enlargement of the EU (see Chapter 8).

---

[1] See also "Conceptualising European Spatial Planning," prepared for the World Planning Schools Congress Shanghai, 11–15 July 2001. It is, in part, based on research done with Bas Waterhout in the context of EURBANET, a project of the Community Initiative Interreg IIC for the Northwest Metropolitan Area. The lead partner was the research institute OTB at Delft University of Technology.

The Nature of the EU

Beyond mentioning in the European treaties that the EU moves toward an "ever closer union," the EU has so far failed to make clear what it is about. The EU is in constant transition, complex and quite unique, so it is only natural that there should be uncertainty about what integration means. Such processes are never easy. The North American reader needs no reminder that this was also true in the process of figuring out what the U.S. is, nor about the fact that a bloody Civil War was fought to sort out relations between the states and the federal union. (For a discussion of the relevance of the *Federalist Papers* for the EU, see Siedentop 2000.)

According to Nugent, when discussing the EU it is only natural to invoke notions of statehood with its features of territoriality, sovereignty, legitimacy and monopoly of governance. If only to a degree, the EU exhibits these features. The reality of statehood is changing, with states becoming looser formations than before, thus making the comparison between the EU and nation states even more plausible (Nugent 1999, 494). It is understandable, therefore, that people should look at the EU as if it were an emergent state, and consequently view European spatial planning as potentially a form of super-planning on behalf of this new formation.

Attitudes differ as to whether this is or would be a good thing. Some are prone to regard this form of planning as a way of overcoming the myopic self-interest of nation states. Banishing the ultimate form of self-interest—warfare—has been a powerful inspiration for European integration. It is worth pointing out that in this the project has been singularly successful. Others fear the influence of remote Eurocrats and thus reject the idea of a European state. In fact no one advocates the EU becoming a fully-fledged state. The specter of the European superstate is a rhetorical device for populists fanning fears, which undoubtedly there are (not all of them groundless) about integration (see Siedentop 2000). Likewise, in the ESDP process, the notion of a European master plan has served as a negative icon for some (Faludi and Waterhout 2002).

If the EU is not a state, not even a nascent state, perhaps it is an emergent federation?[2] Indeed, federal ideas "have always been at the very heart of the debate about the future of West European political integration" (Burgess 1993, 4). As early as 1947, the idea was forcefully expressed by Sir Winston Churchill (1997, 26) in a speech at Zurich on forming a "United States of Europe" modeled on the United States of America. For war-torn Europe, this was seen as an attractive proposition. It soon became attractive to the U.S. as well, which was concerned that a weak and divided Europe might fall prey to communism (see Lieshout 1999).

Confusion exists about the meaning of federalism (Ross 1995, 176). British Euro-skeptics identify it with a European superstate, whereas Germans see it

---

[2] The distinction is sometimes drawn between federation and a federal state; see the speech of German foreign minister Joschka Fischer at the Humboldt University in Berlin, and the discussion in its wake in Joerges, Mény and Weiler 2000.

as a safeguard against such a state emerging. Their experience with checks and balances built into their system gives them confidence that a federal Europe will not necessarily stifle expressions of national identity. Observers of the German scene are more concerned that the EU might fall into the same "joint decision trap" as Germany where, just as the ministers of the member states do in EU decision making, representatives of the *Länder* participate in federal decision making, leading to occasional stalemates (Scharpf 1988).

In his overview, Nugent points out that the EU also falls short of the federal model because member state governments are in control. Under the terms of the "Luxembourg compromise" forced through by French President De Gaulle, member states can invoke an overriding national interest and veto decisions. Thus, they cannot be compelled to accept decisions to which they are fundamentally opposed. In addition, although they are important, supranational EU institutions (the European Commission, the European Parliament and the European Court of Justice) have few independent enforcement powers.

The federal model continues to hold appeal, and not just in the federal states among EU members. Advocates of integration generally see it as an avenue into the future, with former Commission President Jacques Delors seen as a prominent example. As presently constituted, however, the EU is simply not a federation.

If it is not a state, not even a federal state, what is the EU? One answer diametrically opposed to answers of statehood is that it is an intergovernmental organization in which government representatives cooperate on a voluntary basis, but one with little decision-making autonomy and few means of enforcement. Rather than being compared to the U.S., it would be more appropriate to compare the EU with the North American Free Trade Association (NAFTA), or the United Nations.

Unlike other intergovernmental organizations, however, EU meetings of government representatives are frequent and regular. In one of its permutations the Council of Ministers is almost continuously in session, and so is COREPER, the French acronym for a committee of the permanent representatives (in fact, the ambassadors) of the member states at Brussels who prepare the meetings of the Council of Ministers. There are also untold committees of experts working on issues before the decision makers (Christiansen and Kirchner 2000).

The Committee on Spatial Development (CSD) is one of these committees, although it has no formal right to exist. (In Chapter 9, its longstanding member and onetime chairman John Zetter even calls it illegal.) During the preparation of the ESDP, the CSD has met about four times a year, with working parties of various kinds meeting even more frequently. This has generated a dynamic not to be underestimated, taking the ESDP process, like other processes in European policy-making, beyond what would be expected in intergovernmental organization. This process has led to ESDP practices becoming institutionalized, giving them not only a permanent character but also committing participants to common goals. The midrange theories discussed below will be shown to relate to this; they argue that the learning, the convergence of attitudes and the emergence of common discourses are significant factors in their own right.

Another reason the EU is different from other intergovernmental organizations is that none of them has anything like the same range of responsibilities. One argument for spatial planning is that the numerous EU policies affecting territory, so-called spatial policies, need to be coordinated, and that they need to fit into a frame of reference.

Add to this the fact that the EU incorporates supranational characteristics, about which more will be offered below. Finally, passports of member states identify their bearers as EU citizens. NAFTA, by contrast, would not bear North American citizenship. Thus the EU, although less than a state, even a federal one, must be more than an intergovernmental organization such as the World Trade Organization (WTO) or the Organisation of Economic Co-operation and Development (OECD).

The Constitutional Angle

In discussions about the nature of the EU, constitutional issues always lurk in the background. Perhaps the most important constitutional feature of the EU is that it cannot give itself competencies. There is no constitutional assembly, no qualified majority in the European Parliament, no way for the powers of EU institutions to be extended beyond what is already in the European treaties. Member state governments conclude these treaties and their parliaments ratify them. In some member states, Denmark in particular, ratification is then subject to a referendum, thus member states are the masters of European integration. This is why a European Community competency for spatial planning would have to be discussed at an intergovernmental conference.

Three concepts often arise when discussing the constitutional angle:

☐ Sovereignty, referring to the legal capacity to take decisions without external constraints;

☐ Intergovernmentalism, referring to arrangements whereby nation states cooperate on matters of common interest but without sovereignty being impaired; and

☐ Supranationalism whereby states work together in a manner that restricts their control to the effect that ultimately "states may be obliged to do things against their preferences...." (Nugent 1999, 502).

As indicated in Chapter 1, the competency issue relates to the first concept, sovereignty. After all, territoriality—the control over an area of land defined by recognized borders—is one of the features of the nation state. As the ESDP points out, this is an illusion, because European Community policies impact the territories of member states. Furthermore, forces are at work that impair the freedom of choice even of large states. Thus, they are locked in global competition and many developments, like firms locating where the competitive position is optimal (one of the ideas behind the single European market), are beyond their control. The real choice is between alternative paths to meeting the challenge: by voluntary cooperation, as is the case in the ESDP, or by instituting policies that member states are no longer at liberty to ignore and that are in this sense supranational.

This is where the "constitution" of the EU becomes important. Even if there were a European Community planning competency, member states represented on the Council of Ministers in conjunction with the European Parliament would have ultimate say over how it would be used. There is a community method of EU decision making that combines supranational and intergovernmental elements (see Chapter 1). Thus, the European Commission, the European Parliament and the European Court of Justice are supranational bodies, but the Council of Ministers making the decisions represents the governments of the member states and is thus an intergovernmental body. Even where the treaties foresee qualified majority voting, generally considered a step toward supranationalism, attempts are made to preempt voting by seeking consensus (Hayes-Renshaw and Wallace 1997, 18). Thus, the cards are stacked against supranationalism.

Consequently, there must be ways to reconcile the interests of member states and those of the EC, of which "committee governance" (Christiansen and Kirchner 2000) is one, with the CSD seen as an obvious example. Once again constitutional issues arise, in that this type of "infranational" governance threatens to shift policy making away from elected representatives (for a discussion of this concept, introduced by Weiler, see Chapter 5; see also Chapter 7). Thus, it works to increase what commonly is described as the "democratic deficit" in the EU. Other aspects of this deficit relate to the fact that the European Parliament, elected by popular vote, is not the highest source of authority, but rather the Council of Ministers, which strikes deals behind closed doors.

The intergovernmental element represented by the Council of Ministers may be strong, but there are countervailing forces at work. Nugent mentions increasing interdependence and the logic of the EU as promoting supranationalism that here stands for the delegation of powers to supranational institutions in the EU. Among the supranational features, the right of the European Commission to frame the agenda and to operate as a decision maker in its own right, when it comes to secondary and regulatory decision making, is perhaps the most important. For instance, the Commission could prepare and subsequently publish as one of its communications the Europe 2000 (CEC 1991) and Europe 2000+ documents (CEC 1994), and it could also propose guidelines for the community initiative Interreg IIC/IIIB (see Chapter 3).

With every treaty revision, qualified majority voting also becomes more common, and the European Parliament gains in influence, too. Finally, once taken, EU decisions constitute EU law. In a bold move the European Court of Justice has ruled once that EU law takes precedence over national law. Thus supranationalism is present, perhaps even increasing, but not in the ESDP process, where the European Commission has been restricted to offering assistance. Since it is an informal document, all decisions about the ESDP had to be taken unanimously. After all, member states were not even required to participate in this process. By simply walking out, each of them could have stalled the proceedings, which means that none of the member states could ever be over-ruled. Peer pressure was the only form of control applied.

The contribution of the supranational European Parliament, seconded by the Economic and Social Committee and the Committee of the Regions, has been to argue (unsuccessfully) for spatial planning to be brought under the European treaties which would give it limited say in planning matters.

What Nugent writes about integration generally, that "working together results in the EU states becoming ever more intermeshed...." (1999, 505), also applies to the ESDP process. This intermeshing is not so much a cause of a decline in national power but a response to it. The rationale of the EU "lies in the attempt...on the part of member states to increase their control of... a rapidly changing world" (1999, 505–506). This is true for the ESDP process, where member states tried to come to terms with, for instance, global competition. They want to know how the EU as a whole fares, in particular in comparison with the U.S., which boasts four "global economic integration zones" compared to that which Europe has (see Chapter 4). Nugent writes "the discussion about national sovereignty, in the classical sense of the term at least, is no longer very meaningful" (1999, 506). Small member states like The Netherlands (but emphatically not Denmark) have no qualms about accepting this (Martin 2001). In his account of European spatial development in the 2000s, in Chapter 9, John Zetter assumes that the competency issue will simply disappear and that spatial planning, relating in particular to the structural funds, will effortlessly be mainstreamed in routine European Community business.

Grand Theories

The following theories set out to explain the process of European integration. Historically, a theory called *neofunctionalism* came first, followed by *intergovernmentalism*. Here the term stands for a theory of integration and not for a distinguishing feature of EU institutions that represent member state governments. Both grand theories draw on what is called *interdependency theory*, arguing that modernization results in different parts of the world becoming interwoven, thus weakening the position of nation states. A form of interdependency theory focusing on spatial interdependencies provides a rationale for European spatial planning (see Chapter 3).

Neofunctionalism views integration as a seminal process that inexorably proceeds from the modest beginnings of coordinating the production of coal and steel (the European Coal and Steel Community, or ECSC; Lieshout 1999) to engulfing one area of policy after another. The engine behind this is called *spillover*, which stands for supranational powers in one area leading to the successive extension of supranational powers in others. For instance, it is argued that over time the European Monetary Union, now a fact, will inexorably lead to political union.

As a response to the cross-impacts of various Community policies as they manifest themselves in the territories of the member states and their regions, the quest for European spatial planning is a good example of spillover at work. The argument in the ESDP is that EU policies impact each other. This calls for the need for an integrated spatial approach focusing on territories at various scales and on the unanticipated effects of EU policies on them. Those involved see the necessity for taking a spatial approach as one of the key messages of the ESDP (see Faludi 2001b; Waterhout and Faludi 2001).

Under neofunctionalism, integration is seen as largely expert-led since experts are in the best, and therefore privileged, position to identify and analyze spillover. In the early days of the European Economic Community, experts have been a dominant force. Now there are complaints about European integration being a reserve for Eurocrats and about the democratic deficit that this causes (see Chapters 5 and 7).

The other grand theory, intergovernmentalism, sees integration more as a political process than expert-led. Its adherents draw inspiration from international relations theory that is about intensely political processes involving nation states. As one of the approaches in international relations theory, realism centers on nation states and their representatives as the key actors in international affairs. An important variant is liberal intergovernmentalism, which assumes that states are rational actors, that domestic politics explains the formation of state goals, and that governments play a key role in determining relations among states. Albeit implicitly, accounts of the ESDP process often take this position.

On grand theories, Nugent concludes they can be of value in understanding integration (1999, 515). Insights can be drawn from them, even for analyzing something as remote from them as the ESDP process. Nugent is impatient, however, about the jousting between intergovernmentalism and neofunctionalism, and argues the necessity for moving beyond their endless controversies. This is where midrange theories come in.

Midrange Theories

Since the EU fits so uneasily into known categories, a powerful argument is that it is sui generis—in a category of its own. According to Nugent, this argument builds on the "new governance" literature drawing inspiration from research in policy processes and the dynamics of institutions. The same literature also emphasizes the roles of nonstate actors. This "is transforming politics and government at the European and national level into a system of multilevel, nonhierarchical, deliberative and apolitical governance, via a complex web of public-private networks and quasi-autonomous executive agencies..." (Hix 1998, 54, quoted in Nugent 1999, 500). This reasoning suggests where the main thrust of the argument will go.

Concerned with the shop-floor level of integration—the "low politics"—this type of conceptualization sheds more light on the ESDP process than focusing on the "high politics" of the European treaties and the like. As Nugent points out, decision making in the EU is shared among national governments and institutions and actors at other levels. Although intergovernmental, the ESDP has been prepared in close cooperation with the Commission; when applied to the ESDP the term *intergovernmental* means keeping planning outside the bounds of EU decision making. The ESDP thus straddles various levels and is an example of multilevel governance.

> Multilevel governance thus conceives of the EU as a polity…in which power and influence are exercised at multiple levels of government. National state executives are seen as extremely important…but the almost semimonopolistic position that is ascribed to them by many state-centrists is firmly rejected (Nugent 1999, 501).

Multilevel governance as a concept has emerged from the study of EU regional policy (Hooghe 1996; see also Chapter 7). With European spatial planning emerging in the same context, the concept looks promising. In regional policy, however, multilevel governance relates to the interaction of European Community, national and subnational levels of government. Although federal states among the EU members have found ways of involving their regions, on the whole the making of the ESDP has been a closed process, with little participation by regional governments (let alone nongovernmental actors; see Faludi 2001b). Things are different under the Interreg community initiative Interreg IIC/IIIB, set up in the context of the ESDP process (see Chapter 3). Multilevel government may turn out to be a fruitful concept for analyzing Interreg.

Among midrange theories thus addressed, Nugent (1999, 516) focuses on the new institutionalism and the policy-network approach. The former "has at its core the assertion that institutions matter in determining decisional outcomes." Compared to traditional institutionalism, however, new institutionalism defines institutions broadly, including informal procedures and practices. In this vein the ESDP process, which is informal, can nevertheless be seen as entailing the institutionalization of evolving practices. For instance, at a ministerial meeting at Corfu, the CSD agreed to procedures for preparing ministerial meetings. While acknowledging the *acquis communautaire*, the accumulated body of Community legislation, Bastrup-Birk and Doucet (1997) spoke of the CSD developing its own acquis (see also Christiansen and Kirchner 2000, 10).

The policy network approach can be thought of as an application of new institutionalism to describe and analyze policy processes and outcomes. Thus, "policy networks are arenas in which decision makers and interests come together" (Nugent 1999, 517). Networks can be arranged on a continuum. At one end are the integrated policy communities in well-established EU policy areas (like agriculture), and at the other end loosely integrated issue networks in areas where (as in spatial planning) the debate is still fluid. Because of the informal nature of much EU policy making, the many interests involved and the technical nature of policies that give experts and bureaucrats the edge, and since the Commission deliberately employs networking as a strategy, the EU lends itself to the application of the policy-network approach.

For interpreting the ESDP process, midrange theories look promising. The next section draws on a wider range of works than Nugent's alone. They attempt to invoke midrange theories, not only for interpreting spatial planning, but also a related field of EU environmental policy.

Examples of Midrange Theories

In environmental policy, networking that leads to consensus about current problems has formed the object of indepth studies. *Ringing the Changes in Europe* (Héritier, Knill and Mingers 1996), for example, points at "regulative competition" and all that goes with it in environmental policy. The authors analyze institutional structures and informal interactions, exchange and negotiating strategies along with problem-solving cultures similar to those employed in the ESDP process. They observe that interaction brings about changes in the structures and strategies of all participants, which is why this approach goes beyond the realist tradition in intergovernmentalism described above. That this interaction brings about changes in the perceptions of participants could as well be said about the ESDP as about environmental policy (Faludi 2001c; Faludi and Waterhout 2002).

The approach taken in Héritier, Knill and Mingers (1996) rests on a view, like that in the governance literature, of the state relying on voluntary cooperation of other actors. This applies with even greater force to the European Commission, whose resources, it has been emphasized, are so weak that it must rely on national experts. European networks that emerge have specific characteristics, among others their high policy segmentation, with the Commission as the only one to identify itself with Europe. Segmentation "is due in part to the often technical and highly complex nature of the matters to be dealt with. Also important is the institutional circumstance that, in contrast to national policy networks, no policy integration via party platforms or coalition agreements takes place..." (Héritier, Knill and Mingers 1996, 9). This is because there is no real European polity.

This relates once again to the "democratic deficit" mentioned above. Scharpf (1997, 212) argues that the opposite—democratic accountability—presupposes an orientation of voters toward the common interest. The emergence of such an orientation depends on "a competitive European party system, of European media, and of Europe-wide political controversies in which a democratically accountable European 'government' would have to hold its own to survive the next elections." What the advocates of more democracy—for instance in the European Parliament—forget, is that these preconditions are not in place. And, Scharpf continues, "even if it could be created...democratic legitimacy presupposes a *collective identity* and public discourses about common interest and rules of fair distribution based on that common identity...."

The absence of a European polity is one difference from the U.S., where a polity clearly exists. This does not mean that such a polity cannot emerge; over time, identification with the EU may increase. Such considerations add significance to Ole Jensen's claim of the implicit rationale of the ESDP as fostering a European "territorial identity." If it were possible for spatial planning, through the use of metaphors and spatial imagery (see Chapter 6) to define the European territory as having an identifiable shape, then planning would be related to the core business of European integration. (For the same argument, see also National Spatial Planning Agency 2000.)

Héritier, Knill and Mingers (1996) do not engage in such speculations. Rather, they discuss the "strategy of the first move" used by member states in regulative competition over environmental planning. One is reminded of France taking the initiative in the ESDP process to shape it according to French preferences. This strategy requires the support of the Commission as the gatekeeper. Indeed, the Commission is often characterized as a "political entrepreneur" (Kohler-Koch 1999, 18). Atkinson (2001, 397) makes the same point about urban policy, a field closely related to both spatial planning and environmental policy. If the Commission takes up a proposal, this arouses fears of "unilateral adjustment" among other member states, which is what has happened when Germany opposed Commission initiatives as smacking of French-style planning. After all, if one's proposal gains approval, the first mover has the advantage. "The strong interest in the policy proposal generally goes hand in hand with a high degree of national expertise..." (Héritier, Knill, Mingers 1996, 13). In the ESDP process, French experts were appointed to the Commission early on, and the Dutch have benefited throughout from their reputation as planners, based on their acclaimed and effective commitment to keep their country in shape. Low-regulation countries are more likely to sit on the fence (Héritier, Knill, Mingers 1996, 15). Thus, southern Europeans have done so, to the extent that, with the exception of Spanish opposition to the ESDP, there is not much to report about their role.

In the drafting phase of a policy, another pattern manifests itself: problem solving characterized by mutual learning. "Especially when committees are longer lived, common learning processes are set in motion that lead to cognitive rapprochement among national experts and to the development of 'epistemic communities'..." (Héritier, Knill and Mingers 1996, 16). Mutual learning has also been a prominent feature of the ESDP process. Faludi, Zonneveld and Waterhout (2000) have sought to interpret the CSD as a network in which learning takes place. Faludi (1997) has described the "roving band of planners" that make the ESDP an "epistemic community"; and Hajer (2000) and Richardson and Jensen (2000; see also Chapter 5) identify various discourses in European spatial planning, including the discourse on European identity referred to above.

Discussing "network governance," Kohler-Koch (1999) comes to similar conclusions. Network governance rests on self-interested actors perceiving a common interest through negotiations and joint learning. Readiness to participate in problem solving depends on the match of systems. Policies become effective, not by imposition but by means of negotiations, which, in the European context is considered the most effective way of bringing about change. Another way is that of attraction by disseminating best practices. In such ways, the "formulation of European policies enmeshes national and Community actors in a complex discursive process. It incorporates a shared understanding of the basic rationale of the aims and purpose of European political regulation" (Kohler-Koch 1999, 29). Now that it is on the books, one way the ESDP works is by disseminating the spatial planning approach, with the Interreg community initiative seen as a powerful vehicle (Faludi 2001b; Waterhout and Faludi 2001). Thus, in Chapter 9, John Zetter expects Interreg to generate a powerful lobby of spatial planners, with positive effects on the ESDP process.

The conclusions by the editors of *The Transformation of Governance in the European Union,* which contains Kohler-Koch's chapter, likewise emphasize the importance of common concepts (Kohler-Koch and Eising 1999, 270). The European institutional setup differs from that of member states, in that supranational policy actors are largely restricted to agenda setting and policy formulation. In all this, as Héritier, Knill and Mingers (1996) have also argued, there is a need for guiding principles overriding the differences among various national positions. In Chapter 4, Bas Waterhout has made use of their work by showing that in the ESDP process polycentricity has formed a bridging concept fulfilling this function. Even if fuzzy, or perhaps precisely because they are ambiguous, bridging concepts can form the basis for further cooperation.

Arthur Benz, an author who comes from the integration literature, applies himself specifically to the ESDP. His sources of inspiration are game theory and theories of multilevel governance (see Chapter 7, where he shows how to tackle the coordination challenge arising in European spatial planning). Even environmental policy, which has a clear mandate to coordinate other areas of EU policy, finds it difficult to meet this challenge (Bomberg 1998, 179). According to Benz, coordination must focus on what is necessary and feasible. Thus, planning at the EU level should address genuine transnational concerns and leave the autonomy of national and regional authorities as far as possible intact. Keeping planning levels apart, however, is difficult, so Benz looks for other ways of reducing the problem of coordination. Drawing inspiration from empirical research on European regional policy (Benz 2000; see also Benz and Eberlein 1999), he explains that where arenas are loosely coupled, decisions in one arena do not impose unnecessary constraints on decisions in others. Under these circumstances Benz suggests that where those affected have a right of appeal, the ESDP could be turned into a binding framework.

Benz draws on the German political scientist Scharpf, who has not only explored game theory but has also developed an "actor-centered institutionalism." This concept sees situations in which policy actors operate as game-theoretical constellations, the latter in turn being shaped by institutions. By institutions Scharpf means "systems of rules that structure the course of action that a set of actors may choose. In this definition we would, however, include not only formal legal rules but also social norms that actors will generally respect and whose violation will be sanctioned by loss of reputation, social disapproval, withdrawal of cooperation and rewards, or even ostracism" (Scharpf 1997, 38).

Scharpf presents a conceptual framework for policy analysts to map substantive policy problems onto the constellation of policy actors involved (Scharpf 1997, 46). Constellations are anarchic fields, networks or joint decision systems, associations or organizations (including the state). Modes of interaction available to actors range from unilateral actions over negotiated agreements and majority voting to the issuing of directives. Some of these modes are appropriate within certain constellations but not within others. Thus, anarchic fields allow only for unilateral action and, at most, negotiated agreements. At the other end of the scale, all four modes are available in an organization.

With this in mind, Faludi (2000a) discusses the ESDP process where the initial situation resembled an anarchic field, with uncertainty about content as well as the positions of the various actors. Over time, however, what has emerged is an "epistemic community." Now there is an ESDP and perhaps even a planning community. People have come to know each other, and there is an element of mutual trust. Thus, the constellation has changed. This is another example of midrange theories being applied to the interpretation of the ESDP process.

Implications

Nugent thinks there can be no single comprehensive theory of integration. In particular the neofunctionalist assumption of a semiautonomous movement toward integration has been proven wrong. In spatial planning the move, logical though it may have appeared, toward underpinning EU spatial policies with a spatial perspective also has been stalled. European planning does not come about from necessity. Rather, individuals from national planning establishments, who see opportunities for improving their situation, have set the process in motion. This has led to significant change over time. It is clear, therefore, that the midrange theories of European integration that focus on interactions among actors in the field offer better opportunities for understanding European spatial planning than the "grand theories."

Nugent's overview ends on an upbeat note and with a warning that is also relevant for the future of the ESDP process. The EU has a role in the shaping of Europe. "It is approaching this task in a proactive manner, but it will need to be extremely careful.... Most importantly, perhaps, the EU will need to strike a sensitive and appropriate balance between its own needs and...those of prospective member states..." (Nugent 1999, 528). Already forming the topic of one short chapter in the ESDP itself, enlargement is the object of continuing discussions among European planning circles (CEC 2000b; Biehl 2001; see also Chapter 8). Indeed, as Husson (2000) argues, the pursuit of what he calls "territorial cohesion" is central to the success of enlargement.

Territorial cohesion is also a major issue in Unity, Solidarity Diversity for Europe, its People and its Territory: Second Report on Economic and Social Cohesion" (CEC 2001), in which the European Commission sets out its view of the future of regional policy, in particular in relation to enlargement. There the Commission seeks to formulate an agenda for a time after the programming period of the structural funds has ended, in 2006. With the ascendancy of regional policy, territorial cohesion may become even more important (see Chapter 9, which has shown that the budget allocation of agricultural policy is expected to fall below the 50 percent mark in favor of regional policy). Territorial cohesion can be translated into policies for sustaining the polycentric system of towns and cities in Europe. Thus, albeit under a different guise, spatial planning may move to the center stage of European integration.

The full meaning of European spatial planning is far from a settled issue. Where enlargement is concerned, this is true even in a literal sense. As Jean-François Drevet has shown (Chapter 8), how and where the process will end is uncertain. If the Russian federation joined the EU, only the Bering Strait would remain between the EU and U.S. territory.

Chapter 1 discussed competing views of spatial planning, whether evolving around land use and regulation or around spatial strategies, in a context that is becoming more complex, more Europeanized and more globalized. This concluding chapter has added an awareness of uncertainty about the very meaning of European integration. Since there is no immediate prospect of the underlying grand issues being settled, European planners need to live with this situation. They also have to live—nay, to anticipate—enlargement as a huge spatial project.

In this uncertain situation about the context of European spatial planning, planners can take comfort from the midrange theories focusing on processes on the shop floor of European integration. On the level of day-to-day interaction, integration develops its own dynamics, not totally divorced from the grand issues, but still with a momentum of its own. Networking, the formation of an "epistemic community," of a common language and, in the case of spatial planning, a sense of a European "territorial identity" are clearly important.

Interreg IIC/IIIB is the most prominent vehicle for this, but the ESDP process, although vulnerable, must also continue. Chapter 3 has presented two scenarios, one assuming a modicum of recognition of the supranational element in European planning more hopeful than the other. The point is not to give the Commission say over the territory of the EU—the point is to give it enough incentive to stay in the complex game that is the ESDP process. Otherwise, it might sideline the ESDP, the ministerial meetings and the CSD.

The agenda for further research derives from all of the above. Interreg IIC/IIIB—as a vehicle for applying the ESDP; as an arena for articulating the discourse; and as a stamping ground for the new breed of European spatial planners—requires attention, and for this the midrange theories appear to be most appropriate. Researchers should also look beyond 2006, however, when the current programming period for the structural funds comes to an end and enlargement (in its first phase) is likely to be a fact. The focus may then have to shift again to the institutional architecture of European spatial planning. Next to empirical work, conceptual work needs to be done to prepare the ground for a more permanent solution for spatial planning in an even more diverse, changing EU.

Epilogue

Implications for American Planners

Robert D. Yaro

The European Union is transforming its 15 member countries into an increasingly integrated economy and society. With expansion into Central European countries expected within the next few years, the new integrated Europe will stretch from Ireland to Estonia and from Portugal to Finland. Growing numbers of people now think of themselves not only as Germans or Italians or Scots, but also as Europeans—citizens of this larger place.

In this book, Andreas Faludi and his colleagues describe the parallel process that is occurring in the planning world, where planners are creating new forms of spatial planning and a new intellectual and professional framework for regional planning practice across the continent. As Faludi has noted, one of the essential roles of effective regional planning is to redefine attitudes around a regional outlook. In that sense, the emerging practice of European spatial planning can be considered an integral and essential part of the process of creating both the new reality of an integrated Europe and the new European consciousness that is the prerequisite for this integration.

Faludi has worked for more than a decade both chronicling and helping shape this emerging practice. Faludi and his coauthors bring this new world to the attention of American planners and land use professionals. The implications of recent European innovations in spatial planning for the United States could be profound, potentially having the same strong influence on American planning in the early twenty-first century that European planning had on American planning in the early twentieth century.

The Rosetta Stone of European spatial planning is the European Spatial Development Perspective (ESDP), adopted in 1999 by the European Union's planning ministers. ESDP focuses in particular on three areas of the EU's activities: (1) the structural funds by which the EU advances regional economic development in its less developed areas; (2) the trans-European networks, or key infrastructure systems linking all of Europe into a unified whole; and (3) environmental policy. ESDP proposes that these policies be further integrated to create improved spatial coherence and functional synergies from the EU's policies and investments. In effect, spatial development is meant to put a geographic "spin" and a planner's integrating outlook on the European Union's programs.

Essentially, with the adoption of ESDP, North America's largest competitor in the global economy is now utilizing planning to advance its economic and transportation advantages, improve its quality of life and reduce inequities among its subregions. These innovations should open up a range of new possibilities for American planners, causing us to consider rethinking how we plan for metropolitan areas, natural resource systems and larger urban regions.

Imagine what the impact would be were the federal government to provide powerful financial incentives for U.S. states and metropolitan regions to collaborate across borders and issues to integrate transportation, economic development and environmental strategies. Were this to happen, the goals of smart growth, intermodal transportation and sustainable development movements might be advanced rapidly.

If this approach were adopted in places like the Northeast Corridor, stretching from Richmond, Virginia to Portland, Maine, for example, one could imagine major changes: the federal government investing in world-class, high-speed rail and goods movements systems; regional economic development strategies being adopted in Philadelphia, Baltimore and many second-tier cities served by new high-speed services to capitalize on resulting access improvements; and the introduction of resource protection and reclamation strategies in the region's Appalachian highlands, coastal estuaries and former industrial brownfields. Similar strategies could be adopted in other urban regions: the Cascadia region, stretching from Portland, Oregon to Vancouver; the urbanized region of the midwest, stretching from Cleveland to Minneapolis; and the Atlanta-Chattanooga region in the southeast. This approach to regional planning should also inspire us to think creatively about the future of both fast-growing and declining rural regions across the U.S.

Most of these places span a number of cities, counties or even states, and face a wide range of urgent transportation, environmental and economic development challenges, requiring that we create plans that also span these borders. Inspired by the knowledge that their European counterparts are now building effective plans and institutions across national boundaries, planners in New York City, for example, might find it possible to collaborate with their counterparts in New Jersey, less than a kilometer away across the Hudson River.

This book should also help stimulate a fresh look at the longstanding debate in the U.S. about the need for more effective greater-than-local planning programs at the regional, state and national levels. In effect, we need to strike a better balance between bottom-up and top-down planning, as Europeans are striving to do (and succeeding in ways that most areas in the U.S. have not).

Learning from foreign planning experience does not come naturally to American planners. Over the past few decades American planning and land use regulation have become increasingly insular and introspective. Occasionally, we have been known to reach beyond the narrow confines of our own municipal or state planning and zoning system to learn about the latest state or regional smart growth innovations in some far away, exotic place, say Oregon or Maryland. But seldom do we feel the need to look beyond the seas to learn from the innovations in other countries.

It wasn't always this way; through much of the late nineteenth and early twentieth centuries, European planning practice had an important influence on American planners and plans:

- ☐ Frederick Law Olmsted's parks, parkways and city plans were inspired by his visits to Liverpool's Prince's and Sefton Parks in the 1850s.
- ☐ From 1890 to 1910 American planners adapted European Beaux Arts city plans to create the American City Beautiful movement, in the process transforming Washington, Chicago, Philadelphia, San Francisco, Buffalo and dozens of other cities with new civic centers, plazas and boulevards.
- ☐ Later, pioneering American planner Edward Bassett adapted German land use regulatory practices to create New York City's landmark 1916 Zoning Resolution.
- ☐ In the early 1920s Bassett led then-U.S. Commerce Secretary Herbert Hoover's effort to create the model State Zoning Enabling Act, making this adaptation of German zoning principles the national standard for U.S. land use regulation.
- ☐ Early- and mid-twentieth century British new towns inspired two generations of new American communities, and even today these precedents inspire America's new urbanism movement.
- ☐ Finally, Thomas Adams, co-founder of Britain's Royal Town Planning Institute, came to New York in the 1920s to lead the Regional Plan Association's effort to create the country's first regional plan, inspiring metropolitan plans across the country through the first half of the twentieth century.

In the post–Second World War era, however, Americans lost interest in European planning, except for a brief dalliance with new communities in the 1960s and early 1970s, inspired by the postwar British new towns movement. While millions of Americans toured the European countryside and well-preserved historic towns and cities, and admired the results of effective national or regional planning, only rarely would they contemplate adapting these precedents to their own country.

It is significant that European spatial planning focuses on planning, not regulation. But it does rely on the presence of strong central governments administering planning controls and the EU's investments in infrastructure, regional development and environmental protection. Beyond our recent reticence to adapt European planning innovations, there are a number of fundamental impediments to adapting many of these practices, given the political, legal and cultural differences between the U.S. and Europe:

- ☐ The U.S. was founded on the basis of widely held disdain for distant central government, making national and regional planning a contentious issue in most parts of the country. (Given these deeply engrained attitudes, it would be difficult to imagine Americans embracing a new U.S. version of DG XVI—Directorate Regio, the directorate of the European Commission responsible for spatial planning and regional development concerns.)
- ☐ Despite recent smart growth innovations, most states continue to delegate virtually all planning responsibilities to municipal governments, making it

politically difficult to reclaim planning and regulatory responsibilities at the regional or state level. Further, only a handful of state smart growth programs include major commitments to infrastructure systems and urban reinvestment.

☐ Concerns about the Takings Clause of the U.S. Constitution and attacks by the wise use movement have placed a chill on land use planning and regulatory systems that attempt to severely restrict property rights.

Despite these constraints, however, the innovations described in this book could inspire a new generation of American planners to consider new ways to improve planning for major U.S. metropolitan regions, large natural resource systems, especially in those places that straddle regional, state or transnational borders. In the same way that our federal system reserves planning responsibilities to the states (similar to the European concept of subsidiarity), except where a compelling national interest exists, a limited ceding of authority to a higher level might be justifiable in these cases.

Transnational Planning in North America

At the transnational level, planning has already begun to strengthen links between San Diego and Tijuana, including proposals to build a new international airport spanning the border. These efforts have been set back temporarily by post–September 11 security concerns, but given the growing economic, social and environmental integration of the two cities, regional planning across the border is bound to continue.

Similar initiatives are needed in other metropolitan regions that span the Canadian and Mexican borders, in such places as Buffalo-Toronto, Detroit-Windsor and Seattle-Vancouver. However, at present, regional plans in Vancouver, for example, look like pre-Columbian maps of the world—the area south of the border is mapped as a kind of terra incognita, to the disadvantage of both Vancouver and Seattle.

Planners in Buffalo, for example, have for years discussed the potential benefits associated with strengthening ties to Toronto, one of North America's great world cities. Given the kinds of innovations being adopted in Europe, including expedited border crossings and high-speed rail links, the two cities could easily be less than an hour apart, creating economies of scale and synergies between their economies. Ironically, NAFTA remains a major impediment to these links, with its focus on goods movement rather than expanded links for service industries and the professionals who run them. The informal process leading to the ESDP (involving the work, in Faludi's term, of a "roving band of planners") might also be applied to promote these strengthened cross-border links. In the long run, perhaps it would be appropriate for the federal government and its Canadian and Mexican counterparts to initiate EU-style discussions on comprehensive strategies to improve transportation and economic links in transnational border communities in all three countries.

National Planning

European efforts to create more integrated, continent-scaled transportation, economic development, environmental protection and other strategies could inspire a fresh look at national planning in the U.S. Although we have gotten out of the habit of thinking about an appropriate federal role in this area, it turns out that the U.S. has a long and rich heritage of national planning, dating back to Thomas Jefferson's national plan in the early nineteenth century. His plan proposed a series of transportation improvements to promote development of the west and strengthen ties among the country's far-flung regions, leading to construction of the nation's nineteenth-century networks of canals, roads and railroads.

A century later, Teddy Roosevelt promoted development of a natural resource-oriented national plan. This effort, coordinated by Gifford Pinchot, inspired creation of the national forest systems and major river development and conservation projects on the Colorado, Mississippi and other rivers. Later, Franklin Roosevelt promoted a broader set of regional economic and conservation programs, leading to creation or expansion of the Tennessee Valley Authority, Bonneville Power Administration and Colorado River Project, and similar initiatives in other places. During the Great Depression, Roosevelt's National Resources Planning Administration promoted state planning and public works construction across the country. These efforts created the infrastructure (and vast quantities of cheap power and water) needed for rapid development of wartime defense industries in the southwest, southeast and other Sunbelt regions, setting the stage for the growth of these regions in the postwar period.

Even Dwight Eisenhower got into the national planning business with his 1956 National Defense Highway Act, and the resulting 19,000-mile Interstate Highway system, one of the world's largest public works projects. Unfortunately, the road builders studiously ignored the land use implications of their actions, with the result that the interstates transformed metropolitan America in ways that virtually no one anticipated at the time.

Almost a half-century later, after unleashing a wave of unplanned sprawl, the capacity of the metropolitan links of the Interstate system is virtually used up, and new strategies are needed to provide metropolitan America with capacity for mobility and growth in the twenty-first century. Through the ISTEA and TEA-21 transportation funding programs, the federal government has provided significant new financial resources to address these concerns. But the federal government continues to lack any commitment to effective regional land use planning, with the result that the planning response from metropolitan planning organizations (MPOs) in most regions has been limp at best, with only a handful of them making connections between transportation, economic and land use concerns.

European planners face many of these same concerns in metropolitan regions that are also choking on sprawl and congestion. But they are moving aggressively to build trans-European high-speed rail networks and new regional rail systems that will both integrate larger urban regions and create alternatives to crowded highways. Their American counterparts are handicapped by lack of public support and funding for similar improvements.

State Plans

More than a dozen states have adopted some kind of smart growth program, creating greater-than-local growth management processes. Most of these programs are incentive-based or advisory only, and it is still unclear whether they will be able to fundamentally alter the patterns of metropolitan sprawl that are undercutting both urban and rural regions. With the exception of New Jersey's new state plan, these programs also lack a real spatial planning element that could delineate and map growth centers and growth corridors, conservation areas and infrastructure strategies.

Learning from European practice, perhaps the next generation of smart growth strategies could incorporate these planning elements, and in the process expand both their effectiveness and levels of public understanding and support for their implementation. Inspired by ESDP, the federal government could provide financial incentives to the states to strengthen integrated smart growth, transportation and environmental protection strategies.

Regional Planning

Major urban corridors, such as the Northeast Corridor, stretching from Richmond to Portland, are choking on congestion. While new plans are needed to strengthen the regional transportation and economic links that tie these places together, the planning response to these challenges has been virtually nonexistent.

The U.S. economy and population are increasingly concentrated in large metropolitan regions, where four out of five Americans now live. The northeastern U.S., for example, with an economy larger than Germany's, is one of the world's largest urban regions. But its competitiveness is undermined by frayed transportation links and the decline of many of its urban areas. Interstate-95 and the region's airports remain overloaded, but no comprehensive strategies have emerged to address current or future transportation needs. Amtrak has been disinvesting in the northeastern rail corridor for decades, and its new Acela high-speed service is hampered by archaic rights-of-way that limit speeds to a fraction of its European counterparts. And, while the Boston, New York and Washington areas are burgeoning, Philadelphia, Baltimore and smaller cities in the corridor have been underperforming for decades.

The Northeast's large natural resource systems—the Appalachian highlands and the Atlantic barrier beach and estuary systems—are also being harmed by unplanned sprawl. Finally, the Northeast would benefit from regional strategies to address brownfields, air and water quality, waste management, sprawl and other common concerns affecting the whole region.

A regionwide spatial plan, similar to those being developed in similar extended urban regions in Europe, could provide answers to these vexing challenges and build support for public policies and investments needed to address these needs. The region would benefit from plans and investments that could help achieve the same kind of synergies among New York, Boston, Philadelphia, Baltimore and Washington that European planners are creating among London, Brussels, Paris, Frankfurt, Cologne and Amsterdam.

Large rural regions of the country, in such places as the High Plains, the Rio Grande Valley, the Mississippi Delta and the Appalachians, face equally daunting challenges, in many cases related to continuing economic and population decline. With the exception of the Appalachians, none of these regions have regional planning institutions or processes in place. Integrated transportation, economic and social development, and environmental protection and restoration strategies, similar to those being implemented in underdeveloped areas of Europe, could fundamentally alter the prospects of these regions.

Here again, regional planners could learn from the European experience in preparing and implementing regional economic development plans and providing tens of billions of dollars in structural funds to promote their implementation. Through these strategies, the European Union has successfully promoted economic development and integration strategies in less-developed regions of Europe. The EU can be expected to embark on a new generation of these plans in the newly admitted, and mostly underdeveloped, Central European states. The economic and social transformation that these programs helped to create has been remarkable in such places as Ireland, Spain and Eastern Germany, and they could provide a roadmap for similar initiatives in the U.S. Finally, as noted above, this country has implemented similar successful regional policies in the past; inspired by the success of European practices, we could consider adopting them again.

At the metropolitan level over the past decade both civic and public planning groups have developed a new generation of regional plans in such places as New York City, Chicago, Portland, Southeastern Florida, Seattle and Salt Lake City. Civic-led planning groups have been organized in more than 30 regions, most of them members of the newly formed Alliance for Regional Stewardship. These groups could become a focal point for a new generation of regional plans based on European best practices. It must be noted, however, that regional planning in most of the U.S. remains largely advisory, and most of these plans lack the clout of their European counterparts.

Finally, it should also be noted that the social and demographic challenges facing European regions are quite different than those facing their U.S. counterparts. Europe is experiencing a significant decline in population, due to low levels of immigration and declining fertility rates. Planners in Europe are looking at ways to anticipate continued population decline and avoid its potential negative impacts on both urban and rural regions. The U.S., on the other hand, faces challenges related to significant population growth resulting from both continued rapid immigration and rising fertility rates. For this reason, American planners will need to develop regional plans that create the capacity for growth across the country, particularly in those places that have been bypassed by the growth and prosperity of the past few decades.

Conclusion

Given all of the obstacles facing American planners, how can we begin to learn from and adapt the best practices being proposed and implemented by European spatial planners? We could begin by initiating planning processes outside official channels, perhaps through initiatives led by the civic sector or university-based planners. In so doing, we can learn from the experience of Faludi's "roving band of planners" who helped initiate ESDP, operating largely outside official planning channels (but with informal support from national planning ministers and the European Commission) to create these innovations.

The impetus for these plans could come from several sources:

☐ The "1000 Friends" groups operating in most smart growth states could provide the impetus for more effective regional and state planning, perhaps even developing these plans themselves.

☐ Civic-led planning groups, including the members of the Alliance for Regional Stewardship, could play a similar role in metropolitan regions.

☐ University-based urban and rural centers could initiate regional strategies, perhaps in partnership with other civic-led planning initiatives.

☐ Regions could become laboratories for innovation. In some places, metropolitan planning organizations could lead regional planning efforts, in some cases in partnership with civic planning groups. The Southern California Association of Governments, the Los Angeles region MPO, is initiating such a process in partnership with a new civic group, the Southern California Transportation and Land Use Coalition.

Although it may seem unlikely that our federal government could embrace a U.S. version of ESDP in the short run, the American public is beginning to demand solutions to the problems of congestion, sprawl, environmental degradation and economic decline in many areas of the country. Our elected leaders should be either chastened or inspired by the fact that our biggest economic competitor, the European Union, is actively promoting spatial development strategies as a means of addressing these problems, making it possible to at least begin the debate here.

We should look to the growing number of civic-led planning groups who are promoting regional solutions to these problems to begin these innovations. These groups are planning for the future of metropolitan areas or bioregions, such as watersheds, and in many places are gaining the support of state governments. Inspired by the success of these initiatives, the federal government might eventually get into the act, playing the indispensable role here that the EU is playing in utilizing improved planning to address some of Europe's most pressing needs.

References

Ache, P. 2001. The global economic integration zone—European spatial planning suspended between image and production and real substance? Paper for the first World Planning Schools Congress. 11–15 July, Shanghai.

Albrechts, L. 2001. How to proceed from image and discourse to action: As applied to the Flemish diamond. *Urban Studies* 38(4):733–745.

Alden, J. 2001. Devolution since Kilbrandon and scenarios for the future of spatial planning in the United Kingdom and European Union. *International planning studies* 6(2):117–132.

Allen, D. 2000. Cohesion and structural funds. In *Policy-making in the European Union, fourth edition*, 243–265. H. Wallace and W. Wallace, eds. Oxford: Oxford University Press.

Anderson, B. 1991. *Imagined communities. Reflections on the origin and spread of nationalism.* London: Verso.

Anonyme. 1997. European Union: Integration and enlargement. Irish National Economic and Social Council, 101. Dublin. March.

ARL—Akademie für Raumforschung und Landesplanung. 1996. Europäische Raumentwicklungspolitik; Rechtliche Verankerung im Vertrag über die Europäische Union, Arbeitsmaterial Nr. 233. Hanover: ARL.

ARL and DATAR—Akademie für Raumforschung und Landesplanung and Délégation à l'Aménagement du Territoire et à l'Action Régionale, eds. 1994. Institutionelle Bedingungen einer europäischen Raumentwicklungspolitik. Hanover: ARL.

Atkinson, R. 2001. The emerging urban agenda and the European spatial development perspective: Towards an EU urban policy? *European Planning Studies* 9(3):385–406.

Bach, M. 1992. Eine leise Revolution durch Verwaltungsverfahren: Bürokratische Integrationsprozesse in der Europäischen Gemeinschaft. *Zeitschrift für Soziologie* 21(1):16–30.

Bachtler, J. 2000. *Transition, cohesion and regional policy in Central and Eastern Europe EPRC.* Aldershot: Ashgate.

Bastrup-Birk, H. and P. Doucet. 1997. European spatial planning from the heart. In *Shaping Europe: The European spatial development perspective*, A. Faludi and W. Zonneveld, eds. Special issue. *Built Environment* 23(4):307–318. Oxford: Alexandrine Press.

Belgian Presidency of the Council of Ministers. 1993. For a significant step towards a co-ordinated planning of Europe's territory. Presented 13 November at Liège informal Council of ministers responsible for regional policy and regional planning. In *Les cahiers de l'urbanisme, revue de l'administration wallonne de l'aménagement du territoire, du logement et du patrimoine, tiré à part.* Special issue (translation into English) 11, Hiver 1993–1994:33–45.

Bengs, C. and K. Böhme, eds. 1998. *The progress of European spatial planning—facing ESDP.* Nordregio (1). Stockholm: Nordregio.

Benz, A. 1994. *Kooperative Verwaltung. Funktionen, Voraussetzungen und Folgen*. Baden-Baden: Nomos.

————. 1998. Postparlamentarische Demokratie? Demokratische Legitimation im kooperativen Staat. In *Demokratie—Eine Kultur des Westens?* M. Th. Greven, ed., 201–222. Opladen, Germany: Leske und Budrich.

————. 2000. Two types of multilevel governance: Intergovernmental relations in German and EU regional policy. *Regional and Federal Studies* 10(3):21–44.

Benz, A. and Eberlein, B. 1999. The Europeanization of regional policies: Patterns of multilevel governance. *Journal of European Public Policy* 6(2):329–348.

Biehl, D. 2001. Plädoyer für eine europäische Raumordnungskompetenz unter besonderer Berücksichtigung der Ost-Erweiterung. In *Europäisches Raumentwicklungskonzept (EUREK), Forschungs- und Sitzungsberichte 216*, K. Wolf, G. Tönnies, eds., 38–79. Hanover: Akademie für Raumforschung und Landesplanung.

BMBAU—Bundesministerium für Raumordnung, Bauwesen und Städtebau. 1995. Grundlagen einer Europäischen Raumentwicklungspolitik; Principles for a European spatial development policy; Principles pour une politique d'aménagement du territoire européen. Bonn: Selbstverlag der Bundesforschungsanstalt für Landeskunde und Raumordnung.

————. 1998. German delegation to the Transnational Seminar on the ESDP. For a new urban-rural partnership. Discussion paper. 15–16 October. Salamanca, Spain.

Böhme, K. 1998. Northern impressions of the ESDP. In *The progress of European spatial planning*, C. Bengs and K. Böhme, eds. Nordregio (1):77–86. Stockholm: Nordregio.

————. 1999a. Interdependencies of spatial planning in and for Europe. Presented at the XIII AESOP Congress. 7–11 July. Bergen, Norway.

————. 1999b. A northern view on the ESDP. *North* 9(4/5):1, 31–34.

Bomberg, E. 1998. Issue networks and the environment: Explaining European Union environmental policy. In *Comparing policy networks*, D. Marsh, ed., 167–184. Buckingham: Open University Press.

Brenner, N. 1998. Between fixity and motion: Accumulation, territorial organization and the historical geography of spatial scales. *Environment and planning D: Society and space* 16:459–481.

Brunet, R. 1989. Les Villes Européennes, Rapport pour la DATAR, Délégation à l'Aménagement du Territoire et à l'Action Régionale, under the supervision of Roger Brunet, with the collaboration of Jean-Claude Boyer et al., Groupement d'Intérêt Public RECLUS. Paris: La Documentation Française.

Brzezinski, Z. 1997. *Le Grand Echiquier: l'Amérique et le reste du monde*. Paris: Pluriel, Hachette.

Burgess, M. 1993. Federalism and federation: A reappraisal. In *Comparative federalism and federation: Competing traditions and future directions*, M. Burgess and A. G. Gagnon, eds., 3–14. New York and London: Harvester Wheatsheaf.

Castells, M. 1998. *The information age: Economy, society and culture, volume three: End of Millenium*. Oxford: Blackwell Publishers.

CEC—Commission of the European Communities. 1991. *Europe 2000: Outlook for the development of the Community's territory*. Luxembourg: Office for Official Publications of the European Communities.

————. 1994. *Europe 2000+: Cooperation for European territorial development*. Luxembourg: Office for the Official Publications of the European Communities.

————. 1996a. Prospects for the development of the central and capital cities and regions. Luxembourg: Office for Official Publications of the European Communities.

———. 1996b. Communication to the member states laying down guidelines for operational programs which member states are invited to establish in the framework of a Community Interreg initiative concerning transnational cooperation on spatial planning (96/C 200/07). *Official Journal of the European Communities*, July 10, C200:23–28.

———. 1997a. The EU compendium of spatial planning systems and policies (Regional Development Studies 28). Luxembourg: Office for Official Publications of the European Communities.

———. 1997b. European Spatial Development Perspective: First official draft (presented at the informal meeting of ministers responsible for spatial planning of the member states of the European Union, Noordwijk, 9–10 June). Luxembourg: Office for Official Publications of the European Communities.

———. 1998. Decision C(1998)1206 concerning the granting of assistance from the European Regional Development Fund (ERDF) to an operational programme under the Community Initiative INTERREG IIC in favour of areas eligible under Objective 1, 2 and 5b and outside Objective areas in Belgium, France, Germany, Ireland, Luxembourg, the Netherlands and the U.K. June 3.

———. 1999a. European Spatial Development Perspective: Towards balanced and sustainable development of the territory of the EU. Luxembourg: Office for Official Publications of the European Communities.

———. 1999b. Report on Community policies and spatial planning. Working document of the Commission services. Presented at the ESDP Forum. 2–3 February. Brussels.

———. 2000a. On integrated coastal zone management: A strategy for Europe. Communication from the Commission to the Council and the European Parliament COM(2000) 547 final. Luxembourg: Office for Official Publications of the European Communities.

———. 2000b. Services of general interest in Europe communication from the Commission, COM (2000) 580 final, Brussels.

———. 2000c. Communication from the Commission to the member states, 28 April, laying down guidelines for a Community initiative concerning trans-European cooperation intended to encourage harmonious and balanced development of the European territory—Interreg III (2000/C 143/08). *Official Journal of the European Communities*, May 23, C143:6–29.

———. 2000d. The sixth periodic report on the regions. Luxembourg: Office for Official Publications of the European Communities.

———. 2001. Unity, solidarity, diversity for Europe, its people and its territory: Second report on economic and social cohesion. Luxembourg: Office for Official Publications of the European Communities.

CEMAT—European Conference of Ministers Responsible for Regional Planning. 2000. Guiding principles for sustainable spatial development of the European continent. Adopted at the twelfth session of the CEMAT. 7–8 September, Hanover. Strasbourg: Council of Europe.

CGP—Commissariat Général au Plan. 1999. L'élargissement de l'Union européenne à l'est de l'Europe: des gains à escompter à l'Est et à l'Ouest. Paris: La Documentation Française.

Christiansen, T. and E. Kirchner. 2000. Introduction. In *Committee governance in the European Union*, T. Christiansen and E. Kirchner, eds., 1–22. Manchester and New York: Manchester University Press.

Churchill, W. S. 1997. Speech in Zurich, September 1946 (Document 10). In *Building European Union*, Salmon, T. and W. Nicoll, eds., 26–28. Manchester and New York: Manchester University Press.

Committee on Spatial Development of the Baltic Sea Region. 1995. Vision and strategies around the Baltic Sea region (VASAB) 2010: Towards a framework for the spatial development in the Baltic Sea region. Karlskrona, Sweden: Secretariat Vision 2010.

———. 1997. Visions and strategies around the Baltic Sea (VASAB) region 2010: From vision to action 1997. Karlskrona, Sweden: Secretriat Vision 2010.

Copus, A. K. 2001. From Core-periphery to polycentric development: Concepts of spatial and aspatial peripherality. *European Planning Studies* 9(4):539–552.

Council of Europe. 1978. Analysis and prospects of European co-operation in regional planning. Activity Report of the Committee of CEMAT Senior Officials, 1976–1978. Strasbourg.

———. 1980. Prospects of regional planning in Europe. Conference report. Fifth CEMAT. Strasbourg.

———. 1984. European regional/spatial planning charter (Torremolinos Charter). Strasbourg.

———. 1985. Conference reports. Seventh CEMAT. Strasbourg.

CSD—Committee on Spatial Development. 1998. *European Spatial Development Perspective: Complete draft*. Presented at the informal meeting of ministers responsible for spatial planning of the member states of the European Union. Glasgow, June 8, CSD.

Czada, R. 1997. Vertretung und Verhandlung. Aspekte politischer Konfliktregelung in Mehrebenensystemen. In *Theorieentwicklung in der Politikwissenschaft—Ein Zwischenbilanz*, A. Benz and W. Seibel, eds., 237–259. Baden-Baden: Nomos.

Damette, F. 1997. Wie steht es um das Europäische Raumentwicklungskonzept? *EUREG* 6: 17–22.

DATAR—Délégation à l'Aménagement du Territoire et à l'Action Régionale. 2000. Aménager la France de 2020. Mettre les territoires en mouvement, Paris: La Documentation Française.

David, C-H. 1998. Europarechtliche Auswirkungen auf die Raumplanungsrechtsentwicklung in der Bundesrepublik Deutschland. In *Das Recht in Raum und Zeit (Festschrift für Martin Lendi)*, A. Rucht et al., eds., 47–66. Zürich: Schulthess, Polygraphischer Verlag.

Davoudi, S. 1999. Making sense of the ESDP. *Town and Country Planning*, 367–369.

DETR—Department of the Environment, Transport and the Regions. 1998. *Modernising planning: A statement of the minister for the regions, regeneration and planning*. London: DETR.

———. 1999. *Subsidiarity and proportionality in spatial planning activities of the EU*. London: DETR.

———. 2000. *Peripherality and spatial planning*. London: DETR.

DGXVI—Directorate General XVI of the European Commission. 1998a. Program for the transnational seminar on the ESDP. Conference on the European Spatial Development Perspective. 27-28 April, Berlin.

———. 1998b. Report on the contribution of the transnational seminars to the improvement of the European spatial development perspective. Brussels: European Commission, DGXVI.

Dieleman, F. M. and A. Faludi. 1998. Polynucleated metropolitan regions in Northwest Europe: Theme of the special issue. *European Planning Studies* 6(4):365–377.

Draus, F. 2000. Un élargissement pas comme les autres, réflexion sur la spécificité des pays candidats d'Europe centrale et orientale. *Notre Europe, études et recherches* (11).

Drevet, J-F. 1997. *La nouvelle identité de l'Europe*. Paris: Presses Universitaires de France.

———. 2000. *Chypre en Europe*. Paris: Éditions de l'Harmattan.

———. 2001. *L'élargissement de l'Union européenne–jusqu'où?* Paris: Éditions de l'Harmattan.

Dühr, S. 2001. Cartographic visualisation in European spatial planning. Presented to the World Congress of Planning Schools. Shanghai. Bristol: University of the West of England. June.

Eising, R. and B. Kohler-Koch. 1999. Governance in the European Union: A comparative assessment. In *The transformation of governance in the European Union (ECPR Studies in European Policy Science* 12), B. Kohler-Koch and R. Eising, eds., 267–285. London and New York: Routledge.

ERIPLAN—European Research Institute for Regional and Urban Planning. 1975. Prospective study on physical planning and the environment in the megalopolis in formation in Northwest Europe. Submitted to the Commission of the European Communities. The Hague: ERIPLAN.

Eser, Th. W. 1996. *Ökonomische Theorie der Subsidiarität und Evaluation der Regionalpolitik.* Baden-Baden: Nomos.

———. 1997. The implementation of the European spatial development policy: Potential or burden? Trier, Germany: TAURUS Diskussionspapir 1.

Eser, Th. W. and D. Konstadakopulos. 2000. Power shifts in the European Union? The case of spatial planning. *European Spatial Planning* 8(6):783–798.

Faludi, A. 1997. A roving band of planners. In *Shaping Europe: The European spatial development perspective.* Special issue. A. Faludi and W. Zonneveld, eds. *Built Environment* 23(4): 281–287. Oxford: Alexandrine Press.

———. 1998. Polynucleated metropolitan regions in Northwest Europe. *European Planning Studies* 6(4):365–77.

———. 2000a. Strategic planning in Europe: Institutional aspects. In *The revival of strategic spatial planning,* W. Salet and A. Faludi, eds., 243–258. Amsterdam: Royal Netherlands Academy of Arts and Sciences.

———. 2000b. The European spatial development perspective—What next. *European Planning Studies* 8(2):237–250.

———. 2001a. European spatial planning: A contested field. In *Regulatory competition and co-operation in European spatial planning.* Special issue. A. Faludi, ed. *Built Environment* 27(4):245–52. Oxford: Alexandrine Press.

———. 2001b. The application of the European spatial development perspective: Evidence from the Northwest metropolitan area. *European Planning Studies* 9(5):667–679.

———. 2001c. Der EUREK-Prozess. In *Europäisches Raumentwicklungskonzept (Forschungs- und Sitzungsberichte 216),* ARL, ed., 14–37. Hanover: Akademie für Raumforschung und Landesplanung.

Faludi, A. and W. Korthals Altes. 1994. Evaluating communicative planning: A revised design for performance research. *European Planning Studies* 2:403–418.

Faludi, A. and J. Peyrony. 2001. The French pioneering role. In *Regulatory conflict and co-operation in European spatial planning.* Special issue. A. Faludi, ed. *Built Environment* 27(4): 253–62. Oxford: Alexandrine Press.

Faludi, A. and A. J. van der Valk. 1994. *Rule and order: Dutch planning doctrine in the twentieth century.* Dordrecht: Kluwer Academic Publishers.

Faludi, A. and B. Waterhout. 2002. *The making of the European Spatial Development Perspective: No masterplan!.* London and New York: Routledge.

Faludi, A. and W. Zonneveld. 1997. Introduction. In *Shaping Europe: The European spatial development perspective.* Special issue. A. Faludi and W. Zonneveld, eds. *Built Environment* 23(4):257–266. Oxford: Alexandrine Press.

Faludi, A., W. Zonneveld and B. Waterhout. 2000. The committee on spatial development: Formulating a spatial perspective in an institutional vacuum. In *Committee governance in the European Union,* T. Christiansen and E. Kirchner, eds., 115–131. Manchester and New York: Manchester University Press.

Federal Ministry for Regional Planning, Building and Urban Development. 1993. Guidelines for regional planning: General principles for spatial development in the Federal Republic of Germany. Bonn: Selbstverlag der Bundesforschungsanstalt für Landeskunde und Raumordnung.

Fischler, F. 1998. Die Zukunft gestalten. Speech given on the ESDP-Seminar, Cooperation in spatial development planning in the context of an enlarged EU, 25–26 November, Vienna.

French Presidency. 2000a. French presidency of the European Union. Spatial development. Summary report. Synthesis, 4 December, 2000. Paris: Délégation l'aménagement du territoire et l'action régionale (DATAR).

———. 2000b. Contribution to the debate on the long-term ESDP polycentric vision of Europe. Elaboration of a long-term polycentric vision of the European space. Final report, volume 2. Paris: DATAR.

Fürst, D. 1997. Auf dem Weg zu einer europäischen Raumordnung und die Rolle der Regionen in Deutschland. *DISP* 33(130):47–54.

Fürst, D., E. Güldenberg and B. Müller. 1994. Handbuch für Raumplanung; erarbeitet im Auftrag des Bundesministeriums für Raumordnung, Bauwesen und Städtebau. Essen: PLANCO Consulting GmbH.

Gendebien, P. H. 1983. Towards a European scheme for spatial planning. European Parliament, document 1–1026/83.

Giannakourou, G. 1996. Towards a European spatial planning policy: Theoretical dilemmas and institutional implications. *European Planning Studies* 4(5):595–613.

Graute, U. 2001. Kooperation in der Europäischen Raumentwicklungspolitik. Mehrebenenkoordination in komplexen Politikprozessen analysiert am Beispiel der Formulierung und Implementierung einer Politik zur integrierten Entwicklung des europäischen Raums; Ph.D. dissertation, FernUniversität Hagen.

Groth, N. B. 1999. The Baltic Sea region: A region covered by two transnational perspectives. In *From trends to visions: The European spatial development perspective*. K. Böhme and C. Bengs, eds. Stockholm: Nordregio.

Guigou, J-L., ed. 2002. Aménager la France de 2020: Nouvelle édition revue et augmentée. Paris: DATAR—La documentation Française.

Habermas, J. 1996. *Between facts and norms. Contribution to a discourse theory of law and democracy*. Cambridge: Polity Press.

Hajer, M. 2000. Transnational networks as transnational policy discourse: Some observations on the politics of spatial development in Europe. In *The revival of strategic spatial planning*. W. Salet and A. Faludi, eds., 135–142. Amsterdam: Royal Netherlands Academy of Arts and Sciences.

Hajer, M. and W. Zonneveld. 2000. Spatial planning in the network society: Rethinking the principles of planning in the Netherlands. *European Planning Studies* 8(3):337–355.

Hallin, G. 2000. A Europe of nation states. *North* 11(5/6):28–30.

Harvey, D. 1996. *Justice, nature and the geography of difference*. Oxford: Blackwell.

Hayes-Renshaw, F. and H. Wallace. 1997. *The council of ministers*. Houndmills, Basingstoke, London: MacMillan Press Ltd.

Hedetoft, U. 1997. The cultural semiotics of European identity: Between national sentiment and the transnational perspective. In *Rethinking the European Union: Institutions, interests and identities*, A. Landau and R. Withman, eds., 147–171. Houndmills, Basingstoke, London: MacMillan Press Ltd.

Heinelt, H. and R. Smith, eds. 1996. *Policy networks and European structural funds*. Aldershot: Avebury.

Héritier, A. 1996. The accommodation of diversity in European policy-making and its outcomes: Regulatory policy as a patchwork. *Journal of European Public Policy* 3(1):149–167.

———. 1999. *Policy-making and diversity in Europe—Escaping deadlock.* Cambridge, New York, Melbourne: Cambridge University Press.

Héritier, A., C. Knill and S. Mingers. 1996. *Ringing the changes in Europe: Regulatory competition and the transformation of the state. Britain, France, Germany.* Berlin and New York: Walter de Gruyter.

Hix, S. 1998. The study of the European Union II: The new governance agenda and its rival. *Journal of European Public Policy* 5(1):38–65.

———. 1999. *The political system of the European Union.* Houndmills, Basingstoke, London: MacMillan Press Ltd.

Hoogerwerf, A. 1984. Beleid berust op veronderstellingen: De beleidstheorie. *Acta Politica* 19(4): 493–531.

Hooghe, L., ed. 1996. *Cohesion policy and European integration: Building multi-level governance.* Oxford: Clarendon Press.

Hooghe, L. and G. Marks. 2001. *Multi-level governance and European integration.* Lanham, Maryland: Rowman & Littlefield.

Houtum, H. and A. Lagendijk. 2001. Contextualising regional identity and imagination in the construction of polycentric urban regions: The cases of the Ruhr area and the Basque country. *Urban Studies* 38(4):747–767.

Hudson, R. 2000. One Europe or many? Reflections on becoming European. *Transactions of the Institute of British Geographers* 25:4.

Husson, C. 2000. L'europe des territoires ignores: Le concept de cohésion territoiriale. Etude réalisée pour la DATAR dans le cadre d'un contrat avec les Entretiens Régulier pour l'Administration en Europe. Europa.

Hüttmann, M. G. and M. Knodt. 2000. Die Europäisierung des deutschen Föderalismus. Aus Politik und Zeitgeschichte, Beilage zur Wochenzeitschrift Das Parlament B 52–53:31–38.

Inforegio News. 1999. Newsletter No. 65, June. DG XVI.

Informal Council of Spatial Planning Ministers. 1994. European spatial planning. Results of the meeting. 21–22 September, Leipzig, Germany.

International Working Party NWE. 2001. Sustainable territorial development in the northwest of Europe—Towards long-term transnational co-operation. INTERREG IIIB Community Initiative Program. Seventh draft. London.

Jensen, O. B. 1997. Discourse analysis and socio-spatial transformation processes: A theoretical framework for analysing spatial planning. Working paper no. 61. Newcastle: Department of Town and Country Planning, University of Newcastle upon Tyne.

———. 1998. The re-making of Europe—New visions for spatial planning in Denmark and the European Union. XII AESOP Congress, 22–25 July, Aveiro, Portugal.

Jensen O. B. and I. Jørgensen 2000. Danish planning. The long shadow of Europe. *Built Environment* 26(1):31–40.

Jessop, B. 1990. *State theory. Putting capitalist states in their place.* Cambridge: Polity Press.

Joerges, C., Y. Mény, J. H. H. Weiler. 2000. *What kind of constitution for what kind of policy?* Florence: European University Institute.

Joerges, Ch. and J. Neyer. 1997. Transforming strategic interaction into deliberative problem-solving: European comitology in the foodstuffs sector. *Journal of European Public Policy* 4: 609–625.

Jørgensen, I. and R. H. Williams. 1998. Europe of the regions and the regions of Europe: The challenge of transnational spatial planning. Paper for the XII AESOP Congress: Planning, Professionals and Public Expectations. 22–25 July, Aveiro, Portugal.

Kamann, H-G. 1997. *Die Mitwirkung der Parlamente der Mitgliedstaaten an der europäischen Gesetzgebung*. Frankfurt a.M.: Peter Lang.

Karl, H. 1996. Bedarf die europäische Integration einer europäischen Raumordnungspolitik? In *Die zukünftige Ausgestaltung der Regionalpolitik in der EU* (Hanns-Seidel-Stiftung, Berichte und Studien, Reihe Wirtschaft, Band 71), W. Gick, ed. München: Hanns-Seidel-Stiftung.

Kayden, Jerold S. 2001. National land-use planning and regulation in the United States: Understanding its fundamental importance. In *National-level planning in democratic countries: An international comparison of city and regional policy-making*. Rachelle Alterman, ed. Liverpool: Liverpool University Press.

Kistenmacher, H., G. Marcou and H.-G. Clev. 1994. *Raumordnung und raumbezogene Politik in Frankreich und Deutschland* (ARL-Beiträge 129). Hanover: Akademie für Raumforschung und Landesplanung.

Kloosterman, R. C. and S. Musterd. 2001. The polycentric urban region: Towards a research agenda. *Urban Studies* 38(4):623–633.

Kohler-Koch, B. 1999. The evolution and transformation of European governance. In *The transformation of governance in the European Union* (ECPR Studies in European Policy Science 12), B. Kohler-Koch and R. Eising, eds., 14–35. London and New York: Routledge.

Kohler-Koch, B. and J. Edler. 1998. Ideendiskurs und Vergemeinschaftung: Erschließung transnationaler Räume durch europäisches Regieren. In *Regieren in entgrenzten Räumen (PVS-Sonderheft 29)*, B. Kohler-Koch, ed., 169–206. Opladen: Westdeutscher Verlag.

Kohli, M. 2000. The battlegrounds of European identity. *European Societies* 2(2):113–137.

Kokkonen, M. and Å. Mariussen. 2001. Ex ante evaluation of Interreg IIIB, North Sea program, final report. Stockholm: Nordregio.

Krätke, S. 2001. Strengthening the polycentric urban system in Europe: Conclusions from the ESDP. *European Planning Studies* 9(1):105–116.

Kunzmann, K. R. 1998. Planning for spatial equity in Europe. *International Planning Studies* 3(1):101–120.

Kunzmann, K. R. and M. Wegener. 1991. *The pattern of urbanisation in Western Europe 1960–1990*. Dortmund: Institut für Raumplanung Universität Dortmund (IRPUD).

Laffan, B. 2000. The big budgetary bargains: From negotiation to authority. *Journal of European Public Policy* 7(5):725–743.

Laitin, D. D. 2000. Culture and national identity: The East and European integration. EUI Working papers RSC no. 2000/3. Florence: European University Institute.

Landau, J. M. 1995. *Pan-Turkism, from irredentism to co-operation*. London: Hurst and Cy.

Lax, D. A. and J. K. Sebenius. 1986. *The manager as negotiator. Bargaining for cooperative and competitive gain*. New York: The Free Press.

Lehmbruch, G. 2000. *Parteienwettbewerb im Bundesstaat. Regelsysteme und Spannungslagen im Institutionengefüge der Bundesrepublik Deutschland, third edition*. Opladen, Germany: Westdeutscher Verlag.

Lieshout, R. H. 1999. *The struggle for the organization of Europe: The foundation of the European Union*. Aldershot: Edward Elgar Publishing, Inc.

Linberg, L. N. 1963. Political integration: Definitions and hypotheses. In *The European Union: Readings on the theory and practice of European integration, second edition*, B. F. Nelson and A. C-G. Stubb, eds. 1998. London: Macmillan Press.

Marks, G. 1993. Structural policy and multilevel governance in the EC. In *The state of the European Community, volume two, The Maastricht debates and beyond*, A. Cafruny and G. Rosenthal, eds., 391–410. Boulder, Colorado: Lynne Rienner.

Martin D. 1992a. Europe 2000: Outlook for the development of the Community's territory. *Town and Country Planning* 61(1).

———. 1992b. Europe 2000: Community actions and intentions in spatial planning. TCPSS proceedings. Summer school 1992. November.

———. 2000. Les Pays-Bas dans le territoire européen: un petit pays central face à l'internationalisation de l'aménagement du territoire. *Territoires 2020: Revue d'études et de prospective* (1):80–91.

———. 2001. The ESDP from a Dutch point of view. In *Regulatory competition and co-operation in European spatial planning*. Special issue. A. Faludi, ed. *Built Environment* 27(4):263–268. Oxford: Alexandrine Press.

Martin, D. and H. Ten Velden. 1997. Extra options as optional extras: What ideas are behind the ESDP. In *Shaping Europe: The European spatial development perspective*. Special issue, A. Faludi and W. Zonneveld, eds. *Built Environment* 23(4):267–280. Oxford: Alexandrine Press.

Massey, D. 1993. Power, geometry and a progressive sense of place. In *Mapping the futures. Local cultures, global change*. J. Bird et al. eds., 59–69. London: Routledge.

Mehlbye, P. 2000. Global integration zones—Neighboring metropolitan regions in metropolitan clusters. Informationen zur Raumentwicklung, Special issue. *Europäische Metropolregionen* (11/12):755–762.

Meinig, D. W. 1998. *The shaping of America: A geographical perspective on 500 years of history, vol. 3, transcontinental America, 1950–1915*. New Haven and London: Yale University Press.

Ministers for Spatial Planning and Development 1994. Visions and strategies around the Baltic Sea 2010. Towards a framework for spatial development in the Baltic Sea region. Third Conference of Ministers for Spatial Planning and Development. Tallin, Estonia. 7–8 December.

Ministers Responsible for Spatial Planning and Urban/Regional Policy. 1999. ESDP action program. Final version, 18 September.

Ministry of Housing, Physical Planning and the Environment. 1988. *Vierde Nota over do Ruimetelijke Ordening*. The Hague: Sdu Uitgevers.

———. 1988. Fourth National Spatial Planning Report. The Hague: National Physical Planning Agency.

———. 1991. Urban networks in Europe: Contribution to the third meeting of the ministers of the EC member states responsible for physical planning and regional policy. The Hague: National Physical Planning Agency.

Mudrich, G. 1987. European regional and spatial planning policies: Questions and answers. *Netherlands Geographical Studies* 44:135–143.

Nadin, V. 2000. European spatial planning: What it means in principle and practice. Presented to the European Council of Town Planners Congress. London.

Nadin, V. and D. Shaw. 1998. Transnational spatial planning in Europe: The role of Interreg IIc in the U.K. *Regional Studies* 32(3):281–99.

———. 1999. *Subsidiarity and proportionality in EU spatial planning activities affecting the UK*. London: The Department of Environment, Transport and the Regions.

———. 2000. Transnational collaboration in the Atlantic region. In *Atlantic cities: Peripheral towns or metropolitan cities for tomorrow? Problems and policies*, S. Farthing and J-P. Carrière, eds., 15–41. Éditions Publisud, ISBN 2-86600-741-7.

National Spatial Planning Agency. 1978. Ruimtelijke Ontwikkelingen in Europa [Spatial developments in Europe]. Annual report. The Hague: Staatsuitgeverij, 9–40.

————. 2000. *Spatial perspectives in Europe, Spatial reconnaissance's 1999*. The Hague: Ministry of Housing, Spatial Planning and the Environment.

Needham, B. 1988. Continuity and change in Dutch planning theory. *The Netherlands Journal of Housing and Environmental Research* 3(3):5–22.

Netherlands Scientific Council for Government Policy. 1999. Spatial development policy. Summary of the fifty-third report. Reports to the government 53. The Hague: Scientific Council for Government Policy (WRR).

Newmann, P. 2000. Changing patterns of regional governance in the EU. *Urban Studies* 37(5–6): 895–908.

Nilsson, J. 1998. Tal i Lille, Frankrik. Speech for the transnational seminar on the ESDP. Lille. 22–23 June.

Nordregio. 2000a. Study programme on European spatial planning: Conclusions and recommendations. Stockholm: Nordregio (4).

————. 2000b. Study programme on European spatial planning: Final report. Stockholm: Nordregio.

Nugent, N. 1999. *The government and politics of the European Union, fourth edition*. Houndsmills, Basingstoke, London: Macmillan Press Ltd.

NWMA (Northwestern Metropolitan Area) Secretariat. 2000. *Compendium of approved projects 1998–2001*. London.

NWMA (Northwestern Metropolitan Area) Spatial Vision Group. 2000. A spatial vision for Northwest Europe: Building cooperation. The Hague: Ministry of Housing, Spatial Planning and the Environment.

Oates, W. E. 1972. *Fiscal federalism*. New York, NY: Harcourt, Brace, Jovanovich.

Oregon Chapter of the American Planning Association (APA). 1993. *A guide to community visioning*. Chicago: Planners' Press.

Østergård, N. 1998. Note concerning urban systems. Paper for the transnational seminar on the ESDP, Lille, 22–23 June.

Oswald, E. 1998. Die Zukunft gestalten: Das Europäische Raumentwicklungskonzept—Auf dem Weg zu einer gesamteuropäischen Politikstrategie, Eröffungs-statement auf der Konferenz Berlin 27–28 April, Bundesminister für Raumordnung, Bauwesen und Städtebau.

Pedersen, O. K. ed. 1994. *Demokratiets lette tilstand [The lightness of democracy]*. Copenhagen: Spektrum.

Pond, E. 2000. Come together: Europe's unexpected new architecture. *Foreign Affairs* 79(2): 8–12.

Pope, N. and H. Pope. 1997. *Turkey unveiled, Atatürk and after*. London: John Murray.

Portuguese Presidency. 1992. The spatial development of Community territory: The case of transeuropean networks. Meeting of Ministers of the EC member states responsible for regional policy and physical planning, Lisbon. 15–16 May.

Presidenza consiglio dei Ministri. 1990. Dipartimento per il Coordinamento delle Politiche Comunitarie. Objectives and agenda for the Meeting of EEC Ministers, on new problems of territorial planning and balanced regional development connected with the implementation of the Single Market, Turin, 22–24 November.

Pröpper, I. M. A. M. and D-D. Reneman. 1993. De reconstructie van de beleidstheorie als argumentatie: een toepassing op het verkeersveiligheidsbeleid. *Beleidswetenschap* 7(3):238–256.

Read, R. 2000. Chances and potentials of networks in supporting future-oriented development in metropolitan regions. *Informationen zur Raumentwicklung, Special Issue Europäische Metropolregionen* (11/12):737–743.

Regional Plan Association. 1996. *A region at risk: The third regional plan for the New York-New Jersey-Connecticut metropolitan area.* Washington, DC: Island Press.

Richardson, T. 2000. Discourses of rurality in EU spatial policy: The European Spatial Development Perspective. *Sociologia Ruralis* 40(1):53–71.

Richardson, T. and O. B. Jensen. 2000. Discourses of mobility and polycentric development: A contested view of European spatial planning. *European Planning Studies* 8(4):503–520.

Robert, J. 1976. Municipal financing and the implementation of physical planning objectives. The Hague.

———. 1979. Issues related to the concretisation of European spatial planning: Prospects and constraints for the elaboration of a European spatial scheme. Presented at the round table on a project for a European spatial scheme. Strasbourg: Council of Europe.

———. 1979. The impact of international economic changes on development trends in Europe's regions. Strasbourg: Council of Europe.

———. 1979. Long-range forecasting and regional disparities in Europe. Strasbourg: Council of Europe.

———. 1980. Problems and perspectives in regional planning in Europe in the 1980s. Prepared for the fifth CEMAT. Strasbourg: Council of Europe.

———. 1980. The Pyrenees: Their role in European integration and the requirements of trans-frontier cooperation. Strasbourg: Council of Europe.

———. 1981. *Physical and regional planning problems in the Dutch border regions and in adjacent regions of Belgium and Germany.* The Hague: National Spatial Planning Agency (RPD).

———. 1982. Mobilising the indigenous potential of disadvantaged regions: A new dimension of regional planning. Strasbourg: Council of Europe.

———. 1982. Socio-economic development and planning in European coastal regions. Strasbourg: Council of Europe.

———. 1985. The statutory powers of national governmental authorities in the field of spatial planning and their implementation tools. Strasbourg: Council of Europe.

———. 1985. The problems of regional and local authorities involved in planning policies. Strasbourg. Council of Europe.

———. 1996. *Finland in Europe.* Helsinki: National Association of Finnish Regions.

———. 1999. Vers un développement intégré et durable de l'Arc Latin. Perspectives thématiques et options de coopération pour Interreg III en matière de développement économique/hautes technologies. Nice.

Robert, J. and W. Istel. 1980. *Spatial planning on both sides of the borders of the Federal Republic of Germany with other West-European states.* Hanover: Akademie für Raumforschung und Landesplanung.

Ross, G. 1995. *Jacques Delors and European Integration.* Cambridge: Polity Press.

RPD—Rijksplanologische Dienst. 1978. *Jaarverslag 1978.* Den Haag, Netherlands: RPD.

Rusca, R. 1998. The development of a European spatial planning policy. In *The progress of European spatial planning*, (Nordregio report 1), C. Bengs and K. Böhme, eds., 35–48. Stockholm: Nordregio.

Salet, W. and A. Faludi, eds. 2000. *The revival of strategic planning.* Amsterdam: Royal Netherlands Association of Arts and Sciences.

Saretzki, Th. 1996. Wie unterscheiden sich Argumentieren und Verhandeln? Definitionsprobleme, funktionale Bezüge und strukturelle Differenzen von zwei verschiedenen Kommunikations-modi. In *Verhandeln und Argumentieren*, V. Prittitz, ed., 19–40. Opladen, Germany: Leske und Budrich.

Sassen, S. 1995. Urban impacts of economic globalisation. In *Cities in competition: Productive and sustainable cities for the 21st century*, J. Brotchie, M. Batty, E. Blakely, P. Hall and P. Newton, eds. Melbourne: Longman.

———. 2000. *Cities in a world economy, second edition*. Thousand Oaks, CA: Pine Forge Press.

Sayer, A. 2000. *Realism and social science*. London: Sage.

Scharpf, F. W. 1973. Komplexität als Schranke der politischen Planung. In *Planung als politischer Prozeß*, F. W. Scharpf, ed., 73–113. München, Germany: Suhrkamp.

———. 1988. The joint-decision trap. Lessons from German Federalism and European Integration. *Public Administration* 66:239–278.

———. 1992. Koordination durch Verhandlungssysteme: Analytische Konzepte und institutionelle Lösungen. In *Horizontale Politikverflechtung*, A. Benz, F. W. Scharpf and R. Zintl, eds., 51–96. Frankfurt a.M. and New York: Campus.

———. 1994. Community and autonomy: Multi-level policy making in the European Union. *Journal of European Public Policy* 1:219–242.

———. 1997. *Games real actors play. Actor-centered institutionalism in policy research*. Boulder, Colorado: Westview.

Schindegger, F. 2000. Vison planet: Proceedings of the Conference on Spatial Visions, Bratislava. January. Vienna: ÖIR.

Schmidt, V. and M. Sinz. 1993. Gibt es den Norden des Südens? Aspekte regionaler Wettbewerbsfähigkeit in der Europäischen Gemeinschaft. *Informationen zur Raumentwicklung* (9/10): 593–618.

Schön, K. P. 2000. Einführung—Des Europäische Raumentwicklungskonzept und die Raumordnung in Deutschland. *Informationen zur Raumentwicklung* (3/4):I–VII.

Selke, W. 1999. Einbindung in die Bundesraumordnung und in die europäische Raumordnungspolitik. In *Grundriß der Landes und Regionalplanung*, Akademie für Raumforschung und Landesplanung, ed., 115–130. Hanover: Akademie für Raumforschung und Landesplanung.

Shipley, R. 2000. The origin and development of vision and visioning in planning. *International Planning Studies* 5(2):225–236.

Shipley, R. and R. Newkirk. 1999. Vision and visioning in planning: What do these terms really mean? *Environment and Planning B* 26(4):573–91.

Siedentop, L. 2000. *Democracy in Europe*. London: Allen Lane, Penguin Press.

Siedentopf, H. 1994. Institutionelle Bedingungen einer europäischen Raumordnungspolitik. Vergleich und Ergebnisse. In *Institutionelle Bedingungen einer europäischen Raumentwicklungspolitik*, ARL/DATAR, eds., 208–226. Hanover: Akademie für Raumforschung und Landesplanung.

Solop, F. 2001. Survey research and visioning in Flagstaff, Arizona. *Planning Practice and Research* 16(1):51–58.

SPESP—Study program on European spatial planning. 2000. Draft final report. 3 March. *http://www.norregio.a.se* (22 August 2001).

Teisman, G. 2000. Strategies for improving policy results in a pluricentric society: An interactive perspective on strategic policy behavior. In *The revival of strategic spatial planning*, W.

Salet and A. Faludi, eds., 229–240. Amsterdam: Royal Netherlands Academy of Arts and Sciences.

Territoires et Synergies (Strasbourg), EURE-CONSULT S.A (Lux), NEI (Rotterdam), Quaternaire (Oporto). 2001. Spatial Impacts of Community Policies and Costs of Non-coordination (ERDF contract 99.00.27.156). Brussels: CEC.

Tönnies, G. 2001. Konzepte und Szenarien zur Raumentwicklung in Europa. Zum konzeptionellen Ansatz des Europäischen Raumentwicklungskonzeptes. In *Europäisches Raumentwicklungskonzept (EUREK), Forschungs und Sitzungsberichte 216*, K. Wolf and G. Tönnies, eds., 109–137. Hanover: Akademie für Raumforschung und Landesplanung.

Turner, F. J. 1996. *The frontier in American history*. New York: Dover Publications.

UEB—Union Economique Benelux. 1986. Esquisse de structure globale Benelux en matière d'aménagement du territoire. Brussels: Secretariat UEB.

———. 1996. Espace de coopération, deuxième esquisse de structure Benelux, projet, Mai. Brussels: Secretariat UEB.

———. 1997. Espace de coopération, deuxième esquisse de structure Benelux, M/RO (97)1 Octobre. Brussels: Secretariat UEB.

Urry, J. 2000. *Sociology beyond societies. Mobilities for the twenty-first century*. London: Routledge.

Verbaan, A., Beek, I. ter, Boasson, D., Lübke, C., Petrus, P., Schenk, D. 1991. *Perspectieven in Europa. Een verkenning van opties voor een Europees ruimtelijk beleid voor Noordwest-Europa*. Den Haag, Netherlands: Rijksplanologische Dienst.

Vision Planet Project Panel. 2000. Vision planet: Strategies for integrated spatial development of the Central European, Danubian and Adriatic Area. Vienna: Austrian Institute for Regional Studies and Spatial Planning.

Vries, J. 2002. Grenzen verkend. Internationalisering van ruimtelijke planning in the Benelux. Ph.D Thesis. Delft: Delft University Press.

VROM—Ministerie voor Volkshuisvesting, Ruimtelijke Ordening en Milieubeheer [The Dutch National Ministry for Spatial Planning, Environment and Housing]. 2001. The fifth spatial planning report. The Hague: VROM.

VWG—Vision Working Group. 2000. *NorVISION: A spatial perspective for the North Sea region*. Essen: Planco.

———. 2000a. NorVISION: A spatial perspective for the North Sea region (NSR). Minutes from the seventh workshop meeting with Interreg IIC project leaders and researchers from the NSR, Aalborg 2–3 March.

———. 2000b. NorVISION: A spatial perspective for the North Sea region (NSR). Vision working group with representatives from spatial planning offices from the participating countries and regions. Prepared by PLANCO Consulting GmbH, Essen, Germany. Co-financed by the European Community through the Interreg IIC North Sea Program.

Waterhout, B. and A. Faludi. 2001. Multiple perspectives on polynuclear urban regions. In *Polynuclear urban regions in Northwest Europe—A survey of key actor views*. EURBANET Report 1, D. Ipenburg and B. Lambregts. eds. *Housing and Urban Policy Studies* 18:101–118. Delft: DUP Science.

Weber-Panariello, P. A. 1995. *Nationale Parlamente in der Europäischen Union*. Baden-Baden: Nomos.

Wegener, M. 1995. The changing urban hierarchy in Europe. In *Cities in competition: Productive and sustainable cities for the 21st century*, J. Brotchie, M. Batty, E. Blakely, P. Hall and P. Newton, eds. Melbourne: Longman.

Weick, K. 1985. *Der Prozeß des Organisierens*. Frankfurt a.M: Suhrkamp.

Weigall, D. and P. Stirk. eds. 1992. *The development of the European Community*. Leicester and London: Leicester University Press.

Weiler J. H. H. 1999. *The constitution of Europe: Do the new clothes have an emperor? and other essays on European integration*. Cambridge: Cambridge University Press.

Williams, R. H. 1993. *Blue bananas, grapes and golden triangles: Spatial planning for an integrated Europe*. Newcastle: University of Newcastle.

———. 1996. *European Union spatial policy and planning*. London: Paul Chapman.

Zetter, J. 2001. The British perspective on the ESDP process. In: *Regulatory competition and co-operation in European spatial planning*. Special issue. A. Faludi, ed. *Built Environment* 27(4):287–294. Oxford: Alexandrine Press.

Zonneveld, W. 2000. Discursive aspects of strategic planning: A deconstruction of the balanced competitiveness concept in European spatial planning. In *The revival of strategic spatial planning*, W. Salet and A. Faludi, eds., 267–280. Amsterdam: Royal Netherlands Academy of Arts and Sciences.

Zonneveld, W. and A. Faludi. 1997. Introduction. In *Vanishing borders: The second Benelux structural outline*. Special issue. W. Zonneveld and A. Faludi, eds. *Built Environment* 23(1): 5–13. Oxford: Alexandrine Press.

Glossary and Acronyms

ARL	Akademie fur Raumforschung und Landesplanung (Academy for Regional Research and Regional Planning)
CADSES	Central European, Adriatic, Danubian and South-East European Space
CDRC	Committee for the Development and Conservation of Regions
CEC	Commission of the European Community
CEMAT	Conférence Européenne des Ministres responsables de L'Aménagement du Territoire (European Conference of Ministers Responsible for Regional Planning)
CRONWE	Conference of Regional Development of Northwest Europe
CRP	Committee on Regional Policy
CSD	Committee on Spatial Development
DG	Directorate General
EC	European Community (the Community)
EEA	European Economic Area
EEC	European Economic Community
ERDF	European Regional Development Fund
ESDP	European Spatial Development Perspective
ESPON	European Spatial Planning Observatory Network
ESPRIN	European Spatial Planning Research and Information Network
ESTIA	European Space and Territorial Integration Alternatives
EU	European Union
GDP	Gross Domestic Product
ICT	Information and Communication Technologies
MEDA	Mediterranean Development Action
MEP	Member of the European Parliament
NATO	North Atlantic Treaty Organization
NWMA	Northwestern Metropolitan Area
OAU	Organization of African Unity
OECD	Organisation for Economic Co-operation and Development
TACIS	Technical Assistance to Community of Independent States
TENs	Trans-European Networks
VASAB	Vision and Strategies around the Baltic Sea region
WTO	World Trade Organization

Contributors

Arthur Benz is professor of political science at the FernUniversität Hagen, Germany. Between 1993 and 1995 he was professor for regional policy at the University of Constance, and between 1995 and 1999 he held a chair for government and policy research at the Martin-Luther-Universität Halle-Wittenberg. His research focuses on regional policy, federalism and multilevel governance in the EU. He has published extensively on government and public administration, federalism and multilevel governance.

Armando Carbonell is senior fellow and co-chairman of the Department of Planning and Development at the Lincoln Institute of Land Policy in Cambridge, Massachusetts. He also lectures in Urban Planning and Design at the Harvard Graduate School of Design, and is frequently called on as a design critic and planning advisor. Carbonell was executive director of the Cape Cod Commission, a regional planning and land use regulatory agency, from its establishment in 1990 until 1999. During 1992–1993 he held a Loeb Fellowship in Advanced Environmental Studies at the Graduate School of Design. Carbonell is a member of the American Institute of Certified Planners; of the Salzburg Congress on Urban Planning and Development; a fellow of the Institute for Urban Design in New York, and an affiliate member of the Boston Society of Architects.

Philippe Doucet studied architecture and engineering at the University of Louvain, faculty of Applied Science, where he specialized in urban and regional planning. As a Belgian civil servant, he has been working on secondment since January 1994, first at the European Commission, DG Regional Policies, then as head of the Interrg IIC/IIIB Northwest Europe Program Secretariat. During his four-year term at the European Commission, he was deeply involved in the proceedings of the Committee on Spatial Development (CSD) and the creation of the European Spatial Development Perspective (ESDP). His current duties in the Interreg Secretariat provide him with an excellent opportunity to test innovative ways to implement the ESDP agenda through transnational cooperation on spatial planning.

Jean-François Drevet is an official in the European Commission, in the Directorate General for regional policies and cohesion, responsible for relations with third countries (including enlargement of the EU). Previously he worked on the Europe 2000 program and the preparation of a European policy on spatial planning. Before joining the Commission, he was personal adviser to the French Minister responsible for regional development (1988–1989), and for the International and European Department in the French National Agency for Regional Development (DATAR) (1985–1988). His academic background is in geography and economies (University of Paris, Ecole Normale Supérieure). He has authored numerous articles, both in French and English, and published a number of books in French.

Andreas Faludi is professor of spatial policy systems in Europe at the University of Nijmegen in The Netherlands. Previously, he held chairs at the University of Amsterdam and Delft University of Technology, and a teaching appointment at the Oxford Polytechnic (now Oxford Brookes University) in England. He was a British Council Scholar; an Australian-European Fellow; a Fulbright Scholar at the University of California, Berkeley; a Fellow of the Netherlands Institute for Advanced Study; and an EU Fulbright Scholar at Harvard University. He has written extensively on planning theory and related topics.

Ole B. Jensen is associate professor in planning and sociology at the Department of Development and Planning, Aalborg University, Denmark. His research areas include European spatial planning; the relation between urban planning and transport activity; and the cultural sociology of space. He holds a masters degree in social science and sociology and a Ph.D. in planning and sociology. His Ph.D. thesis was titled "Re-thinking the Urban Systems—Discourse and Rationality in Danish and European Union Spatial Planning."

Derek Martin is head of the International Affairs Division at the Dutch National Spatial Planning Agency in The Hague. He has been involved for more than 20 years in cross-border, transnational and European planning, both at the Agency and in the European Commission. He has worked on the spatial aspects of European environment policy and on setting up spatial planning within European regional policy, which has led to his involvement in both the negotiation and the writing process of the ESDP.

Vincent Nadin is reader and director of the Centre for Environment and Planning at the University of the West of England, Bristol. He has led a number of major international research projects on aspects of European spatial planning, including the EU Compendium of European Spatial Planning Systems and Policies; and Sustainability, Development and Spatial Planning (SPECTRA), both funded by the European Commission. He has also directed Subsidiarity and

Proportionality in Spatial Planning Activities in the EU, funded by the U.K. government; and a Comparison of Environmental Planning Systems for the Royal Commission on Environmental Pollution. He recently led the technical assistance in the preparation of the *Spatial Vision for Northwest Europe*, and he has served as adviser to the OECD and UNECE on spatial planning.

Jacques Robert is director of Agence Européanne "Territoires et Synergies." He is a European planner with broad experience from the 1970s in developing cross-border, transnational and European spatial planning. During this time, Robert has worked mostly as a consultant and adviser for regional and national governments and European institutions. He is the author of numerous articles and publications.

Bas Waterhout is junior research fellow at the University of Nijmegen, The Netherlands. In 1998 he earned a masters (with distinction) in spatial planning at the University of Amsterdam. His thesis concerned the making of the European Spatial Development Perspective (ESDP). Before going to Nijmegen in 1999 he worked for the Netherlands Institute for Spatial Planning and Housing in The Hague, editing a volume on the consequences of European integration for urban and rural policies. He conducts research with Andreas Faludi on the application of the ESDP in The Netherlands, and in the framework of the Interreg IIC project EURBANET in the Northwestern Metropolitan Area.

Robert D. Yaro is president of Regional Plan Association in New York. RPA has worked since 1922 to improve the quality of life in the 31-county New York–New Jersey–Connecticut metropolitan area by creating long-term comprehensive plans and promoting their implementation across political boundaries. Yaro is also a practice professor in city and regional planning at the University of Pennsylvania and he teaches at the Harvard University Graduate School of Design. He was previously the founding director of the Center for Rural Massachusetts and an associate professor of regional planning at the University of Massachusetts, Amherst.

John Zetter is visiting professor at the Bartlett School of Planning at University College London, where he directs a course on European Spatial Planning. He is active in the work of international and national NGOs, being vice-president of the International Society of City and Regional Planners, the International Federation for Housing and Planning, and the Town and Country Planning Association. He is a fellow of the Royal Town Planning Institute, the Royal Geographical Society and the Royal Society of Arts. Between 1990 and 2000 he was the assistant secretary responsible, inter alia, for international planning in the U.K. government's Department of the Environment, Transport and the Regions.

About the Lincoln Institute

The Lincoln Institute of Land Policy is a nonprofit and tax-exempt educational institution established in 1974. Its mission as a school is to study and teach land policy, including land economics and land taxation. The Institute is supported primarily by the Lincoln Foundation, established in 1947 by John C. Lincoln, a Cleveland industrialist who drew inspiration from the ideas of Henry George, the nineteenth-century American political economist and social philosopher.

The Institute's goals are to integrate the theory and practice of land policy and to understand the multidisciplinary forces that influence it. Through its curriculum development, courses, conferences and publications, the Lincoln Institute seeks to improve the quality of debate and disseminate knowledge about critical issues in its departments of planning and development and valuation and taxation, and in the program on Latin America and the Caribbean.

The Institute does not take a particular point of view, but rather brings together scholars, policy makers, practitioners and citizens with a variety of backgrounds and experience to study, reflect and exchange insights on land and tax policies. The Institute's objective is to have an impact—to make a difference today and to help policy makers plan for tomorrow. The Institute is an equal opportunity institution in employment and admissions.

L Lincoln Institute of Land Policy
113 Brattle Street
Cambridge, MA, USA 02138-3400

Phone: 617/661-3016 x127 or 800/LAND-USE (526-3873)
Fax: 617/661-7235 or 800/LAND-944 (526-3944)
Email: help@lincolninst.edu
Web: *www.lincolninst.edu*